T0343654

"Sarah Krasnostein takes us on an unexpected journey through strains of belief that range from dubious to bizarre. It is sometimes disconcerting, sometimes deeply beautiful, and never simple."

—**JAMES GLEICK**,
author of *Time Travel: A History*

"In an era when it often appears as though beliefs are our biggest dividing lines, Sarah Krasnostein's *The Believer* comes as a great tonic—a thoughtfully reported, entertaining, and empathetic examination of the beliefs that sustain yet sometimes dangerously mislead. Exacting yet compassionate, she takes readers deep inside communities and lives that may be distant from us, offering portraits that refract back on our own worlds. The result feels deeply wise. If reading a book can make you more human, *The Believer* does just that."

—**ALEX MARZANO-LESNEVICH**,
author of *The Fact of a Body*

"Sarah Krasnostein's *The Believer* is filled with everything the world needs more of: compassion, curiosity, and tenderness. Krasnostein brilliantly shows us how to look more carefully, listen more closely, and love more expansively. A complicated, lyrical portrait of belief, meaning making, and the stories we tell that might save us."

—**SARAH SENTILLES**,
author of *Stranger Care*

"Sarah Krasnostein holds a mirror to the world we inhabit but don't fully understand, helping us see how our lives are shaped by beliefs at once wholly strange and unexpectedly familiar. Lyrical, haunting, endlessly curious, *The Believer* will restore your faith in the power of stories to bridge the gaps between us."

—**PETER MANSEAU**,
author of *The Apparitionists*

"Compassion and curiosity permeate Sarah Krasnostein's writing. Every few pages there is a line so poignant it takes my breath away."

—**SASHA SAGAN**,
author of *For Small Creatures Such as We: Rituals for Finding Meaning in Our Unlikely World*

THE
BELIEVER

Published by Tin House, Portland, Oregon

Distributed by W. W. Norton & Company

Library of Congress Cataloging-in-Publication Data

Names: Krasnostein, Sarah, author.
Title: The believer : encounters with the beginning, the end, and our place in the middle / Sarah Krasnostein.
Description: Portland : Tin House, 2022. | Includes bibliographical references.
Identifiers: LCCN 2021046861 | ISBN 9781953534002 (hardcover) | ISBN 9781953534071 (ebook)
Subjects: LCSH: Belief and doubt. | Faith. | Credulity. | Skepticism.
Classification: LCC BF773 .K73 2022 | DDC 121/.6--dc23
LC record available at https://lccn.loc.gov/2021046861

First US Edition 2022
Printed in the USA
Interior design by Jakob Vala

www.tinhouse.com

Cover images: © filo / Getty Images; Zamurovic Brothers / Shutterstock

THE
BELIEVER

ENCOUNTERS WITH THE
BEGINNING, THE END, AND
OUR PLACE IN THE MIDDLE

SARAH KRASNOSTEIN

TIN HOUSE / Portland, Oregon

CONTENTS

PART II: ABOVE
HALFWAY HOME · THEORIES OF FLIGHT · THE KINGDOM OF HEAVEN

CODA: HERE

This is a work of nonfiction, researched and written over a period of four years. For privacy purposes, the following names have been changed:

PARANORMAL

Misha / Amber

Lee

Jessica

Evelyn

Paul

Marina

Luke

Bridget

THE DEATH DOULA

Carol

HALFWAY HOME

Lynn

AJ

THEORIES OF FLIGHT

Neil

The great themes are love and death; their synthesis is the will to live, and that is what this book is about.

—John Hersey, *Here to Stay* (1962)

PROLOGUE
SARAH

This book is about ghosts and gods and flying saucers; certainty in the absence of knowledge; how the stories we tell ourselves to deal with the distance between the world as it is and as we'd like it to be can stunt us or save us.

The word "distance" comes from the Latin *distantia*, which means standing apart. We have invented numerous ways of measuring this apartness. There's Euclidian distance (the shortest path between two points assuming the absence of obstacles), Manhattan distance (the number of blocks a taxi must travel to reach a destination in New York City assuming, delusionally, the absence of obstacles), Canberra distance (a less colorful metric for the distance between pairs of points in a vector space) and Chebyshev distance, which concerns itself with the moves of a king on a chessboard. We have painstakingly devised metrics for the distance between notes in a chord, strings of computing code, certain and possible events, periods of time, points in outer space and the magnitudes of removal between ourselves and the actor Kevin Bacon.

Psychological distance is a way of measuring the cognitive separation between ourselves and other people, events or times.

It is the felt experience that something, or someone, is close to or far away from us, here and now. Which is to say that there is not a direct relationship between psychological distance and objective distance—something far away in space or time can feel closer than something right beside us, and vice versa. Psychological distance is our superpower and our Achilles heel, a way of flying or falling.

Before it settled into dailiness, the phrase "socal distancing" would remind me of something I learned years ago about perspective in space while reclined between my husband and our eldest child under the domed roof of a planetarium: wherever plonked down in the vastness of the cosmos, the narration said, the viewer will perceive themselves to be at the center and this means the opposite of how it feels—there is no center, the universe is more immense than we can possibly conceive, and it is moving away from us all the time.

You're about to read six different stories, six different notes in the human song of longing for the unattainable. Their combination is the seventh note.

I didn't set out to find these stories. I stumbled on the first one—a choir in a train station, as absurd as it was beautiful—and this led me to the next and so on. But, of course, while meetings can be accidental, curiosity is not. Until we make the unconscious conscious, said Carl Jung, it will direct our lives and we'll call it fate.

In each case, I needed to understand them, these people I found unfathomable, holding fast to faith in ideas that went against the grain of more accepted realities. It may be accurate to say that I needed to get closer to something, someone, that felt very far away. That I believed maybe I could.

One of the lies writers tell themselves is that all things should be understood.

THE CHOIR

Snow-blinding whiteness does not immediately come to mind when I think about the South Bronx. Once the habitat of the Yiddish-speaking Jews of my maternal grandfather's childhood, the neighborhood has longer been the domain of the Latino and Black families who arrived in search of the same security his father had arrived seeking. But when I climbed the stairs to change trains at 149th Street and Grand Concourse, there it was: an expanse of milky cheeks mottled red, like Cézanne's peaches, and corn-silk braids and platinum beards untethered to mustaches. From their dress, they appeared to be from a different time altogether: a full Mennonite choir, singing. And, despite the startling homogeneity of this choir of men and women, it also appeared as a pastel rainbow. The lavender and lemon, teal and pink of the women's homemade floor-length dresses reflected the sounds they were making, which were their own soft rainbow of harmony.

I stood there, frozen in the summer heat, too transfixed by the sound to wonder why. I could not take my eyes off them, the people of this bizarre choir. How confident they looked. How very nice it must be to stand shoulder to shoulder, to be one of those voices and therefore, somehow, all of those voices.

I was approached by one of the singing women who was, in fact, a blue-eyed girl of fifteen or sixteen, her blonde hair obediently smooth under the tiny white tent of her bonnet. Smiling, she handed me "a tract." And when I took this booklet and thanked her, she said, smiling still, that it was important for me to be prepared. The end of days would come, she assured me, and it was coming.

PART 1
BELOW

And ghosts must do again / What gives them pain.

W. H. Auden, 'The Hard Question' (1930)

1
THE DEATH DOULA
KATRINA & ANNIE

This situation is not common, but it is the most mundane thing imaginable. To knock on someone's door and be let in. To see your photos in their photos (wedding, school, holidays). To look at their teenage son and see your own son a decade on. To sit on their chair, by their fireplace, laughing. To use their bathroom and dry your hands on the towel still damp from their own clean hands.

This is also not common; also the most mundane thing imaginable. Katrina, fifty-nine, has a husband named Peter, three stepsons, one biological son. Katrina has a friend named Carol whom she's known for thirty-five years and on whose lap she is currently resting her blanketed feet. Katrina has a warm home, her own patch of sky over the deck out back, a lounge in which to sun herself, a full fruit bowl in the kitchen, some mild annoyance at Pete being behind with replacing the carpet in the front room. Also: cancer, blurred vision, light sensitivity, a racing heart, extreme nausea, the shakes. Katrina has, if she's lucky, six months left.

This is not common. It has taken a year to make contact with Katrina. It is, as you would expect, difficult to find a patient in palliative care who wants to make time to talk with me.

"Use my name," Katrina says, directing me to throw another pine cone on the fire.

•

The first time I stumbled across the words "death doula" they clobbered me. Strong words made stronger by the drum of their alliteration, but that wasn't it. It was the startling directness about a matter that concerns us all, and which we talk about rarely and only in swerving euphemisms.

Not with us anymore, not long for this world, to pass away, to lose the battle with, to lose one's life . . . as though it were a wallet in the back seat of a taxi driving away.

I liked that frankness and I feared it. Also, I had no real idea what the term meant. I understood vaguely what death doulas must do only because I was familiar with birth doulas: trained professionals who provide emotional, physical and educational support to mothers before, during and after labor. Thirty-eight years old and an entire profession a mystery.

"You know that Leonard Cohen song?" Annie Whitlocke asked me early on. "Where there's a crack that's where the light comes in? Well, where there's a crack—at the hospital, with the doctors, in the family—that's where the death doula comes in."

Annie lives in a suburban house distinguished from its neighbors only by the string of Tibetan prayer flags on the front porch, batting in the breeze like lashes. That, and the fact that the backyard contains an enormous gold-painted Buddha and the living quarters of a senior Tibetan Buddhist monk.

Annie has to tilt her shaven head backward to look up at most people through glasses that magnify her already-large eyes, and has a habit of emphasizing emotionally exciting information with a puff of breath that reminds me of a small child playing with a toy car. This lends weight to her own evaluation of herself: childlike in the Buddhist sense of "beginner's mind." But it is not quite the reason why she will say, at the age of sixty-six, "I don't know the rules of life, how you react, and what you say . . ."

She hates the word client. Finds it extremely hard to accept money for the work she does. On the one hand, she is highly trained and has to be able to support herself if she is to continue providing this type of service. On the other, she would not be as effective at what she does if it was simply a commercial transaction. She is a perpetual intimate stranger.

The boundaries of Annie's work are bespoke to each job, necessarily unclear and always shifting, but most days start the same when she wakes in darkness. Shortly after her alarm goes off at 4:15 AM, Annie says the Buddhist prayer known as the Four Immeasurables. *May all beings have happiness and the cause of happiness. May they be free from suffering and the cause of suffering . . .* Then she listens to public radio while she boils water, squeezes a lemon and prepares for more prayers at her altar, setting an intention for the day, which is to be of benefit to others. By 6:10 AM she is at the park walking the three dogs, Lady—zipping across the football field in a fresh diaper, her hind legs tethered to her dog-wheelchair—and old Bob and Missy limping along under the rising sun.

What follows varies. Yesterday she went to the vet, then dropped the dogs home before driving across town to visit a single mother looking at an early death. Her goal for the young woman: to help her live without thinking of dying so she and her child can enjoy their remaining time together. Toward this end, Annie will teach her mindfulness meditation so that she can just have a bit of a break by resting in the present moment rather than constantly thinking and thinking about the past and the future. Also, Annie will inform her about advance care directives—instructions regarding her medical treatment for when she is no longer able to voice them herself. Having read a book with her son from Annie's vast collection, the woman is now working on creating her own book for the child, intentionally speaking to the stages he will go through without her— some kind of preparation for when the time comes. Annie's goal is to help the woman and her child in whatever way she can in order "to develop a safe place, a healing place within themselves."

"It's just wonderful," Annie explains, and I say something that indicates agreement while inside I experience a racing panic followed by a retreat into a place that feels far away from this woman and her child and their books and Annie's "wonderful," but which I know is not.

On another day, in Annie's colorful and cozy living room, she shows me the Goodbye-box she ordered from a play therapist in the Netherlands. In addition to a coffin smaller than a sandwich, the box contains human figurines of various sizes, miniature flowers, hearts, stars, a candle holder, emotion dice with a different facial expression on each side and a music box. Everything is made from blond wood and hand painted, sparingly, in pastel colors. The medium is the message: the toy's frank utility evidences an organization of mind profoundly different from our prevailing sensibility where death—like sickness and age—only ever comes as a shock, an elevator opening on the wrong floor.

Though she once texted me with an offer to be my death doula should I die in time, and on another occasion discreetly sent through a picture of the flower arrangement on a corpse she had recently "washed and shrouded," Annie's interest in dying and death cannot accurately be characterized as morbid because there is nothing gloomy about her. It's less the case that these are topics she discusses too much; more that we discuss them too little.

"I thought this was just perfect," Annie coos, turning the crank on the music box to release a sweet, but not sad, song before maneuvering a few of the wooden figurines around. "It's for children to play. Mommy's going to stand here, Dad or a friend is going to stand here. We're going to put the flowers over here. They can have the visual, I mean how good is that?" She kneads the emotion dice in her palm, considers its different sides. "So they're feeling sad right now, maybe they're feeling a bit angry or, you know, maybe there's some happiness. In the coffin, we can put flowers, notes . . . It's just beautiful."

To explain how she got into her line of work, Annie says a few different things. That it's hard to know. That there are degrees of loss, death and dying are just another loss, and that it's possible to come to an understanding of it. That she had to question herself, her interest in this work, as part of her clinical pastoral education at Monash Medical. And, finally, that when she was six months old, her parents split up and she was sent away to a home for a couple of years.

"Even at that age, I do remember a loss," she says. She was placed with different carers. She felt unhappy, not safe. Became very ill with scarlet fever and was sent to the Fairfield Infectious Diseases Hospital. High above the Yarra river where branches bend towards the brown water and where one may rent a canoe—that same stretch where sixty years later I regularly take my son to feed the ducks—Annie the toddler sat, terrified, in isolation, her eyes wrapped shut. And when she explains this to me, the quiver in her voice conveys that a part of her is sitting there still. She remembers having no idea what was going to happen next because first she was at her mom's, then she was with this other person who was not good, and then she was placed with a much nicer family only to be ripped away and taken to hospital, where she was left in the dark. When she recovered, she was kept in a cot with another child from whom she caught the measles. So she was removed, again: returned to isolation, where no one was allowed to touch her without plastic gloves.

When Annie finally went home, to her mom and nana and grandpa, she found that her older sister—no longer an only child—perhaps resented her. At first, when she tells me this, I misunderstand the living configuration. I ask whether, when they were placed in care, she and her sister were kept together.

"Oh no," she corrects me, "Mom kept my sister. Because I was the younger one, and my mother had moved in with her own parents . . ." She trails off, starts again. "I was young, and I cried a lot, it appears . . . In those days, mid-last century—" She interrupts herself with a big laugh, saying she sounds like she should be in a rocking chair, but I understand that laugh to be doing something different.

She tries again. "If my mom had gone to the authorities, asked for help, I would have been made a ward of the state and she didn't want that so she had to try and find some way to still keep the family together but at that stage she was unable to keep me." Annie's tone here is official, the voice of the administration telling a serviceable narrative that makes my stomach tighten.

At first, her sister did not know who she was, this smaller child receiving anything she asked for from adults trying to alleviate their guilt. So a rift that's never quite healed developed between them, she explains.

"Okay then, life, life . . ."

Annie says this to speed the narrative along, so we don't get too lost in the morass of detail which is the difference between life and the story of a life but also, I suspect, because of feelings she prefers to keep at bay with the big laugh and the bureaucratic tone. So "life, life" is said in the spirit of et cetera or yada yada, but also with a deeply sorrowing and authentic acceptance which I find so graceful and moving that I have to look past my page and out into the yard, where the gold-painted Buddha is reflecting so much light it appears to be generating it.

2
PARANORMAL
VLAD

One of the problems with ghost research, Dr. Vladimir Dubaj once explained to me, is that "things happen outside of your attention." You can set up cameras and sit there with an intense focus, and nothing will happen. "It's when you're taking a coffee break that something comes up." Once Vlad was standing around with his colleagues on an investigation, having such a coffee, when they all heard a whistle pass through the room. Frustratingly, no one was recording. "It waits till you're not ready," he said.

Vlad is the current president of the Australian Institute of Parapsychological Research, "a non-profit scientific and community society founded in 1977." *Help is Available*, promises the institute's website. It goes on to explain that it has a history of providing support in relation to alleged or actual experiences of a paranormal nature that may require relief of suffering, distress or helplessness. Though paranormal investigation is not Vlad's professional work—his doctorate is in biomedical imaging and he lectures in physiology at a university—one might say that it is his life's work, given the financial, intellectual and emotional resources he has invested in it.

Vlad is hungry for data. While he will unhesitatingly ask those who purport to be psychic what they feel, see or sense, he knows his best chance of establishing proof lies in the physical realm: things that can be quantified and replicated.

"Around thirty percent of people will experience ghost or haunting activity at some stage of their lives," he has stated. "Such a high percentage suggests that science really needs to consider these phenomena seriously."

3

IN THE BEGINNING
THE ARK

It is as advertised: a full-size Noah's ark, built according to the dimensions in the Bible, resting on an endless expanse of grass in the middle of nowhere. The "largest timber frame structure in the world," the ark is as long as a football field. All honeyed timber and strangely pristine, it reaches more than four stories up into the gray Kentucky sky, eloquent in its absurdity, just waiting for the storm.

It's freezing outside in the late autumn wind but warm in the belly of the ark, where a looping soundtrack of snarling and clucking laps against triumphal flutes and drums. Walking across the ark's three long decks, I pass exhibits on Why the Bible Is True and animatronic replicas of Noah's family and his animals—his hippos and horses and stegosauruses all snug in their cages.

Like its "sister attraction," the Creation Museum nearby, the Ark Encounter is the fully realized brainchild of Ken Ham, a former high school science teacher from Queensland and the founder, president and CEO of Answers in Genesis, a nondenominational Christian fundamentalist evangelical ministry. Both the attractions speak to the ministry's mission—the suspension of disbelief, less as a matter of faith and more as a matter of scientific fact, as cold and hard as the planks of the ark now holding me in midair.

Though it feels right, it's wrong to call this the middle of nowhere. The attractions are a short drive from Cincinnati/Northern Kentucky International Airport: a "strategic location," explains Answers in Genesis, "because it is within a day's drive of two-thirds of the U.S. population." So here, down the road from an Amazon "Fulfillment Center" and the town of Rabbit Hash (which has elected a dog as its mayor for the past twenty years) and Big Bone Lick National Park (the birthplace of American palaeontology)—is exactly where the attractions belong. It is the middle of the national Everywhere in a country that values the ostentation of size over the grace of proportion and where its dreams are consequently locked perpetually in the distance. Just out of reach through no fault, it would seem, of one's own.

To get to the museum from the ark, you drive forty-five minutes along a stretch of Interstate 75, the highway that bisects America from the northern tip of Michigan all the way down the finger of southern Florida. You drive past fields and barns and fast food signs on improbably tall poles. You drive past churches that look like houses or warehouses or motels. Past billboards erected at some expense by the "anti-theocracy" Tri-State Free-thinkers. You drive through country where "atheist" occupies the same linguistic terrain previously inhabited by "communist." You drive next to people who don't go to church on Sunday but who will performatively profess guilt about that, putting religion on like pants when they leave the house. People who swap concealed carry gun permits with loved ones for Christmas. People who do not like Donald Trump but feel a little sorry for him on account of his flailing, people who are fine with creationism and evolution being taught together at school, to keep an open mind.

Here, it is easy not to hear how Trump just mixed up his school shootings and instead tune inadvertently into Christian radio stations and get: "It's not the size of your faith that matters, it's the size of your god." You drive past new-built houses and rusting farm machinery, until you turn off into the Creation Museum. *Prepare to Believe*, its motto urges.

4

THE DEATH DOULA
ANNIE

When Annie was seventeen, her husband took the boxes of her childhood books, which she had just moved from her mother's house, downstairs to the furnace, popped them into the chute and burned them.

She learns this while they are unpacking, setting up their new home. She turns to him, saying, I can't find the books. I've gotta go to my mom's and get them.

No, you don't, he replies. I burned them.

The Wizard of Oz, the poems, the books that Nana and Grandpa gave her, all those beautiful books, those building blocks and life rafts—gone. Annie understands this not in punitive terms, but rather because he isn't a reader and cannot conceive of the books' significance to her. They'd just take up room, he says, you've already read them.

I've just married this man, she thinks, standing there, pregnant. And though she is a child still, she sees it with absolute clarity. Fuck. This is gonna be my life.

"From there," she explains to me, "it just went down the sewer."

Annie's schooling was truncated at fourteen. She has been, among other things, a dressmaker, a funeral celebrant and a truck driver, steering a four-ton Ford tray on the roads for eighteen months. She's completed courses in neuroplasticity and pastoral care and grief counseling and mindful self-compassion. She's taught yoga and breath control and meditation. She's written, self-published and sold ten thousand and eleven thousand copies, respectively, of her *Pocket Guide to Positive Symbolism* and *Eastern Gods and Animal Spirits*. She's completed an accelerated freefall, skydiving out of a Cessna 182 from an altitude of fourteen thousand feet. She's had seven surnames, returning last to her first. Her grandfather died in her arms, her baby nephew died in her arms. She's been married six times and tried to kill herself twice. She's had six miscarriages and two live births. And she's died once.

5

PARANORMAL
VLAD

"Has anyone here had a paranormal experience?" the conference organizer asks the group that has gathered on a Friday night for the first session of this weekend's Real Ghostbusters of Australia Conference.

"Kind of comes with the territory," says one of the participants, a professional psychic, with a wry laugh.

We are upstairs at Milano's Tavern in Brighton for a "night of haunted place sensing and ghostbusting demonstration." The building has been reincarnated many times since its first iteration in the 1840s as the Royal Terminus Hotel. It was a pub at the end of the line frequented by outlaws, perhaps a brothel too, then a seaside sanatorium for the wealthy unwell.

Despite its age and the dark of the night, my first impression of the building was the diametric opposite of fear on account of the pinging of slot machines and the posters advertising the upcoming performance of an Abba cover band. Online reviews were divided on the freshness or failures of the bistro's calamari. None, however, mentioned Tilly, the ghost of a woman said to have been murdered on the premises in the 1840s, who has been encountered by various people over the years and by the staff as recently as last Wednesday, when two waitresses on the second floor, where we are now gathered, reported hearing a disembodied voice and went running downstairs.

The Bayview Room just hosted a wake for a twenty-six-year-old. Still-full wine glasses on soiled white tablecloths and a strong scent of perfume and cigarettes brought to mind a suddenly abandoned cruise ship as we threaded into the room and congregated around a table at the back. A pubful of ghost hunters.

In addition to the five parapsychological professionals who will be presenting at the conference this weekend, there are ten participants who've come along not so much for a bit of fun as from a solemn curiosity and the organizer, who does not turn on the lights.

The young woman who just spoke goes by the alternative names of Misha/Amber. She does readings and house clearings, she explains, and releases spirit attachments. The conference presenters joining us tonight are Vlad (*interested in investigating haunting and poltergeist activity*) and Rob Tilley from Sydney (*decades of experience "clearing" homes and people of psychic distress*). Also, Johann and Karen, a ghostbusting couple from Perth, and Brett, a clinical hypnotherapist and spirit-release therapist, who specializes in "taking entities out of people who are possessed."

Earlier, Vlad learned that Brett's introduction to the paranormal stood in stark counterpoint to his own inasmuch as it involved Brett walking into a room where the ghost of an elderly woman jumped on him in fright. "I don't know how that works but that's his introduction," Vlad told me, as he pondered it gravely. "He can see these things, he can interact with these things. I have no intuitive element whatsoever."

Technically, Vlad's main interests—out-of-body experiences, near-death experiences, ghosts, poltergeists—are adjacent to "true parapsychology," which encompasses phenomena of the mind like ESP, telekinesis and clairvoyance. "Survival of consciousness is a little bit on the borders," he explained to me the first time we met, in a café at Monash University, where we both earned our doctorates. He spoke in a soft voice and his face was open and earnest beneath a pale, broad forehead.

Empirical evaluation of spontaneous out-of-body experiences is tricky. For one thing, it is challenging to find someone who can have them on demand. Most of the research these days, Vlad said with some frustration, is qualitative. Sending questionnaires out to a thousand people and asking how many have had an out-of-body experience, how they would describe it, things of that nature. Vlad, on the other hand, was initially interested in hands-on research of the style that had been funded in academic eras long gone: getting people into the lab to measure their brain activity or test whether they could see an object around the corner and so on.

Faced with the improbability of obtaining funding for such experiments, he asked himself what would be the next best thing. The answer was: ghosts. "It's very easy to find a location and you don't need ethics approval."

You don't generally talk seriously about ghosts in academic circles. "Interesting thing, though," he said, "when you do, no one says much until after they've got you alone and then it's 'Guess what? Such and such happened to me . . . .'"

Vlad started a research group with a colleague about ten years ago and, once the website was up, calls started coming in. "I would like to think that the only difference between my research and mainstream science, or a skeptical researcher, is that I don't dismiss *all* of the activity as being made up or fake," he said. "I go in there with the idea that something's happened that we can't explain, and I try to filter out all the noise to get to the signal."

From Vlad's experience, ninety to ninety-five percent of claims can be dismissed by a mundane explanation, and the majority of mundane explanations are psychological. But he has found that other claims cannot be so easily dismissed.

•

Streetlamps soften the darkness in the Bayview Room as Lee, a young man with his own paranormal investigation group, takes out a device I believe at first to be a buzzer for an order of food downstairs at the bistro. It turns out to be a K-II electromagnetic frequency meter. He places it on the tablecloth in front of him and peers into it with a satisfied smile as its lights go off.

Vlad extracts a yellow rubber ducky from his bag and places it next to his own EMF meter. The duck of Dr. Dubaj contains a mechanism that, when thwacked with some force, causes a light to go off inside its sunny abdomen. Vlad uses it as a trigger object. The parlance of paranormal investigation can be opaque to the laywoman, so he explains that a trigger object is any tool that can clearly signal changes in the environment while ghost hunting. You can choose "whatever you think might interest the entities." Unlike pricier, purpose-built products like BooBuddy—marketed as *an attractive, talking bear trigger object* that responds to changes in temperature and EMF energy *with a friendly voice*—the duck was purchased from a two-dollar shop. Its lights have gone off, unthwacked, only once in the course of Vlad's paranormal investigations and they will not go off tonight. But the duck is there for the purposes of preparedness. As Vlad has said, "The scientific community devotes little attention to ghost and haunting phenomena due to its unpredictable and spontaneous nature." He is nothing if not prepared.

"Allow the spiritual eye to start observing . . ." Brett says, starting off the night with an opening meditation. We breathe deeply. He cautions us not to question ourselves if we see something in this altered state of consciousness by thinking that it can't be true, because it's precisely the suspension of the analytical mind that allows the spiritual vision to arise. Also, not to worry if anyone feels they've got something attached to them at the end of the night; there's plenty of people here who can sort that out.

I close my eyes, I go along with it. I feel the cold air coming down from the vents above my left shoulder. A tingling down the right side of my face. A heaviness on the back of my head as though it is being subtly pushed forward. A thump sounds, like the emergency exit door in the room's bar area has opened and closed.

At the conclusion of the exercise, Misha/Amber shares with the group that she is sensing the presence of a man who died as violently as he lived. Sees him hogtied, wriggling as he is killed by his fellow criminals.

"Haunted people, haunted places, it's the same problem," says Rob Tilley, a tall man of seventy in a leather jacket, with the wild white hair, rosy cheeks and jovial laugh of a muscular Santa. "You ask the good spooks to come in and take care of it. You don't take an interest in them 'cause that's what they want! You just cut 'em off and say, 'You're a bloody nuisance, go to the light,'" he explains, waving one large hand as though shooing off an invasive seagull.

"Do you ever find," Vlad asks Rob, "that some people just don't want to let go? Like the occupants of the house subconsciously actually want the attention?"

"Yeah, those are the ones you can't help," Rob replies, before regaling the group with the story of a case he had in Brisbane. A woman who was fascinated and frightened in equal measure by the poltergeist haunting her home. With frustration, he explains how he told her to just leave it alone but that she kept pulling it back in, undoing his work. "That's a psychological problem," he says, shaking his head.

Brett chimes in with a similar case—a house clearing he did for a man "of Chinese origin" necessitating the incidental removal of a dragon from the kitchen. The man later requested its return, explaining that it had been benevolent. Brett explains that in his effort to accommodate the request, he summoned a dragon while in a trance state that was larger than the original one and would not fit in the kitchen. So he left it curled around the house, protecting the property and those inside: an outcome that happily exceeded his own expectations.

Vlad's EMF meter emits the type of theremin sound you hear in old horror movies. "It's showing lots of background activity," he notes briskly. "Looks like the wiring isn't shielded properly."

Before we adjourn to explore the rest of the floor, Brett mentions that he senses "an energy" nearby, watching over what we are doing from a corner up against the ceiling. It's not a deceased person, he explains, rather it's a form of energy that has never been human, probably an ancient energy, attached to this location before they built the pub around it.

A woman inquires whether we might be on an Aboriginal sacred site.

"Could be," he replies. It's here in the room now, and he believes this is where it will permanently stay. Having communicated with it, he found it to be a frightened entity, asking that it not be made to leave. He warns that "if we rush over there in a group we'll scare the hell out of it."

"As I was walking around in here earlier on, it was so packed with dead people, I could feel them passing through my body," Rob says brightly, pushing his chair back to stand. "So you can try that when we get up and move around. See if you can sense that."

"I feel nothing whatsoever," Vlad notes, still seated, chewing his gum with his arms crossed over his chest and the light from outside clouding his glasses.

As a younger man, Vlad would watch American ghost-hunting shows where something astonishing, or at least weird, happened in every episode. It gave him a false impression of the field. "It's a lot of waiting around not really experiencing anything at all," he told me earlier. "My personal experiences aren't particularly remarkable. Certainly, I've spoken to a lot of people who've started their own research groups and every one of them has had a very dramatic experience which really triggered them to research it. They've seen full-blown apparitions in front of them and started questioning reality. I, on the other hand, have not had that experience but probably the most interesting one—because I haven't been able to explain it—has been seeing the orb."

Vlad saw this orb while on an overnight vigil at the site of the former Ararat Lunatic Asylum, which started accepting patients—then called inmates—in 1865 and closed in 1998. The site he selected for investigation was J Ward, the former town jail co-opted by the asylum in 1886 to house the criminally insane.

It was around three in the morning when Vlad and his colleague saw the glowing orange ball in the doorway. "We automatically assumed it was someone trespassing who had a torch," he explained, "so we actually went looking around. Nothing there." They returned on successive occasions to eliminate potential causes. They thought it could have been an electric light, but there was no electricity in the building. They thought it could have been a car auto-lock, but the car light didn't have that effect. "We don't know what caused it, so we just assume it was something genuinely paranormal," he said. "But it didn't feel particularly paranormal."

Recently, he fell asleep in a cell while on another overnight vigil at J Ward. "It was so quiet," he shrugged.

The beam from Vlad's torch caresses a coffee urn in the Bayview Room as I pad after him in the dark. Pictures of the original ironstone building indicate that the section where we find ourselves is fairly unchanged: two walls of windows, a balcony facing the water.

"I felt something; I don't normally feel something," Vlad says evenly as the EMF meter in his hand releases a crispy static. He peers through the glass doors leading out onto the balcony:

empty except for a larval cluster of cigarette butts, a few broken glasses, the wind blowing over the dark water of the bay.

"There's a lot of things we don't know, a lot of stuff we don't understand," Vlad had explained to me. "If you look at astrophysics and cosmology, in essence, they've found that our understanding of the whole universe is made up of visible matter plus dark matter plus dark energy.

"Dark matter and dark energy—things we can't physically measure with our equipment—makes up about ninety-seven percent of the universe, according to their estimates. And the rest of the physical matter that we *do* understand—the stuff that we're made of, and the stars and the planets—that makes up about three percent of the universe as it's known to us."

He considered this for a moment. "But that argument seems a bit of a cop-out. To say we can't explain ghosts so it must be quantum physics or it must be dark matter—something that we can't physically detect or measure—it seems like almost a religious cop-out, so to speak, to default to something mystical, something beyond our comprehension . . .

"I don't disagree with the scientists, but to say, 'I can't explain ghosts, so I'll just put it over there and deal with it later' . . ." He paused. "My whole interest in this is people have reported ghost activity for thousands of years, even in the Bible it's been reported. And when it interacts with us—it must physically interact with the material world."

Something that can physically interact with the world should be able to be recorded and measured; it may even have repeatability.

"You hear mediums and psychics talking about the energy not being strong enough," he continued. "I don't know whether that's true or not, but they'll say some ghosts don't have the energy to interact properly with the world so they need to build up more energy before they do that. Quite often, it's reported that right before something occurs you have this sudden cold and then you experience something weird. That implies the idea that as it gets cold, they're drawing the energy to do something with it. Or some people have reported electrical problems, batteries draining from their phones or from their cameras just before something occurs."

Vlad talked about ghost researchers who have recorded electromagnetic responses at the time of a ghost experience. "So, if there is activity there, I want to know in what part of the electromagnetic spectrum it actually occurs. People have reported everything from audio, temperature, magnetic fields, visible, infrared, thermal, all the way up to radiation, they've even had Geiger counters going off in one or two examples. It's all through the spectrum, but nothing consistent. So the question is: what are the ideal conditions, and if we can find the ideal conditions can we reverse the process? Can we actually make an environment perfectly suitable for something to occur?"

The answer, he acknowledged, is not straightforward. "The problem is, the more you work in the field, the more you realize that it's not just physics. It's physics plus the psychology of whatever might be there, and a lot of these things don't necessarily want to play by the rules."

Hands clasped behind his back, Vlad meanders away from the balcony and down a hallway. I follow and am immediately hit by a wave of nausea. As Vlad disappears around a corner up ahead, I feel a fear so enormous that for one moment I cannot bring myself to follow or retreat, both ways being equally dark and empty. I do not sense a ghost but, often, absence is more terrifying than presence.

I am standing in a hallway above a bistro that smells of fried foods, but suddenly my mind is in Charlottesville, Virginia, where I was born. My maternal grandparents' farm was my first home, and where I returned with my parents on weekends and holidays throughout my childhood until we moved to Australia, where my father was from, when I was a teenager. There were barns and paddocks. A goat that I fed from a baby bottle. A lake ringed by deep forest, where I would walk next to my grandfather as he whistled around a toothpick eternally clamped between his teeth.

Their house was beautiful from the outside and, probably, from the inside, but my memory of it is mostly a memory of fear. It wasn't the sweeping spiral staircase, so high and so polished that I clung to the railing like a bird on a perch, convinced I would slip off at any moment and fall forever. It wasn't the dim rooms looming off to each side, their deep corners like wells I might drown in. It wasn't the locked door of my grandmother's bedroom, or the edgeless solitude radiating all around.

What terrified me was the constant expectation that I was about to see a ghost. And by that I do not mean the monsters or bogeymen of every child's nightmares. I mean the finely drawn, white, spectral body of Mrs. Peters, the former owner of the property, whom my mother and both of my grandparents habitually spoke about as though she were a malicious neighbor popping by uninvited.

6

IN THE BEGINNING
THE MUSEUM

Why do we have to die?

The question is written across a wall inside the Creation Museum next to a black-and-white photo of a mother and child staring at a coffin. There are other images around it—a man in a wheelchair, someone crouching in a corner, a flooded town.

Why do I suffer? Why am I here? Is there any hope? Am I alone?

The Creation Museum's parking lot is immense and to walk across it is to travel back in time. This is less about the fossils displayed inside and more about the fact that the people who work here speak and think as though they are living in feudal times and waging—in a world of iPhones and heart transplants—a medieval war. Which is also, of course, what makes them so perfectly modern.

They're just finishing their morning prayer meeting, a black-clad, armed security guard informs me. When they open the museum doors, they are smiling and adorable. Also, multitudinous: old and young, many of them volunteers, they stand alone or in groups, ready to help and watching.

It feels nice in here, I won't lie. Sweet and wholesome, like the numerous diabetes-inducing pumpkin spice lattes I will consume from their coffee shop over the next few days. The vibe is Very Erudite, on account of the numerous mentions of the learned professionals on staff. But it's also a Pretty Fun Place; it is, after all, targeted at children. So, in addition to the multimedia exhibits touting "the evidences for a young earth," deriding "molecules-to-man evolution" and charting the moral decline of society, the Creation Museum features a planetarium, a pizza place, two fudge stands, a mining sluice, a zip line and a petting zoo inhabited by a zonkey and a zorse named, respectively, Cletus and Zoë. There is a chapel in the Creation Museum, and the building is also where the offices of Answers in Genesis are located.

Ken Ham is unavailable to meet on the days I visit but his face appears—smiling or serious under a cap of white hair—on books, DVDs, brochures and the napkin dispensers in the café. Aussie accent largely unaffected by thirty years in the States, he speaks before the films shown in the 4D movie/lecture theater, on DVDs played in the gift shop and from a television dangled delicately between the men's and women's bathrooms. The short syllables of his full name are in everyone's mouths and are spoken with overtones of reverence and awe.

Burdened to tell others the facts supporting a biblical view of creation, Ham's bio explains, he has spent his career promoting, to children in particular, a literal interpretation of the book of Genesis as the basis for biblical authority in all areas of their lives. While I cannot agree with him that authority is accuracy, I see his point: what happens early is, in vital ways, formative.

The first exhibit, in the lobby, is set to an audio accompaniment that sounds extremely close to the *Game of Thrones* theme. This exhibit considers the question of whether dragons were real: *The Bible is authoritative, without error, and inspired by God. While dragon legends may be fanciful retellings of actual events, God's Word tells us about two real dragon-like creatures.*

After I read about the behemoth and the leviathan, the walls narrow, funneling me down a curving hallway past a stand of mobility scooters and strollers for rent and an eye-wateringly expensive souvenir photo booth. Then the walls open out into the Main Hall. Past a woolly mammoth skeleton and a white statue of Mary, Joseph and Jesus, I see a bucolic tableau of dinosaurs and cave people cavorting beneath a real waterfall: everyone together as the "PhD scientists" on staff here will assure you it was at the dawn of time, six thousand years ago.

Deeper in the museum, two plastic palaeontologists stand over a simulated dig, dinosaur bones at their feet. Their dialogue comes alive on the screen above them, where a white man in fieldwork gear gestures to the Asian man beside him and explains how they interpret their findings differently. Kim, his colleague, thinks the Spinosaurus died over a hundred million years ago and was covered by sediment caused by a local flood. But our white guy sees something different. "I believe this animal died in flood, but it wasn't a local flood," he says, augustly. "It was a massive flood that covered the earth. Noah's flood."

He explains that, according to the Bible, that was about 4,300 years ago and that's how old he believes this fossil to be.

"We come to different conclusions because we have different starting points. I start with the Bible and my colleague doesn't." At this point, the camera zooms in and lingers on Kim's face. "We all have the same facts, we merely interpret the facts differently because of our different *starting points*."

Walking on, I reach a dim but luscious Eden, branches curving over a winding path. Frozen gazelles to the left, mountain goats to the right; a great comingled congress of big cats and zebras, llamas and kangaroos and a stegosaurus. Adam nestles in a flower patch with Eve. Thick ropes of root spiral upward to form an enormous tree trunk with apples bobbing enticingly overhead. Through concealed speakers: *From the tree of the knowledge of good and evil you shall not eat, for in the day that you eat from it you shall surely die.*

Through a dark archway, I too am ejected from the Garden, left to twist down the path towards Corruption. Large black-and-white photos line the walls. A woman screaming in labor. A pile of skulls and bones. A man tightening a tourniquet around his arm. A sea of gravestones like small, white teeth. A plaque informs me that human sin introduced these things into the world: clothing, animal sacrifice, thorns, venom, carnivory, scavengers, cosmic aging, cosmic pain, conflict, poisons, weeds, burdensome work, disease and death. *Sin changed everything. Where there was fellowship, now there is fear . . .*

This is NOT how it was MEANT TO BE!

I am sitting in a circle on the floor of my year two classroom, listening to Mrs. S read us a story. Mrs. S visits each week. She wears much pink. Her hair: a perfect white cumulus above her smile. Kind. Never disciplines us, never has to; we are in thrall to her delight in us. Three decades later, remembering her still feels like curling up next to the heater.

Mrs S was always already more than the black numbers tattooed on her forearm which the bolder among us sometimes asked to see and to touch. I am eight years old and the numbers on Mrs. S's arm are not shocking to me and they never were. They are just What Is, and What Is, to a child, is normal. Unlike my mother's mother, who is not to be asked about the War, Mrs. S will roll up the soft sleeve of her pink sweater for a couple of moments before returning us to the book on her lap. We know that Mrs. S did not want to get this tattoo and that she got it in the Camp where she was called by a number instead of her name. We know a sliver of her sadness; it is always in the room with us.

We know the lesson: Never Again. To learn it is to live, though it is also a falling in the belly, a drop of distance that compresses time and space to a point of singularity.

Understand, "Never Again" is not something we are comforted with; it is a duty we are assigned because our lives depend on it. We are eight years old and this is the water we swim in.

I pause at an exhibit about Ebenezer the Allosaurus. A plaque explains that, having survived the flood on Noah's ark, dinosaurs eventually went extinct for a variety of possible reasons including "a post-Flood Ice Age, or other post-Flood catastrophes, or maybe even because people killed them for food or sport." The rest of the exhibits trace a line from the Corruption of Adam through the Catastrophe of the Flood to the Confusion of Babel.

I walk on through rooms of increasingly sparse and esoteric displays about Cross, Christ and Consummation. It's not all bad news—*God promises that a day is coming when He will judge sin and take away the curse.*

And then I am unceremoniously spat out on the building's lower level with this parting sentiment: *Those who remain in unbelief, rejecting His completed work on the Cross, sacrificial death, and Resurrection from the dead, will suffer eternally in the lake of fire.*

7
THE DEATH DOULA
ANNIE

Annie's father left when she was six months old. As an adult she will meet him only briefly—long enough to be told how pleasing he found his life, his other children. Later, she will be told too long after the fact that he died. But her stepfather, John, is a kind man who works as a funeral director and embalmer in High Street, Northcote. Annie visits his office on weekends and school holidays, taking his lunch to the embalming room where he explains to her about the tubes dangling down from the ceiling that suck liquid from the bodies. He introduces her to the person he is working on, addressing them all the while, calling them by their name. *I'm just telling my stepdaughter what happened to you, Tom.* Whenever he goes silent for a day or so, she knows it means a baby came through.

She is about to turn sixteen when a vet hires her as a nurse. She learns as she goes; it is work she both loves and hates—like the vet himself, a real bastard she comes to admire enough to name her first child after. She is made tall by his trust even as she deals with his temper and his alcoholism, and a streak of something she can't quite put her finger on. It materializes in the scalpel he throws at her face in frustration one day. And again the time she assists him with a hysterectomy on a bloated German shepherd and he instructs her to take the dog's uterus outside and stick a scalpel in it. I want to understand what's inside, he explains. She solemnly carries the dish outside, places it on the ground near the gully trap, crouching over it with the knife. There is one moment of serious inquiry before stinking black pus squirts over her face, her hands, her clothes.

"Of course he told me to take it outside. He knew what was going to happen," Annie says, in her living room. "I still . . . I still . . . I could smell it for days, weeks, afterwards." She can summon a memory of the smell even now because it was very similar to an elderly lady she worked with—much later, during her years as a medical practice manager—who had bowel cancer. "The husband was so old, he couldn't look after her but he did his very best. I'd go out to the car, pick her up and bring her in. Once she leaked all over me, and it was the same smell."

This reminds Annie of a third olfactory link: a crow she found in the gutter, barely alive. She picked it up, planning to find a box to put it in. "And it defecated on me," she explains. "Same smell. It was so repulsive, something that I wanted to run away from, but I couldn't. I was holding it. Just like that old lady, I was holding her."

Annie was fourteen when she met the boy who would become an adult before her, and later her husband. He was three years older, over a foot taller. A police cadet at the time. She was fifteen when she had an abortion. Sixteen when she broke up with him and her mother pressured her to return to him.

I'm not interested, she replied. But he kept coming round and speaking to her mother, who was a sucker for the approval of men. And so Annie agreed to hear him out. Met up with him in his car.

I can't have this baby, she thought, a few months later. She was referred for an abortion but the doctor in Collins Street said he couldn't touch her. A growth in her abdomen made the procedure too dangerous. Nothing he could do. You've made your bed, her mother said, now you've got to lie in it.

In fifty years, Annie will not be too sure of where the marriage took place but she will remember vividly how his family wanted nothing to do with her and she will remember the pain that throbbed all through those months. How she became huge with the baby and the cyst that grew alongside it. How her husband was a policeman by this stage, working shifts. How deeply unhappy the marriage was.

She is alone when her water breaks. Hobbles to the telephone booth on the street, calls an ambulance. Spends thirty hours in labor, delivering her ten-pound son. Holding him, she feels a self-surprising but deep call to have the child circumcised. Some strong attachment to the religion her grandmother had instructed her always to hide.

She tries to leave her husband, takes the baby. She ends up returning to the house, becoming pregnant with her second son.

One weekend, her husband is at work and the boys—not yet school-aged—are at her in-laws' house where they are welcome but she is not. She knows that she must leave and that this is her chance to do it. She goes to Southland shopping center, sits in the sleek foyer, people shoaling around her. She sees a young man with long hair, a bit of a hippie. Approaches him, though she feels so shy. Oh . . . excuse me but I need a place to stay, she says. I'm leaving my husband and I need help.

This stranger drives her to the apartment he shares with his girlfriend above a butcher shop. They lend her their bed, their little Volkswagen. From this sanctuary, where she cannot sleep for missing her children, she writes to her husband. Tells him that she has left him and will be seeking custody of the boys once she has a job and a place to live. Next day, she borrows the car and finds full-time work as an assistant accountant. Replying to an ad in the local paper, she rents a room in a house with three aeronautical engineers who agree to let her pay her share of the rent whenever she gets her first pay. Under the same terms, she purchases a cheap but functional car. When she tells her family about her plans, her mother—perhaps desperate to distinguish her own act of child abandonment—tells her that what she's done is shocking, disgraceful.

Her husband asks her to come by the house. Says they need to talk. She arrives to find two of his mates there, policemen in uniform. You try and get custody, they say, and we'll go to the court and testify you had sex with both of us. Once again she returns.

When the boys are old enough to go to school, Annie leaves her husband for good. It means surrendering custody of her children but she reassures herself with the thought that their father loves those boys, she will see them when she can and perhaps one day they might understand.

At twenty-six Annie gets remarried, to an abusive alcoholic who dies six months later in a car crash on the Nullarbor with the baby-sitter by his side. She goes to the morgue to identify his body. Looks down at him, the stitches where his head has been opened. Sits on the floor, back against the wall. The young man, gone. And her still here, warm in the cold room.

The growth in her abdomen sends her repeatedly back to the doctor, doubled over with pain that goes not merely undiagnosed but entirely dismissed (psychosomatic) until she requires a hysterectomy at the age of twenty-eight.

At twenty-nine she marries a telephone repairman. A nice guy but not a great match. They divorce three years later.

At thirty-three she marries a postman. He wants children and she is done having babies. They divorce after two years.

At forty she marries a younger man from China. They travel between the two countries, start a business and buy the house she still lives in today. They divorce eight years later.

At forty-eight, she marries a con man from Colorado with significant debt. Six months later, they divorce.

Marriage certificates, divorce certificates, passports with different surnames. Annie's relationship history has been reduced to paperwork but paging through it still feels profoundly sad. Addiction is the word I think of. To something we are physically built to be addicted to: love, the security of attachment. The diminishing returns are less interesting to me than the prenup she wisely made the last guy sign before she married him with girlish braids in her long blonde hair. So although there is a strong sense of futility and of history repeating in this file of personal documents, there is also, in the accounting of his meager assets and sizable debts, an undeniable sense of something slowly rising.

Radical acceptance of uncertainty and impermanence is what one may expect of a person who shares her home with an enormous gold Buddha and a monk, who is currently eating his lunch out back. But Annie's focus is less on letting go and more on letting in; finding language for everything stifled by the dark silence that society insists on draping over the dying and those they leave behind.

Take the luxuriantly thick washcloth that she is handing over to me so I too can have a fondle. "You can wash the body, or just the face or hands, the feet," she says, explaining that she chooses to do so without gloves. "As you're washing, *talk* about things: what did these hands do when that person was alive? These feet? And the stories start coming up and laughter and tears." She explains that whether the time you had with that loved one was long or short, remembrance is about connection. "These are things that can be done when your baby has died. Some ritual, some little ceremony."

She holds up a wool bundle cinched with pink ribbon: a mock-up baby carrier she is trying to present to hospitals to help grieving parents connect with their dead babies.

"It's soft," she explains, holding it like a football and giving it a good squeeze. "When a little baby has died and it's just in a blanket, it's so fragile, you don't want to hug it.

"But that child can come home, and the other children can hold it, or the extended family, because everyone is touched by that."

After the death of her newborn grandchild, Annie saw that people simply did not know what to say. And that silence is to grief what petrol is to fire. "We're not told about how to respond to a situation like that," she explains.

And we don't necessarily do it any better at the other end of the age spectrum. She cared for her auntie who was in her late seventies. Stage four pancreatic cancer. Annie's mother warned her, "Now, don't talk about all your death stuff with Betsy, we don't want to upset her."

So Annie went into the bedroom, where she saw that her aunt was in pain.

"How you going?" Annie asked.

"Good, I'm fine," Betsy replied, from bed.

"So what do you know about your situation?" Annie asked.

"Well, I know that I'm dying."

"Do you want to talk about it?"

"I *do* want to talk about it," Betsy said, "but people won't let me. They keep saying, 'You'll get better.'"

So they started talking.

Like all socialized silences, the one around death doesn't do what we think it does. Doesn't make anything easier. Breeds only disconnection, isolation, fear.

"What do you want to tell everyone?" Annie asked her auntie.

"I want everyone to be kind to each other," Betsy replied.

"This is one of the things I've learnt," Annie says to me. "Everything that was so important—we've gotta do this, we've gotta achieve this—when faced with our mortality, the simplest things become the most significant. Kindness. Patience. Gratefulness. And that doozy of all things: forgiveness."

Betsy felt that she was a failure as a mother, in her life she'd been a failure. That she could have done things better. In her auntie's bedroom, Annie started pulling items out of a box of Betsy's memorabilia. Things that had been completely forgotten, things that reminded Betsy of her successes. "The victories that she'd had in her life that she had totally trivialized because the negative things were just taking over her attention. Which is quite common, isn't it?"

8

IN THE BEGINNING
GEORGIA

"Many of us have become accustomed to images of the ark that look like this," says Dr. Georgia Purdom, clicking to a slide showing a cartoon Noah's ark stuffed with smiley animals. "As soon as that wave hits, that ark is *gone*, okay? It's gonna capsize and considering there's animals sticking out of everywhere, it's not gonna be a good thing."

After killing some time in the gift shop looking at books (*The Purpose & Meaning of Life*; *Dinosaurs of Eden*; *God's Word on Gay "Marriage"*), I settled into the Creation Museum's 4D movie/lecture theater to watch Dr. Purdom, a microbiologist with a doctorate in molecular genetics from the Ohio State University, give her second lecture of the day.

Purdom is a very busy person who says things like, "Relaxing or resting is sort of hard for me, I figure I'll do that later when I get to Heaven." Having read years' worth of her blog before I see her lecture, I find her voice familiar: a strident didacticism containing both the martial and the folksy.

"Now, the thing is, the world mocks the ark," she continues, looking out at the audience from under the convex curtain of her auburn fringe. "Many say it's just a story. We help the world when we show them pictures of the ark like this. Like, no wonder they make fun of us, right?

"We know exactly how big the ark was from Scripture. The length was to be three hundred cubits, the width fifty cubits, and the height thirty cubits. A lot of large-scale ancient construction projects used a cubit of 20.4 inches, that's what we used for Ark Encounter. It's sometimes known as the Hebrew long cubit," she adds casually. "That's about a football field and a half long. It's about two school buses wide, and it's about three giraffes stacked. Its volume is equivalent to about five hundred semitrailers. So whatever you can fit in five hundred of those, you could fit in the ark," she continues. "Now, it's not as big as the *Titanic* or the *Queen Mary II*. But remember those are steel boats and leisure cruisers. Noah didn't need a golf course, okay? What Noah needed was a cargo ship and that's exactly what he had.

"Of course it's perfect, right? Because God designed it, and He knew exactly what the dimensions should be."

Perfect is a word I hear a lot at the museum. It's a word I love (or so my self-punitive interior monologue would suggest) but which I am teaching the larger part of myself to hate. Perfectionism is a lie that brings us the opposite of the protection we crave.

"Almost without fail in our modern culture, the ark is shown as fairytale-like . . ." Purdom continues. This is a problem, she says, because it promotes the idea that the flood was fiction. "The fact is that Satan is saying, 'If I can convince you that the flood was not real, then I can convince you that Heaven and Hell are not real.' That's what Satan does throughout time, right? Is to get people to question God's word. So that's why it's so important that we portray the ark accurately, especially to our children."

To sit in this lecture is to experience a great untethering from what Hannah Arendt called "the human world." By this she meant a shared world of stable processes, laws and institutions which create the conditions for social negotiations and the pursuit of common goals in an environment that values human diversity.

In Arendt's words: "The more peoples there are in the world who stand in some particular relationship with one another, the more world there is to form between them, and the larger and richer that world will be." Because of this emphasis on plurality, the human world is polyphonic, inherently conflicted; confusing, even. Less immediately satisfying in these respects than tidier "pseudo worlds," which offer synthetic, ideologically consistent ways of being "whose inner coherence defies all factual evidence." Beware the perfect is, therefore, the lesson of the human world. As in the natural world, we tolerate violence towards its ecosystem at our own risk.

"Now, what animals do you think I get asked about most when it comes to the ark?" Purdom is saying.

"Dinosaurs," intones a dutiful chorus. My fellow audience members, who remain gravely attentive, largely comprise what I have started to think of as The Demographic: white heterosexual retirees in pairs and young white heterosexual couples with little children.

"And I say: 'Of course!' Because it says: *Every living thing of all flesh, animals after their kind will come to you to keep them alive*. So there's no doubt that they were on the ark."

The Titanosaur. That's what this reminds me of. A dinosaur so grandiose in its construction that it could not stand up once it fell. An arrangement of facts so contingent that one misstep was death. And I am on edge in this audience as though I'd just seen a spider at the edge of my vision; a reflexive fear of certain forms.

We may be the only animals who can think about our thinking, but that doesn't mean we can be relied on to do it particularly well. The only discomfort we tolerate worse than not knowing is knowing. A cognitive bias is a pattern of deviation from rational judgment and the list of our deviations is long. No one is exempt.

We privilege information that confirms our preconceptions (confirmation bias), react to disconfirming evidence by strengthening our pre-existing beliefs (backfire effect), ignore the obvious (ostrich effect). We prefer consensus to critical evaluation (conformity bias), refuse to mentally metabolize that which has not yet happened to us (normalcy bias). We assume the world is fundamentally just and rationalize injustice as something the victim deserved (attribution bias) but we become more sympathetic as our similarity to the victim increases, the pain of others flashing past us and into the distance like a siren in the night (egocentric bias). And all while thinking that we alone see reality as it is, unbiased and objective.

Reality is a shelter that we continuously augment with distraction and deception, insistence and belief. This landed us on the moon but it could kill us before our time.

In 1963, Arendt wrote about how evil is so much more mundane, more banal than she had assumed, and therefore all the more fearsome. This was after recognizing Adolf Eichmann's "quite authentic inability to think." It is thinking—in the specific sense of an honest interior conversation that tries to distinguish between right and wrong, both factually and morally—that anchors the human world.

Arendt speaks of the willingness to hold these inward inter-rogations as the disposition to live with oneself. If we can't be trusted to live with ourselves, we can't be trusted to live together, as James Baldwin—writing about racism in America—told us in 1962. This is because the roiling discomfort that lies beneath this type of inner willful blindness too easily gets redirected as external violence. "It is this individual uncertainty on the part of white American men and women, this inability to renew themselves at the fountain of their own lives, that makes the discussion, let alone elucidation, of any conundrum—that is, any reality—so supremely difficult," Baldwin wrote. "The per-son who distrusts himself has no touchstone for reality—for this touchstone can be only oneself."

•

"Some people have problems with: how could animals that size fit on the ark?" Georgia Purdom says. "I hate to break this to you, but the ones they show on *Jurassic Park*? That's *Hollywood's* version. Most dinosaurs are not that big. In fact, the average size of a dinosaur is a buffalo, okay? So we're talking cow-size, right? Really not that big. It's not an issue. And probably it was the older dinosaurs that they show in *Jurassic Park*. Noah needed to take juvenile dinosaurs. That makes the most sense, because they had the longest reproductive life after the flood. Even dinosaurs start small, okay?

"And some people say, 'What did T. rex eat?' Well," she sighs, "again, this is about *survival*, this is not about *leisure*. Some animals can survive on vegetarian diets for a certain period of time. The other possibility is that Noah took dried meat for carnivorous dinosaurs. But I tend to think it's more that they just survive on a vegetarian diet . . ."

9

PARANORMAL
VLAD

At the end of the dark hallway, Lee stands on the threshold of a small room, enthusiastically explaining how he was physically pushed out of it moments ago by an invisible entity with a touch that felt like a hand on his skin.

I walk into the room, which is oddly shaped and brightly lit. It contains nothing much—a table, a mirror. Standing there, I feel a coldness on one side of my face, my neck, my arm. Not a cold wind, just . . . cold. I look around for an air vent, find none. Besides that, nothing remarkable.

Just outside the door, two participants, both self-described mediums, chat like they're waiting for the bathroom at a party. One explains that she senses the spirit of a large, bossy lady. Perhaps the madam of a brothel that may have operated on the premises. Also some barrels, potentially of beer. Lee heads off to get something from his bag in the Bayview Room. Others wander over. Snatches of conversation float into the room:

"I found myself in bed, *behind* my sleeping body . . ."

"Is that like astral traveling?"

"Sort of, but I didn't go anywhere. When I went back into my body, it was just like a cold lump of meat. I thought, 'Now I understand why people don't want to come back.'"

"There's more to it than this. The whole world doesn't exist for us to live and die . . ."

Vlad is inspecting the evenness of the floor in this, the oldest part of the building. He notes the potential neurophysiological impact of the physical environment: how even subtle changes in the gradient of the floor can contribute to a perception that something is not quite right. "Walk down that hallway," he says when I join him outside the room, "and tell me if your feelings change." I tell him I did that just before and felt extremely nauseous.

"Yeah?" He nods with interest. "At what point?"

I gesture towards the spot, and he heads over, EMF reader extended before him.

Nearby, the mediums start discussing an image they are getting of a young girl. Vlad, returning, asks if they have a sense of what her name is.

"Something like Annabelle or Mary Belle . . ." one replies.

The other chimes in: "She keeps saying something like, 'I had no choice in the matter . . .'"

The first one nods. "And it's like she just gave up on life."

"And you're feeling that here?" Vlad asks, a wrinkle like a hinge appearing between his eyebrows.

Lee returns to the threshold of the small room holding a thin reed of bent metal in each fist.

"Cool." One of the mediums nods approvingly.

"I've been doing these since the nineties," Lee explains. He turns and walks very slowly into the small room, concentrating in an effort to keep the rods evenly aligned in their cylindrical metal handles. "Cross for yes, open for no," he instructs the ether, his hands visibly shaking. "If there's anyone in this room who'd like to talk to us, it's cross for yes, open for no."

The rods cross.

"Okay, ah . . ." His voice is tighter now and slightly breathless. "Are you the one who pushed me out of the room before?"

The rods cross again.

"Can you point with the rods where you are right now?"

Both rods swing to the side of the room where I felt the cold.

"So you're over in that corner," he says. And then to the rods: "Okay, you can go back to normal now." The rods straighten out. He swallows with visible effort. "All right. I'm not feeling very good now, do you want me out?"

The rods cross.

"That's a strong yes."

The mediums laugh.

"I want you to push me out," Lee says with an excitement that borders on the erotic.

Nothing happens, which feels just.

I ask Brett whether, if this is indeed the room of a traumatized ghost, there might be a more respectful manner of interacting. He replies yes, but that the entity would be so damaged they would not be able to appreciate it, being trapped between the desire to be left alone and the desire to be in control.

Rob Tilley enters the room as Lee exits. "What's going on here, gang?" he says.

"She didn't want me here," Lee says dolefully. "She just didn't want me."

"Female, is it?" Rob booms.

"Yeah," Lee says. "Didn't like me."

"Well, a girl was raped in here, so …" says one of the mediums.

I ask about the rods, and Lee lets me hold them.

"I can't control them, I cannot control them," he says. "I've had them dancing to music, and I've told them to stop and they've *stopped*. I've had them in really, really strong wind at a cemetery and I've said, 'Move the rods to where you are' and they went against the wind. Strong wind. I could not believe where it was going."

"Does it need you to hold them?" Vlad asks. "Like, could you put them on a tripod?"

"I dunno," Lee replies. "I've never done it."

"I suppose it's like the glass, isn't it, when you're doing a séance," says one of the mediums.

"Or table tipping," Vlad offers, explaining for my benefit how people sit around a loose tabletop, placing their hands on it lightly to feel but not influence its movement. "That's interesting, I've felt it. When it moves by itself … it's different. It glides. I've only experienced very subtle sensations but it is … unusual."

I have a sudden memory of sitting on the floor of my bedroom across a ouija board from a friend, arguing about who moved the planchette, both of us certain that we hadn't. Scientists call this the ideomotor response—a phenomenon where thoughts, beliefs or expectations influence muscular movement without perceived conscious control. An illusion of self-stillness, of passivity.

"So, did we find anything?" Vlad asks as we all reconvene in the Bayview Room.

"There was some energies around, nothing that would cause any drama," says Johann. A young man describes his throat going ever so slightly dry. A woman reports that she felt nauseous in the hallway, the same spot where it hit me. Lee recounts his experience of being pushed out of the small room and one of the mediums says she picked up that someone had been locked in there, assaulted, then let out as though nothing had happened. A silence settles over the table.

Though the information is freely available on the internet, the organizer does the big reveal of the stories associated with the building. A suicide in the 1800s. A rumor that someone died in a brawl. The story of Tilly, said to have been raped and murdered on the premises in the 1840s, her body dragged through a tunnel running between the building and the shore. Tilly, the staff say, is merely mischievous with the ladies but hates the men.

Sometimes, if I am not careful, I miss what people are saying because I am watching their faces, their hands, their habits. Not just singly: a group of people is like a person itself, though any two members are as different as their DNA. This is in my mind as I watch the mediums talk shop, referring casually to poltergeists and attachments and dragons as though they were doctors comparing patients.

This, for me, is the extreme weather in the room. And it comes from people with puffy jackets and car keys in pockets and illuminated photos of children or partners or pets on finger-smeared iPhone screens, with laundry to do and money worries and tremulous wonder at how fast this year is passing, how is it May already?

They chat about tomorrow's conference sessions and the night is about to end when I say it. I'm not sure why.

Earlier, I had felt strong disgust when Lee demanded to be physically pushed out of a room in which he understood himself to be unwelcome, but I hadn't seen anything the others purported to see, hadn't been scared, in that hallway, of anything all that specific. Maybe it has something to do with the simple fact that our bodies are here and will be gone—same as those who gathered for the wake 180 minutes ago and those who drank and laughed and fought here 180 years ago. No wonder, then, the urge to see their faces slipping past the windows, to hear their voices in our ears, feel their hands brushing our skin. I am trying to explain that I think I say it more for us than for them. At any rate, it comes out awkwardly in a voice too small: "Should we do . . . like . . . a cleansing . . . a closing . . . Whatever the opposite meditation is to the one we started with?"

Rob emits a big chuckle, and I understand that he is not mocking me, the only admitted non-psychic in the group, but rather showing some measure of pride at my efforts. There is general agreement and it is entrusted to Brett to end the night with a closing meditation.

"First off, we should say thank you to these spirits here that we tested somewhat, a couple of whom really didn't want us around," he says. "I'd like every person to give themselves a shower of light: imagine light sweeping and washing away any dark energies."

Even purely as a cognitive exercise, this is valuable. I imagine next, as instructed, a psychic sieve going through my body, filtering out any energies that are not mine. It feels like a yoga class. Just people, together, more united by our physiology than divided by our varying credulities and doubts.

"And then finally," Brett continues as I soften into my breath, "imagine that powerful light of Christ energy coming down . . ."

As the only Jew in the Christ-lit circle on a night that had previously lacked religious overtones, I want to ask why the energy is Jesus-specific but after someone says, "Good work!" the circle applauds and the group swiftly dissipates.

Before I head out to the parking lot, I speak to the manager downstairs, a tidy man with snow-white hair who looks to be in his sixties. Sitting in the now-empty bistro he explains that two weeks ago he went up to the second floor to get some papers. "I honestly felt something," he says. "There was no one there but someone touched me. I came down and made a joke about it, but something did touch me."

"Would you go up there alone now?" I ask.

"No. No no no no no no," he replies, unsmiling. "Anything I have to do up there, I get done before six o'clock."

I get into my car and plug in my phone to map my way home. It fails to connect. I try to call home but, for the first time in the life of this phone and this car, hands-free doesn't work. I try to play music from the phone itself, but the speaker doesn't work. I capitulate and turn the car radio on instead. The radio doesn't work. For reasons I do not articulate to myself I urgently open the windows of the car and let the passing world stream in.

10

THE DEATH DOULA
ANNIE

Having died once already, Annie feels that she knows a little about what it will be like when it happens for good. She was in her mid-twenties, drowning in pains both physical and emotional, and she swallowed too many pills. Ended up in the intensive care unit, where she was informed that she had been dead for about three minutes. Forty years later she remembers how she looked down at herself lying in the hospital bed as doctors and nurses raced to resuscitate her. Their frenzied, shouted orders did not disturb her sense of peace, although she felt some dismay at what they were doing to the body down on the bed, thinking, "Leave her alone!"

"It was only years later that I realized, of course, that wasn't my body up there, that was just my consciousness," she explains. "I'm just a wisp. I'm nothing. I wasn't aware of the ceiling or walls. All I know is I felt so at peace."

I think of Annie weightless at a great height, hovering near the ceiling like steam from a kettle. I think about how Milan Kundera wrote that anyone who aims at something higher must expect some day to suffer vertigo. Which, he explained, was not fear of falling but rather the voice of the emptiness below tempting us: "It is the desire to fall, against which, terrified, we defend ourselves."

Suddenly, Annie found herself returned to her body in a hospital bed on a floor of what, for a time, was the tallest building in Melbourne. Sealed once more inside her terrestrial casing, her mother next to her wailing rhetorically, How could you do this to me!

You're a very lucky girl, the doctor told her. You died. Do you realize that?

Yes, she thought. Yes. That was the whole idea.

He asked if she would return to speak about it, this dying, to the staff. But she didn't. Couldn't put this experience into words. She was part of the walls, part of the ceiling, it was such a long way away and she just felt so . . . at peace.

Looking back at this time from the other side of her life, Annie feels no less wondrous, and what she wants me to know is this: during those moments in which she remembers looking at herself, she was almost entirely disembodied. Untethered not only from her physical form, but even from an individualized consciousness. There was barely any "she" that existed separately from the "we" that constitutes the greater sum of energy in the universe.

They call it emptiness and it's fascinated Annie for the thirty years of her Buddhist practice.

"It's the true nature," she explains. Free of all the encumbrances put upon us by ourselves and our social structures. "*Shunyata* it's called, it's the thing we meditate on. It's about impermanence—how everything will diminish and eventually disintegrate. You will. I will. The dogs will." I take a long look at the dogs, two of whom will be dead within the year, now snoozing on the floor. "Our clothes will, the mountains will. Everything."

When Annie speaks she uses her hands freely and the shapes they make emphasize both the words she says and the ones she leaves unsaid. Sometimes they form fans, fingers radiating into the room. Other times, one hand might undulate gently in the space immediately before her like the ocean calming. To make a point she touches her ring finger to her thumb, and to make a bigger point she curves both hands into Cs as though holding a beach ball in front of her face. My favorite gesture, though, is when she is detailing something that almost escapes language. In these moments she cups her palms together as though cradling a baby bird.

"That helped me in so many ways, understanding that nothing is fixed or permanent. And it also helped in all my marriages." She laughs loudly and then her voice softens. "I used to think, 'Ah, love . . .' I really wanted to have love in my life and I realized that it's so conditional. So, yeah. That was a good teacher."

Annie is a woman of unnerving enthusiasms and when I hear her reverently call someone or something "a great teacher," my blood runs cold. Physical pain is "a great teacher": the lesson is to find comfort in discomfort. Death is "a great teacher": the lesson is impermanence. Josef Fritzl, who raped his daughter and imprisoned her and their seven children in his basement for twenty-four years—"another great teacher."

At first, I think the lesson is about injustice, but listening to Annie that's not quite right.

"That was the most horrific thing," Annie says. "I had to learn to forgive him." The bridge to forgiveness, she explains, is to understand that a person was not capable of behaving in any other way because of their own circumstances, locked in their own subjectivity. And this is the world as it is.

"In Buddhism, there's a thing called *Tonglen*. It's not recommended for the weak of heart. It's strong," she says. "Strong" is another word which makes me internally wince when Annie drops it into conversation.

"People think, 'Oh yeah, Buddhism is about loving everyone, being compassionate, helping everyone.' It's so much more than that. When you actually practice it, it's tough. It's easy to be nice to the people who are nice to you. You try being nice to the people who are horrible to you."

Her first husband was "such a great, great teacher." Though she found it uncomfortable at first, it has now become normal for her to spend Christmas each year with him and their grown sons, his current wife and the grandchildren.

"And so, *Tonglen*—there's various ways you can do it. One thing is that I see you and your suffering. Okay. So I'm with you. Perhaps we're talking. But what I'm doing is I'm inhaling your pain and your suffering. I take it into me. I welcome it into me. And I'm exhaling healing or calm or peace. It's nothing you can verbalize. It's very private.

"But it changes me and hopefully it may have some impact on you. I don't know, the jury's still out on that one but it's my practice to take in your pain and suffering and to wish you well."

Annie was in her twenties when she read her first book on Buddhism. *Grist for the Mill* was written in 1976 by the spiritual teacher and clinical psychologist who was born Richard Alpert to a Jewish family in Massachusetts and who returned from a trip to India as Ram Dass, which means servant of God. This book, which changed Annie's life, was written ten years before Ram Dass opened the Dying Center in New Mexico, the first residential facility in the United States where people came to die consciously. In it he wrote that faith is a journey "that has taken us from primary identification with our body and our psyche, on to an identification with God, and ultimately beyond identification."

This intrigued Annie, and when Annie gets intrigued she goes all the way. So, perhaps inevitably, she got into Tibetan Buddhism, "because it's so in your face." She loved how it was deeply confronting. When she tells me this, I think of something I once read about bones. Bone reacts to its environment in one of two ways: by removing some of itself or by creating more of itself. In every home she had ever known, Annie was diminished, erased or expendable. There was something, I think, in this school of thought—new to her—that said that she could find presence in absence, ground in groundlessness; that she could hold on to the thought of being attached to nothing. Somewhere in those pages lay an inviolable security, something that could not be taken away from her and burnt in a furnace.

Throughout her thirties, in her reading—which was, and remains, voracious—and in her yoga practice—which progressed swiftly to the level of teaching—Annie was becoming better at finding comfort in discomfort. Practicing the counterintuitive art of moving towards the things that scared her so they became known: "maybe a not-so-close friend." There was a story she read once about two men installing forty-foot telephone poles and the younger one, the apprentice, joked that if the thing started to lean he'd be off running. No, his older colleague replied, the safest direction would be closest to the pole; if you've got your hands on it, you know where it's going.

The Buddhist approach, she was learning, was not merely to acknowledge suffering and loss. It was to be well with it. To accept that suffering—both the cruel infliction of it and the painful experience of it—comes about because we exist physically in arrangements of bodily senses, trapped inside our subjective perception. "Buddhism," she says, "taught me that it's not about me."

When asked about self-care, Annie waves the question away. Says she is elevated rather than depleted by the nature of her work. When pressed on the point, however, she mentions her books and meditation practice, her various pets and the family members in her life. She adds: "I've also got this monk that I care for. He has health issues and I take him to his appointments. So that's great."

This monk is a "spiritual architect for the Dalai Lama"; a senior Gyuto monk without a monastery named Thubten Khedup, whom Annie refers to deferentially as Khedup La. Having come to Australia to help with the building of the Great Stupa of Universal Compassion in Bendigo, he currently serves as a ritual master for the Tibetan Buddhist Community.

When she was younger, Annie studied with a variety of revered monks, some of whom are still around while others are dead or diminished by accusations of sex with their students.

She took what she could use, left the rest. So while she never accepted any of them as her leader, including the one on whose door we are currently knocking, she considers herself closest to him. She has housed him for the past ten years and has put something aside for his care in her will should she predecease him. Friends jokingly refer to Khedup as Annie's husband and Khedup jokingly refers to Annie as Mom.

Khedup's living quarters are clean and cozy with a spacious adjacent room that he keeps as a temple. To take off your shoes and walk into that sacred space is to pass from a suburban apartment into another dimension. It is perfectly silent and spacious, radiantly colorful. The floor is where Khedup sits on a navy cushion, alone or leading students, in meditation and prayer.

"I can discuss things with him about certain issues," Annie once explained. "And he says, 'Pshh, don't worry about that one, it's not important.'" I try to imagine how reassuring this would be, to have authoritative spiritual advice on tap from a senior religious official in a deeply felt religion of one's choosing. I don't succeed, lacking the requisite respect for authority, but it strikes me that this dynamic sounds very much like the deepest comfort offered by simple friendship.

In six months' time Khedup will chant the prayers over Annie's dog Bob, lying wrapped in a blanket on her kitchen table. Now, however, he declines Annie's suggestion that Lady might enter with us, and she takes the diapered dog back across the small yard to her living room. I chat with Khedup about his childhood in Sikkim, where his parents, Tibetan refugees, worked breaking stones. And about the teachings he has been studying since he entered the monastery in Dharamshala as a boy.

Suffering exists. Suffering has a cause (the unrestrained mind). Suffering has an end. Suffering has a cause to bring about its end (ways of seeing past the conditioned nature of our reactions). Your mind is your greatest teacher, he says, your mind is your best friend, everything is solved in the mind. Just as we all have egos—which are responsible for our drives towards pleasure and away from pain—we also all have the seeds of something else inside us.

"Remove the 'I' and all good things are coming," he continues, flexing his feet inside his cherry-red socks. "Good practice requires you to lose yourself. Lose your pride, your money, your certainty. Only then can the mind training work."

Khedup enjoys creating mandalas from colored sand, cosmograms representing the world in perfect harmony. Traditionally, monks work together for weeks, moving grains of sand across tiny distances to build the intricate detail of the geometric Sublime, before ceremonially reducing the whole thing back into its constituent parts to demonstrate the relationship between possibility and impermanence.

Khedup stands up, wants to show me something. Reaches towards the ceiling, takes a large framed image from the wall. A beautiful mandala he made. The grains stuck to the paper with glue, sealed behind glass. He points to his name written in the bottom left-hand corner, gestures for me to take a photo.

Annie once told me about the day Khedup's mom died. How, in relaying this news, he had said to her, with some measure of surprise after a lifetime of training in nonattachment, "I cried."

"You're human, you know," Annie told him. "Welcome."

•

I am boarding a plane when Annie texts me photos of the suicide notes from her second attempt twenty years ago. They were written late at night during a period of deep depression, after a day with her mother. Blue pen on unlined white paper. There is one letter each for her mother, her children, her grandchildren and her boyfriend at the time, and one page entitled *My Wishes*. The fact that we have taken off and I am unable to text Annie back after I realize what they are, dovetails with the fact that I do not yet know what to say about them. And both of those things make me deeply anxious as the plane lifts above the clouds. I am grateful that she shared them with me. Their intimacy reveals much about her state at that time, and makes her deeply vulnerable still.

Beyond that, I do not know what I am feeling. Except that they remind me of a dream I once had. I was on one small planet in space, a rock really, like in *The Little Prince*. My mother was on another such planet. And that's all there was in the universe. Longing and distance and the impossibility of bridging it. Such a spare dream. In direct contrast, the panicked grief it made me feel—in the primal sense of frantic psychic pain rather than a more refined cognition of loss—was overwhelming then, and is overwhelming still.

Later, Annie will explain her reaction on rediscovering what she had written. "I went into that black hole, I embraced it, did backstrokes," she will say. "My gosh, look at that, I thought I had everything under control. Powerful lesson for me."

The notes do bring to mind a black hole—what is left when a star of certain mass burns through its fuel and there is no remaining force sufficiently strong to resist the inward influence of its own gravity. But gravitational collapse is also the primary means of structure formation in the universe.

Now I can say that the sadness of the notes is not that Annie forgot the lesson of thirty years of study: the fact that everything changes is the knife of the world but also its gift. Our brains, favoring certainty, seem built to forget even that; especially that.

The sadness of the notes is that there was no one there to remind her when she could not remind herself.

11

IN THE BEGINNING
GEORGIA

From her blog on the Answers in Genesis website, I know that Georgia Purdom is thrifty (makes homemade gifts) and a good planner (Christmas shopping done before December). She is a big fan of "fictional Christian romance/mystery/action novels" generally and *Deadly Disclosures* by Julie Cave specifically. She used to attend a church near Henpeck, Ohio; she and her husband honeymooned in Tennessee; they adopted their daughter, whom Purdom homeschools, from China. She has suffered from progressive hearing loss since high school and now wears a cochlear implant which aids her greatly, though imperfectly. And she describes herself as "inherently impatient," a good multitasker, a "type-A personality."

I wait for Purdom in the lobby of the Creation Museum, watching turtles swimming through the water churned by the waterfall, an artificial system sufficiently supported to approximate the real thing. She materializes from a doorway that leads into a rabbit warren of the Answers in Genesis workplace, through which she ushers me to her windowless office.

"It's definitely put me in a unique position," she replies to my question about her experience as the only female scientist on staff. "It gives me a way to minister to people that maybe before would have been difficult with a male speaker." The answer succinctly demonstrates the difference between "scientist" and "creation scientist."

"There isn't really a lot out there—or at least in Christendom—that is apologetics specifically focused on women," she says. "And because most women are mothers, or taking care of children in some capacity, I think it's really important that they know how to defend their faith so that they can teach that to their children."

Purdom is the Ministry's "content administrator" and she sits on its editorial review board. She was the only woman in her graduating class to complete a PhD, and the only female biology professor at the Christian college where she taught. In her blog she has written, *I am one of the very few female creation scientists and the only one in the US who I am aware of speaking and researching on creation full-time.*

Given this, I ask whether she would describe herself as a feminist.

"No-o-o," she intones, her voice falling then rising in the way one might warn a dog away from the trash. "If you mean, like, what feminists want, which is usually pro-choice as far as abortion goes.

"In our culture there seems to be a lot of . . ." She pauses for a moment. "People wanting *sameness*. Not equality—just everybody being the same. And I don't understand that from a Christian perspective because God made both man and woman in His image and they display that image differently and that's a *good thing*. That's a design thing. I'm for what Scripture says, not for what the feminists say because they're thinking apart from Scripture."

Here in the room with Purdom's coffee machine and her jar of healthy nuts and her daughter's finger-painting and her framed degree and her map of the Galapagos Islands: "Christendom," "apologetics," "defending the faith." On her blog: the importance of *wifely submission*, a critique of the ads during the Super Bowl that *mocked God's design* by positively portraying *homosexuality, bestiality, and alcohol consumption*. Out in the lobby, the plaques pitting *God's Word* against *Human Reason*. Burning words. Time machines. Terrifying, to hear them rolled out casually in conversation with cubicles and calendars and coffee mugs all around.

Purdom grew up in a "very strong Christian home" where she knew from a young age that she wanted to be some sort of scientist or doctor. At university she was drawn to microbiology.

"I really liked studying DNA because, to me, DNA is the level where everything *happens*." She explains that her goal in getting her doctorate was to go into teaching rather than research, her lab experience being isolating and difficult to balance with her family commitments. So she taught for six years at a small Christian college and it was there that she saw some students trying to reconcile what they had been raised to believe with what they were learning.

"I really saw a lot of Christians struggling with creation versus evolution and what was true. I'd always believed what the Bible said, hadn't doubted it even though at Ohio State obviously they were gonna teach evolution and all of that. I was like, 'Okay, I'm a molecular geneticist studying DNA and these amazingly complicated genetic structures and there's no way this came about by chance. There's just no way. It had to have been design.' That was never a question for me."

The issue that she did struggle with, however, was the age of the earth. Not being an expert in geology, she didn't know whether to trust "conventional" dating methods, didn't know how to reply when her students asked her about it. "I didn't have a strong apologetics, so to speak," she explains.

"One of my verses is First Peter 3:15, to *be ready to give a defense and answer for the hope that is in you*. And I didn't have that as strongly as I wanted it to be, so I started researching, really looking for those answers."

There were "two big pivotal points" in resolving her struggle. The first was coming to genuinely believe that the six days of creation described in Genesis referred to literal twenty-four-hour days. She explains to me that this was on account of how the Hebrew word for day, *yom*, was used in a specific context—"with morning, evening and a number." This put to rest her uncertainty regarding the age of the earth.

"The biggest thing, though, was the death before sin issue," she says. "If God used evolution over millions of years, then there would be millions of years of death and suffering *before* Adam and Eve came into existence to sin."

On this logic, rather than being a punishment for sin, death was around before sin.

"Theologically, that's totally inconsistent with the Bible. And so that was like a big lightbulb that went on in my head. I thought, 'I never thought about that before!' And it's *plain*, it's in *Scripture*, it's not rocket science."

12

PARANORMAL

ROB

At the Abbotsford Convent it is a morning cold enough for gloves, which I wish I brought as I cross the lawn. One of the oldest Catholic institutional complexes in Victoria, the building has a history dating back to the 1860s of providing food and shelter to those in need. People love the Convent. There are festivals and farmers' markets here, barista coffee and baked goods to enjoy on the lawn, studio space for rent.

I have never liked it here. Always found it deeply unsettling, even before I learned about the history of its Magdalen Asylum and Laundries: "two hundred penitents . . . rescued from lives of sin by the good sisters." Young girls laboring in silence, excluded from the education offered to other children on the premises, whom they could hear as they worked too-long hours for no pay, their hands cracked red and raw. Today's Ghostbusting workshop—led by Rob Tilley (*Poltergeist disturbances and hauntings—how to clear the space*)—will be held in the Linen Room.

I recognize Lee (of the divining rods), Misha/Amber and two of the women who were on the haunting excursion. After Rob urges us to pull our chairs in a circle, one of the women pulls out a notebook on which is printed, *Believe that you can and you're halfway there.*

•

Recently retired from his day job running a business that repaired nursing-home equipment, Rob has cleared haunted houses for thirty years. On this morning he has an ear infection that has affected his ability to hear but left his attentiveness and good cheer undented.

"Has anyone done a haunted house job before?" he starts off, perched majestically on a plastic chair, looking both crisp and rugged in tan jeans, a chambray shirt over a white T-shirt and shiny brown boots.

"Well, we *think* we did," Lee replies tentatively. The client never called back to confirm whether he and his colleague were successful in their use of sage in and around "a portal" found in her home.

"Sage, is it?" Rob says, loudly.

Lee explains that they had asked the light to take the particular spirit away, then suddenly a window made a sound like it was cracking although he could see no evidence that it had. "Maybe it tried to get out," he shrugs. "But we didn't have any feedback so I don't know if we cleared it or not."

One of the women, a professional psychic, explains how she went to help someone who had seen a shadowy figure in her home. There, she connected with a male spirit in the bathroom whom she understood to be distraught over losing contact with his child. She believed he had died by suicide.

"How did you actually clear that?" Rob inquires, turning to-wards her with interest. "Did you get the good spooks to come in?"

She replies that in this instance she communicated directly with the spirit, persuading him to go towards the light, but that she occasionally calls on angels "who basically just manhandle the entity," taking them to "the lower realms" if they can't be convinced to go upward.

"And it was completely successful?" Rob asks.

"Yeah," she replies, with the caveat that there was some-thing about the people in that house, how they held their energy, that was attracting the problem so it won't be a per-manent fix. Satisfied, Rob starts his session in earnest.

"If you're gonna have contact with spooks," he says, looking around the circle with his sharp blue eyes, "just have contact with good spooks. Be absolutely clear about that in your own mind.

"If you're gonna clear haunted houses, good spooks won't work with you unless you're a good person. Be clear in your mind that you're in the world to increase the amount of good in it and you have a duty of care obligation to always act in the best interests of anyone who asks you for help."

He doesn't know who these good spooks are, their names or their faces. Just recognizes their energy. It feels like a good presence when they arrive. There's one behind him now, he says, with its hands on his shoulders. "It's all very subtle, it's energy, it's feelings," he explains. "You feel what's about to happen next and the emotion contains the message."

This is what my grandparents told me when I was a child: be-fore Mrs. Peters died she beseeched her son not to sell the house. Then she died, and he did. This was said not to frighten me, but more in the spirit of background information. The tone that was used to tell me about the importance of applying myself at school or the cancer-fighting properties of vegetables was also used to tell me about the time the lights went off in the middle of their Sabbath dinner and how, in that engulfing darkness, the candlesticks were suddenly swept off the table and onto the floor. Or about entering the kitchen one morning to find that all their crockery had inexplicably swapped cupboards. Or about how they sat alone in the kitchen listening to the repeated sounds on the floor above—*thud, step, step*—which was clearly Mrs. Peters, who had required a cane to walk. Or about peering into the kitchen window from outside to see the gauze-like apparition of Mrs. Peters sitting in the rocking chair, a large Bible open on her lap, as had been her custom each morning. Or about waking up in the middle of the night and feeling the weight of her on the bed in the room in which I sometimes slept.

They told me about the pond on the property everyone still referred to as the ice pond, where slabs of ice had once been cut in winter, hoisted onto carts and stored in the nearby ice house. They told me about a woman who, not so long ago, had taken a stroll to that pond and reported feeling hands tightening around her neck, though no one else was there.

These were not appropriate things to share with a child. But they weren't trying to frighten me. Had they wanted to do that, they would have been less cautious with how they spoke about the war: the real ghosts all around us.

"There's memory stored in things," Rob is saying. The first thing he notices when he walks into a room is an energy in the space that he identifies as place memory. "There's memory in body tissue, in bricks and mortar, in keys . . ."

It's cold in the Linen Room. I have not removed my coat. Through the windows, out towards the river, the aspect of gray branches undulates slightly behind the hand-blown glass, largely unchanged since the laundry girls moved in and out of this room, pausing in their work if only for a breath.

Rob did not set out in his life intending to clear houses. He volunteered to give it a go in response to a request for help that had come through the Australian Institute of Parapsychological Research (AIPR), of which he was already a member. To gain the requisite skills, he apprenticed himself to a few older house clearers in the field. He felt that while he had much to learn he was finally on the path revealed to him as a boy when, walking home from school, he was stopped in a park by a spirit who told him that his nascent psychic abilities were extremely important and would be his life's work. He considers himself chosen in this respect. He has only ever found this work extremely interesting and has never had anything he considers to be a particularly bad experience.

Once, after he mentioned that he was seeing some bad spooks in the room we were in, I asked Rob whether he found that frightening.

"What? A couple of bad characters?" he replied, dismissively. "You get that all the time. They move around. They blow in, they go to your house, if they can't get a reaction out of you, they go find somebody else."

"Much like people in that sense," I offered.

"They're just dead people," he said. "Easiest way to think of them. Bad people, narcissistic, they like to control you, frighten you. That's what they get their kicks out of. If you don't respond, they move on."

Rob will travel interstate for certain jobs but he does not like to fly, prefers to drive. An average house clearing takes around two hours. He charges a hundred and fifty dollars for a job. If the client can't afford it, he will work for free. He does not advertise, is largely uninterested in self-promotion. Clients find him through the AIPR website. "Most of our members are PhD psychologists, work in humanities," he says. "The website looks very businesslike. I think it's the only website in the paranormal community that isn't black." He chuckles. "It looks very sober. Most of the people are finding it scary enough—what they're experiencing, who to trust, who to feel safe with."

Although he is the only member at large in the physical world, Rob considers himself part of a team. "I answer the phone and talk to people, do emails and that. I don't get involved in who the bad spooks are or what their problems are. I leave that to the good spooks because they're much better at it than I am . . .

"I score very poor on persuasive skill, I learned that from doing psychology tests. So I'm not good at persuading people. The good spooks know how to do that . . .

"They always have the situation under control. They're far more intelligent, they arrive in sufficient numbers, they've got overwhelming superiority and they get on with it."

Still, it's isolating work. Most of his close friends or family are not psychic. He was mocked when he shared his abilities with schoolmates, couldn't talk to his parents about it.

"It's a lonely business," he says. "But it's very, very interesting and it just comes into my life all the time. So I got used to it, it's just part of my day."

It's like no other conference workshop I've attended, Rob's teaching style being anecdotal in a way that seems only incidentally didactic. In full flight, it's like he's just hanging out at the pub, one-upping himself with tall tales that also happen to be the reality of his professional experience. About ghost children drawing with crayons, leaving little teeth marks on chocolate left out for them. A house invaded by "non-physical animals"; a gryphon-like entity nesting in the child's bedroom, emitting a strong odor when scared. A Catholic woman levitated and assaulted by demons in her home. A long-haul trucker who chose his profession so as not to contaminate the home where his wife and children lived with the demonic entity that had followed him since childhood; how it would occasionally grab the steering wheel of his semitrailer out of his hands.

We hear about a South American woman's incubus. "She loves the sex but she's also frightened by it," says Rob, explaining with some annoyance that he cleared the house but to no avail. "Silly bitch, she can't say no to the sex and then she rings up and says, 'Can you come and rescue me again?' She met some psychic woman who told her the way to stop it was to take all her clothes and throw them into the ocean after the seventh wave." He shakes his head. "Nuts. Just stupid. You can't help those that won't help themselves."

The most recent job he did was about three weeks ago at a house in regional New South Wales where a newborn was found, to the great fright of his mother and great-grandmother, lying on the floor after being inexplicably removed from his stroller.

He discusses a family whose mirrored bathroom would convert into a 1950s hamburger restaurant whenever the teenage daughter would go in there to get ready for school. "She's as psychic as can be," Rob explains with admiration. "I said, 'It's nothing to be afraid of, it's just a psycho-spiritual opening, it's a normal part of life for people like you or me.'" A few days later, the father rang to report it had all stopped after they put towel racks on the mirrored wall.

We hear about scrying, the old practice of peering into something—a mirror or a crystal ball—to receive communications from beyond. Rob explains about the psychiatrist Raymond Moody and his psychomanteum: a small room containing only a chair and a dark mirror for subjects to gaze into in order to make contact with the dead. "Moody said that as a psychiatrist one of the most difficult emotions to deal with is grief," Rob says. The aim was to facilitate a reunion so that the mourner knew their loved one was still, in some sense, present.

"He would have the grieving person talk about the deceased person so they get really emotional—because all the best psychic functioning always has a high emotional content. Then he'd have them go in this psychomanteum room. You sit there, you gaze into the mirror but you can't see your own reflection, so it's like gazing into an open space.

"It's like waiting for a bus; you know sooner or later the bus is going to show up."

•

1988, 1989. A warm day on the slab of old Virginia where my mother's parents lived. My grandmother led me through high weeds into the sky-roofed rooms of a ruined building on the farm known as "the slave house." I remember how she poked at the overgrowth with a branch, the wavy wool of her hair yanked taut into a low ponytail. How shy I felt around her, like the guest I would turn out to have been.

We walked through a gap in the bricks where a door had hung, found a layer of mint carpeting one of the rooms. She triumphantly tore a handful of leaves and munched them like a young goat, green triangles flapping against her lips. I remember the crumbling bricks, their threads of gray cement. A chimney reduced to hearth. Air where there had once been wall. The terror of the fact that whole rooms once there were now gone and of the notion, scarier still because of the casual way in which it was spoken, of a "slave house."

My grandmother standing in the mint would have been able to see the roof of her own house. Perhaps, in the ruins, she saw something of what she left behind as a teenager in Ukraine or Romania or Germany or France. I can't be more specific about the world through her eyes. Information came in grotesque scraps, like the leftovers she could not bear to throw out from her fridge because of the years she had gone hungry. A crumb here, a sliver there.

I was never told where she returned home to the day a boy in her class broke her nose after seeing the yellow star newly sewn on her sweater. I was told, however, that a girl she had been holding hands with was shot while they were running away from something, somewhere. That babies had been buried alive and that they had made the soil move. I knew, too, that her mother had died when she was young, that she believed her stepmother hid her gloves each winter. I knew that she felt she had been the mother to my own mother that she had craved for herself and that my mother had not felt that at all. And I knew, already, from the way I could hold neither my mother's gaze nor her warmth, that I had been born into a line of missing mothers. But I also unknew this. So that when she left—with explanations I did not understand at the time and do not understand now—I did not, at first, believe it. At a loss, perhaps, to account for this and too pained, it would seem, to be reminded of what their daughter left behind, my grandparents thereafter did not reply to letters, hurried off my calls saying only that they loved me, must go, Sarachkoo, goodbye, goodbye.

Decades later, still insisting on some understanding, I will find only crumbs, only slivers. A sound my mother made to soothe me as a baby that I was surprised to hear myself use with my own. My grandmother's Jewish Displaced Person and Refugee Card, an address in Dachau replaced inexplicably with another. Her arrival date in New York Harbor on the *Queen Mary*, that enormous ocean liner's grand return after its storm-colored stint in the war as the Gray Ghost. Her marriage date, remarkably soon after, to my grandfather who was born in the Bronx to a Polish father, an American mother, named, respectively, Abraham and Sarah.

The one room I did not feel scared of at the farm was the kitchen on the ground floor, which doubled as the living room. I remember it as a warm pool of golden light. TV on. My grandfather reading *Time* magazine, red-robed in a rocking chair. My parents giggling at the heavy wooden table where my grandmother turns an apple under a knife, the skin dangling in one continuous pelt. Words are on the air, an entire vocabulary that would disappear overnight; the Yiddish for things, the old jokes, our nicknames. We must live in the warmest rooms of ourselves, and this is one I still visit.

The toilet, however, was one flight up. It required walking into the dark and the possibility of Mrs. Peters' web-drawn body. So I would race there, petrified of resting my eyes anywhere in case they found her. The bathroom was tiny, wallpapered with a forest: silver trees on a neon-green background. In an early nightmare I am in a rowboat, on a lake surrounded by that forest. I am with my mother; we are drinking from my plastic tea set and we are sinking. When I am ten, eleven, that stops and another starts. There's not really a narrative. I'm in the middle of the ocean, treading water. The tip of one toe scrapes something solid and I know it is the bow of a sunken ship, a graveyard; an ocean liner vertical beneath the surface. The sea is an opaque gray. A dark mirror in which I cannot see my reflection.

13

THE DEATH DOULA
ANNIE

Annie is about to speak to students at a course on secular spiritual care for the dying. It's run by Joe Sehee, who started the Secular Spiritual Care Network, now an unaligned charity known as Social Health Australia, based on his experiences as a humanist chaplain at a hospital. This kind of "emotional-existential support" is usually offered to hospital patients according to their religious affiliation. Historically, if you ticked *Not religious* on your admission paperwork, no one would—or even could—offer to come visit you. And, indeed, Sehee will step down from his current patient-support role at the hospital in a few weeks, when the role is confirmed as the exclusive domain of the established religions.

Joe's goal is to make emotional-existential support more accessible. Towards that end, he would like to build a community of secular compassionate carers who can provide support to those with different, or no, belief systems. We do not currently have a bureaucratic vocabulary for this idea, but it is essential for our wellbeing and its further development is why fifteen people are sitting in a semicircle inside a cosy outbuilding of the Habitat Uniting Church on this brisk morning.

Aside from Annie and Joe, they include death doulas, social workers, funeral celebrants and a public servant.

Annie had to take painkillers to make it out of the house today. She's had testing lately to diagnose pain near her stomach and her MRI results came back negative which is all very well but she would like an explanation about why she is feeling so bloody awful. You wouldn't know any of this, though. She looks calm, is focused, peering through her black-and-white glasses at the slide Joe is currently showing:

Why Are We Here?

Because suffering together is an integral part of being human.

He plays a short video discussing Charles Darwin's view of human sympathy.

Adam Gopnik has written about the extent to which a sense of personal loss informed Darwin's *The Origin of Species* (1859). The defining event of Darwin's life was perhaps the death of his daughter, Annie, in 1851. "There is no inherent meaning in Annie's dying at ten," Gopnik writes, "except the recognition that mortality was the role of existence; serenity could be found only in the contemplation of the vast indifference of the universe."

In this light, the ending of *The Origin*—those conceptually stunning last sentences hauled by Darwin from the hull of his grief—demonstrates what Hannah Arendt would later refer to, in a different context, as the difference between truth and meaning, and how they are separate wisdoms:

Thus, from the war of nature, from famine and death, the most exalted object which we are capable of conceiving, namely, the production of the higher animals, directly follows. There is a grandeur in this view of life, with its several powers, having been originally breathed into a few forms or into one; and that, whilst this planet has gone cycling on according to the fixed law of gravity, from so simple a beginning endless forms most beautiful and most wonderful have been, and are being, evolved.

But this wasn't everything. By *The Descent of Man, and Selection in Relation to Sex* (1871), he would argue that sympathy—a term closer in his usage to empathy—is our strongest instinct, stronger than pure self-interest, and that natural selection would ensure communities with "the greatest number of the most sympathetic members, would flourish best." As the attachment psychologist Louis Cozolino would say a century later, we are not the survival of the fittest, we are the survival of the nurtured. Which is to say the sorrows that are inherent to life cannot be eliminated, but they can be alleviated. We are built to share each other's pain.

Sehee clicks to his next slide:

Compassion.

Means: to suffer with or together.

Secular spiritual care for the dying is not "solution focused," Sehee explains. Spiritual pastoral carers are not doctors, they do not view death as a failure. We are not there to pull anyone out of the hole, he says. We are there to sit with them in the hole.

After morning tea, Annie sits in the center of the semicircle and introduces herself to the group, the tips of her yellow brogues pointing at each other. She is sufficiently nervous that she has prepared comprehensive speaking notes. But she is also Annie, a woman with the self-possession to deliberately pause before responding to anything put to her in conversation, so when she starts talking she does so authentically, eloquently, and unaided by those notes. While she is a death doula, she explains, today she'll be talking about her experiences in hospitals as a Buddhist chaplain and spiritual care worker. "So when people are dying or have died, I get called out at any time," she explains, "and sometimes I'll go with a senior Tibetan lama who lives round the back of my place."

The sun is a sharp slice under the drawn blinds, but enough makes it into the room to dance in dappled patches on her scalp while she explains that the people whom she visits will share things with her that they keep from their doctors. How she handles that. She speaks about how she doesn't feel she's there to "cheer up" anyone. Sadness, she says, is not a moral failure and it's not a disease. She has no right to put a cover over that. She's there to be with them in whatever they are feeling at that time. She speaks about the opposite impact, on a person in palliative care, of words from their loved ones to the effect of "don't give up" or "keep on fighting." How some people in the dying phase have expressed to her, privately, a certain guilt at maybe not having tried hard enough.

And then she shares the stories of some of the people she has sat with.

The young woman. End stage. In and out of consciousness. Heavy painkillers. Dark room. Damp air. Tiny voice.

Would you like it if maybe I gave you a hand massage? Annie asked.

Yes, please, the woman replied.

I noticed the blinds are pulled down. It's a beautiful day outside, would you like me to open the blinds so you can have a look?

Yes, please.

It's about seventy-three, seventy-four degrees. Would you like me to open the window so you can have some fresh air?

Yes, please.

Would you like some music? Do you like harp music?

Yes, please.

A young couple whose baby died in the hospital. They were hugging their child, which the woman's mother found distasteful. Holding a dead body. Don't do that, she told them, put it down, they can take it away. This was their first child, Annie says. So she made the point of referring to them as the mother, as the father. No less so simply because their child had died. The woman's mother found this, too, extremely confronting, Annie explains. As the parents hugged the bundle that contained their child's body, Annie gently asked, Would you, too, like to hold your granddaughter? Yes.

"A simple, little thing like that can have a *profound* effect. Actually for generations," Annie says, as rain suddenly buckets down, pelting the window behind her.

Sometimes, at the baby memorial services held at Monash Hospital, Annie will see an older female relative, the grandmother usually, get up and light a candle. And sometimes that woman will later say, extremely softly, to Annie: I had a miscarriage thirty years ago, they told me not to talk about it. I lit this candle for my baby. "This person would've been holding on to that for decades," Annie says. "The courage, the bravery, to get up in front of their family, who knew nothing about it, and light that candle . . ."

An eighteen-year-old girl whose mom was unconscious. End stage, brain cancer. Though they had divorced, the girl's father was planning a religious ceremony in a church for his ex-wife. Mom would hate that, the girl told Annie, Mom would never have wanted something like that. Annie asked whether they had spoken about her wishes before the mother became unconscious. No, she replied. Mom wouldn't. She just kept on thinking she was gonna get better.

A man in his early forties, terminal. His family knew nothing about his wishes. I have tried so many times, he explained, but they won't let me talk about my death.

"We're not going to talk about death," Annie says, zooming out. "'Cause talking about death is going to kill us. Just like talking about sex is gonna make you pregnant, talking about muffins is going to make us fat." The room laughs; needs to.

Another story, another. A young woman, brain dead, car accident. After she died, her father thanked Annie for her help. Annie responded by saying, "Tell me about your daughter." Well. He started talking about things he had never known, how he couldn't believe the stories her friends were calling to share with him. How his daughter had been the wise one in her friendship circle, the go-to, the fixer, the helper. How proud he was of her. How devastated to learn this, to know her truly, only now.

Annie will speak directly to the person even if they are unconscious. She was called in for such a man. Greeted him by name as he lay in his hospital bed. Introduced herself.

He can't hear you, said his wife.

I understand, Annie said, sitting beside her and explaining that, according to Buddhist belief, hearing is the last sense to go.

"It's really important," she tells the group, "to keep speaking even though it looks like the lights are out and no one's home, because we just don't know."

Annie told the man's wife that she could keep talking with him. Share the stories of your family, Annie said, what you've done together. Let him know that these are the lessons that you've learnt, share some of the funny things, just keep talking. Then Annie said some prayers. Excused herself, saying she would be going.

"Martin, I'm leaving now," she told the man from the foot of his bed. "And I'm going to pray for you."

He opened his eyes, looked directly at her. Said very quietly, "Thank you." A perfect example, she tells the group, of how we just don't know.

"How are we going for time?" Annie asks Joe, who gives her a nod. One more. Elderly lady, in her eighties, surrounded by her family, her two strapping sons. Suddenly she says that she wants to get out of bed, needs to get out of bed. Stay there, stay there, urged her children and the nurses. Whatever it is, we'll do it for you. She kept insisting she needed to get out of bed.

Why do you need to get out of bed? Annie asked.

I need to do something important, she replied.

"I may cry," Annie says now, "because this was very powerful for me."

Annie checked with the nurses, they approved as long as the woman was supported. So her sons lowered the bed rail and, in the reversal that is Time, lifted the bundle of their mother out of her cot. I'm going to kneel down now, she told them. This was what she had wanted to do. Touch the ground.

"I'm just thanking the earth," she said. "Because the earth has been so good to me."

Silence while we all breathe together. And then Joe asks where everyone would like to have lunch. "It was raining fifteen minutes ago," he says. "But it's blue sky now, though it's a bit blowy."

A decision is made to eat outside anyway.

14

IN THE BEGINNING
ANDREW

Everyone who works or volunteers at the Creation Museum—from the cleaners to the cashiers at Uncle Leroy's Fudge Stand to the "PhD scientists"—is required to sign the ministry's Statement of Faith. That statement attests, among other things (such "other things" including that God finds homosexuality offensive) that: *Scripture teaches a recent origin for man and the whole creation, spanning approximately 4,000 years from creation to Christ.*

Dr. Andrew Snelling is a geologist and the ministry's Director of Research. Dr. Snelling completed his doctorate—a geochemical study of the Koongara Uranium Deposit—at the University of Sydney in 1980. According to the Answers in Genesis website, Snelling's *research has demonstrated that a global flood about 4,300 years ago explains many rock layers and most fossil deposits found around the world.* His research also indicates, the ministry argues, that *the radioactive methods for dating rocks at millions and billions of years old are not reliable, polonium radiohalos indicate granites and metamorphism of rocks occurred rapidly, and the rock evidence overall is consistent with a young earth.*

I sit down with Snelling the week before he flies to Brisbane to speak at a conference with Ken Ham. Like Ham, he has an Aussie accent undiminished by his time in Kentucky. He presents as perfectly professorial in his lack of enthusiasm for eye contact, the precision of his phrasing and the trajectory of his pointer finger when he speaks. Unlike Georgia Purdom, he has an office with a large window through which I can see a line of trees, their leaves turned yellow and orange. Shelves of journals and books encircle him where he sits. He gestures me towards a chair in front of his expansive desk, on which rests a well-thumbed Holy Bible in a zip-up leather case.

"Do you have any church background at all?" he inquires.

"I'm Jewish," I reply, settling into my chair.

"Okay."

"You could probably put me in a secular humanist Jewish basket," I offer.

"Oh, I don't like necessarily putting people in baskets," he replies somberly, with a touch of the Pooh Bear. "Course, the trouble is you put a person in a basket and there may be all these other things attached to that basket that they don't really hold to. You shoehorn people into a particular slot and you really do them an injustice."

He is, of course, correct both generally and specifically insofar as he demonstrates that it is possible simultaneously to consider Satan your personal spiritual adversary and to stay up to date with the *Journal of Geology*.

As a geologist, Snelling worked for various uranium mining companies, the Australian government agency responsible for scientific research and the Australian Nuclear Science and Technology Organization. "I started working with Ken Ham in Brisbane at the end of 1983 for the forerunner to the min—the

Answers in Genesis organization," he explains, correcting himself when he starts to say "ministry." "I worked for nearly fifteen years for the min—for the organization in Australia."

Snelling first came to the States in 1990 when he went to the Grand Canyon with a geologist from the California-based Institute for Creation Research. He explains that he accepted a role working for that institute from Brisbane, so he would not have to uproot his children, who were young and "finding their wings," a phrase I find moving. Finally, in 2007, he stepped into the role he currently holds.

Boxes of rock samples in chalky plastic baggies populate the floor. Books and journals are heaped everywhere: *The Adelaide Geosyncline*; *The Geology of New South Wales*; *Geology and Mineral Resources of Tasmania*; *The Geologic Time Scale, 2012*; *The Tectonics of the Appalachians*.

The first impulse is to freeze; the second is to grapple for some way out. The continuing impulse is towards control despite knowing it's impossible.

The first time I felt an earthquake I found myself, for too long, vaguely annoyed that our upstairs neighbors had decided to move furniture late at night. "The experience of an earthquake can be destabilising," Geoff Manaugh writes, "not just physically but also philosophically." The idea that the ground is solid—that we can build on it, trust it to support us, he continues, undergirds nearly all human terrestrial activity.

What we call "ground," however, is just the solid crust on a slowly flowing river; a puzzle of tectonic plates drifting on the viscous mantle beneath. When Manaugh made the error of asking a seismologist he was interviewing a question about geology she replied, "I study waves, not rocks."

"We do not, in fact, live on solid ground," Manaugh realized. "We are mariners, rolling on the peaks and troughs of a planet we're still learning to navigate."

Andrew Snelling grew up in a strongly religious house and by the age of five was expected to sit quietly at attention in church. One of the books he read as a boy still looms large for him. "*The Genesis Flood*, published in 1961 by Whitcomb and Morris, was a book that was influential on Ken and it was influential for me," he says. "I looked at that when I was a teenager and he was a young man as well."

Though young Snelling and Ham lived in New South Wales and Brisbane, respectively, they were introduced through Snelling's minister, who knew they were both interested in "this creation flood issue."

The book he is referring to, *The Genesis Flood: The Biblical Record and its Scientific Implications*, was written by John Whitcomb, one of the founders of the modern creationism movement, and Henry Morris, a civil engineer. In it can be found the particular flavor of logic promoted at the Creation Museum and the Ark Encounter, namely the conflicting assertions that "the evidences of full divine inspiration of Scripture are far weightier than the evidences for any fact of science" and that scientific facts support the veracity of Scripture. In 1972, Morris elaborated on his cosmology in *The Remarkable Birth of Planet Earth*, writing that a cosmic battle between Satan and the archangel Michael probably caused the craters of the moon. Ken Ham has called Morris one of his "heroes of the faith," stating that "he is the man the Lord raised up as the father of the modern creationist movement."

Though Snelling's papers took out the first, second and third prizes for technical excellence at the Fourth International Conference on Creationism, he is not one to rest on his laurels. Unlike Purdom (now ensconced in other roles) and Ham (whose five doctorates are honorary), Snelling is an active researcher. Despite some time lost earlier this year resolving an unpleasantness with Grand Canyon National Park, in which his initial application for rock sampling was rejected due to what he calls "world-view discrimination," he now has the requested rock samples and they are in a lab getting thin sections cut. "I'll be studying them under the microscope, photographing features et cetera for publication et cetera . . ." he says.

While his articles are peer-reviewed in creationist journals, Snelling no longer has strong links with non-creationist academics in the earth sciences.

"I did earlier on but because of my focus and because of some of their reactions to what I do, the distance has grown," he explains. "I'm still involved in professional societies but not so much in an active way, per se, in contributing to the life of the society. But I support their work and their journals et cetera. So, no, it's a while since . . . I've had contact with a few people over the years but I haven't maintained those strong links. Because of busy-ness more than anything else . . ."

I ask what initially attracted him to geology as a specialization.

"*Ah!*" He is suddenly animated, explaining that he went to Tasmania on a family holiday when he was in fourth grade and there they visited a mining area. "So I got attracted to the sparkly, shiny minerals and I started picking up rocks!

"And you know what it's like to have show-and-tell at school, I brought my rock collec—my rocks in to tell about them. And it's not long before you know more about these things than anyone else in the class, which of course makes you feel important, so it spurs your interest. By the time I was going to high school, I was convinced that I was going to be a geologist, so it went from there. I was reading everything I could get my hands on."

Later in our discussion, I ask Snelling whether selectively applying the scientific method is as problematic as selectively applying the Bible.

"One of the areas I look at is the Genesis flood," he replies. "You read what the Bible says and you say to yourself, 'If that really occurred, what would be the evidence?' So at one level, yes, you're saying, 'Yes, this is a literal historical account.' But then you're saying, 'Well, okay, if it is a literal historical account, let's test what it claims.' If it says that it *covered all the high hills under the Heaven* then that means that the ocean waters must've flooded over the continents. If they did that, would they not carry creatures that lived in the ocean and potentially bury them up on the continents? So you predict that there would be marine fossils buried on the continents. And you go out, and that's what you find," he concludes crisply.

"It doesn't prove, *per se*, because we weren't there to actually see it happen but it's circumstantial evidence that confirms what you predicted. Yes, it is taking the Bible as an actual historical account, but it's testing it. That's what a forensic scientist does, say, with a crime scene. If suspect A did it, what will link up with what I found at the crime scene et cetera? It's a similar process."

That is the role of an advocate which is, I suppose, the whole point, since his ministry's Statement of Faith holds that "by definition, no apparent, perceived or claimed evidence in any field, including history and chronology, can be valid if it contradicts the scriptural record." Also: "Of primary importance is the fact that evidence is always subject to interpretation by fallible people who do not possess all information."

It is impossible to directly experience the past, the future, alternatives to reality, remote locations or another person's perspective. But we have memories and hopes, plans for the distant future; we speculate about what might have been and we are capable of deep empathy.

The various ways in which something or someone might be removed from us—in time, space, social distance or hypotheticality—are categorized as different types of distance. But social psychologists Yaacov Trope and Nira Liberman found "a marked commonality" in the way people responded to those different categories. They proposed that this was because responding to anything or anyone that is increasingly distant from ourselves requires us to rely more on our capacity for abstract thought and association, and less on our direct experience. It is possible, in other words, to build a cognitive and emotional bridge across distance, but the integrity of that bridge will depend on knowing where we end and the Other begins.

This human ability to both affirm our self and transcend it has always been essential, and perhaps it is becoming increasingly important. "Human history is associated with expanding horizons,"Trope and Liberman write, "traversing greater spatial distances, forming larger social groups, planning and investing in a more distant future, and reaching farther back into the past." *Our superpower and our Achilles heel, a way of flying or falling.*

Unlike Ham, Snelling sees himself returning, eventually, to Australia. "See, it's different," he says, explaining that unlike Ken, his grandchildren do not live in America. "So it makes sense for us to go back, though I would hope to still be able to be writing and things like that while I still have the health."

In the sunlight that filters in through the large window and gets lost in the crevices just above the bridge of his glasses, I can almost see the boy with his rock collection hovering shyly at the edge of the space between us.

I imagine he would say something about the quarantining comforts derived from special knowledge; how it substitutes, poorly but adequately, for a different type of ease and belonging. And, at the same time, this boy contains a bursting to share what he has discovered; carries the love that burns at the heart of close attentiveness.

That boy, who is now grown and finally inhabiting the center of his particular universe, might not fully enjoy retreating from this enabling Eden, with its scholastic superhighways and its multitudes sufficiently large and willing to finance them. But what is distance anyway on a still-new earth where anything, really, might happen?

15

PARANORMAL

THE VIGIL

Where do I start with my night at the Masonic Hall? With the strange mix of boredom and terror? How I regret leaving too early? Maybe the moment when I was so spooked that I hurried from the bathroom, pants still open under my sweater, and scuttled on legs pumping with insectile rapidity back through a dark hallway towards the only inhabited room in the old building where moments before I had sat in inky blackness on "vigil" with members of the Australian Institute of Parapsychological Research before acting on the delusional self-confidence that I might perhaps go to the toilet by myself. Or another moment, weeks later, sitting at my desk. On high alert listening to the audio of that night's events, alive to the information that voices unheard at the time, voices unaccounted for, have sometimes—according to those AIPR members—clearly manifested on tape after the event.

It was a Saturday night, a Sunday morning actually, and I left the vigil at 12:45 AM—which, like I said, I now regret given what happened twenty-six minutes later.

The Yarraville Masonic Hall was suggested as a candidate for paranormal investigation by Misha/Amber, who recently held a workshop here. She did not go into detail, but the possibility of something encysted inside the building's 111-year-old walls was sufficiently intriguing for Vlad to come out tonight, along with three other AIPR members—Paul, a psychologist, Marina, a forensic scientist, and Evelyn, a grandmother in her seventies—as well as Jessica, one of the psychic attendees at the Abbotsford conference, who is in her twenties and currently completing "a diploma of regression," working with those who wish to explore their past lives.

Aside from the Freemasons' lodge meetings that are its raison d'etre, the Masonic Hall hosts a weekend craft market and occasional events like book launches and weddings. Nick the caretaker is giving Vlad the grand tour, snapping on the lights as he goes. I wander into the great hall for a moment with Jessica, our footsteps echoing in the vast space. "It's like an old dance hall," she laughs, looking around before her smile drops like a curtain. "I don't like it."

When I ask what it feels like to "not like" the space, Jessica explains that it's a feeling of *No*, a heaviness in her chest. I'll read later of the send-off that was held here over a hundred years ago for eight local boys going into the First World War. How *a strong ladies committee had made elaborate arrangements—as only ladies can*, giving each of the boys a waist-belt and clasp-knife. How there was dancing until a late hour. But for now there are just the two of us under six ceiling fans inexplicably whirling above the emptiness. To Jessica's surprise, a decision is made to start the investigation in the lodge room rather than in here.

Nick heads off with a wave and the paranormal researchers start setting up their equipment, a process that resembles a band loading in for a gig. Their many cases contain power boards, computers, recording devices and, at various points in the process, it appears as though everyone has at least one tripod. Vlad, returning from his car, hovers over his gear: four metal briefcases, two cloth bags and a plastic crate from which yellow and orange wires explode like viscera. He's unenthusiastic about setting up cameras tonight. "I'm getting more and more of an impression that cameras deter the activity," he explains.

"Well, there's that poltergeist in Humpty Doo . . ." Paul, the psychologist, says. "Similar to the Enfield one, and it didn't want to be recorded. It evaded the cameras just slightly or would do something just out of shot."

"And the same has happened with us," Vlad nods. "In one of the places we went to—the cinema—nothing ever happened in front of the cameras, it always happened when we were on a tea break. You would hear a voice just go through the group—like a whistling noise or exhales and things—and it also somehow damaged the PC recorder twice. Every time I've been there I've had to reformat the disk."

"That's why you bring a lot of batteries, they get wiped out," says Evelyn, holding a headlamp as she surveys the walls for a power point to charge her two sound recorders.

Evelyn specializes in EVP: electronic voice phenomena. She explains that, though she had always been "a sensitive" she knew nothing about EVP until she started hearing voices and became interested in parapsychology later in life. EVP refers to sounds found on electronic recordings that are interpreted to be spirit voices recorded unintentionally or on request. The idea was popularised in the 1970s by the Latvian parapsychologist Konstantins Raudive, who described such sounds as typically brief—usually one word or a short phrase. Besides communication with the dead, other explanations advanced for these sounds have included nature energies, beings from other planets or dimensions, and living humans imprinting thoughts on an electronic medium through psychokinesis.

Two more AIPR members walk into the lodge room—Luke, a young man in a baseball cap who works in IT, and Bridget, an artist. They are a couple and this is their second night out in the two years since their child was born.

"And you chose to spend it here," laughs Marina, the forensic scientist. "I can't remember the last time we all did one together."

The lodge room is a ritual space and its symbols are not readily intelligible to noninitiates. There is a pentagram at the center of a checkerboard pattern on the carpet, a golden G dangling from the ceiling. Ornate chairs of dark wood and navy leather are positioned in front of an open Bible on a stage at one end of the room. To one side, an exhausted Australian flag sags above a desk that looks like it was frozen in time at an accountant's office in 1975. An organ sits at the back of the room beneath two portraits of abundantly white-haired men in suits which Paul is currently wanding with an EMF meter. Marking the baseline readings in a notebook, he methodically raises the device towards the ceiling before lowering it towards the floor as he makes his way around the room.

Setting his laptop on the stage floor, Vlad connects it to a magnetic field spectrum analyzer anchored on a nearby tripod. Then he heads to the grocery store around the corner to stock up on supplies because, like any long game, snacks are an important part of ghost hunting and the night is young.

"Do you ever work off intuition?" I ask Vlad when he returns and we stand for a moment in the large hall, which is freezing. A tiny portrait of the young Queen hangs too high and at a slant on an expanse of cracked wall. The only other decoration is three dingy squares of cardboard decorated like playing cards propped up at various points along the moldings. It looks like something out of a David Lynch film but far less sleek, all the conditions conspiring towards creepiness.

"I *have* no intuition," Vlad replies in a sheepish whisper. "I'm trying to develop some. But I do try to eliminate other influences." He notes how the floorboards in here slope almost imperceptibly down towards the center of the room.

Back in the lodge room, he produces his trigger objects. No rubber duck this time: instead he's brought two soft plastic spiky balls that do the same thing. Each contains a mechanism that, when given a good whack, causes a light to go off at its center. One is neon green, the other is neon pink and shaped like an Angry Bird. He rolls both onto the carpet towards the center of the room before crouching over his computer, where the screen springs to life, displaying a multicolored bar he will use to monitor changes in the magnetic field during the hours that follow. "I generally lean towards lower frequencies—under a hundred hertz," he explains, "but there's no hard and fast rule."

Marina sits down at the organ. She plays a few sustained notes that sound like something from a Hitchcock film and add a certain gravitas to Vlad's explanation.

"Some people think that the Shuman Resonance—7.8 hertz, which is the overall frequency of all the lightning that's occurring around the world—causes this kind of echoing at seven or eight hertz. So some people think that's ghostly or paranormal in some way," he continues.

"There's quite a few papers now out saying that fluctuations of the earth's magnetic field correlate with activity—not just ghosts but extrasensory perception, other things. If that's the case . . ." He sighs. "It'd be very low frequencies. ELF— extremely low frequencies, VLF—very low frequencies. Under two cycles per second. Quite slow."

At the back of the room, Jessica sits with perfect posture, hands neatly folded on the notebook in her lap, long blond hair cascading down her back. She is absolutely still and staring into the middle distance.

"What's the time now?" Luke asks Bridget, peering up from the floor where he is pressing buttons on an audio recorder.

"8:05," Bridget replies.

"Testing," he says into the mic.

"Anybody have the time?" Evelyn asks, holding her own recorder.

"8:06 now," Bridget replies.

"Recording one, Yarraville, September 28," Vlad says into his audio recorder before going to make a cup of coffee. First, refreshments. Then we'll make a start.

Just before 9:00 PM, the AIPR members in their AIPR windbreakers stand in the cold tea room finishing hot beverages or crinkling empty chip packets as Jessica recounts what she's picked up.

"There was a man," she begins.

"Did you get a sense of what he looked like?" Vlad asks. "Caucasian, Aboriginal . . ."

Not really, she says. But he has an adult daughter who is upset by what she believes to be a misunderstanding about the manner of his death. The man wants his daughter to know: it was an accident.

"And how did he communicate this information? Was it just subjective?" Vlad asks.

Jessica replies that it just comes to her. He nods. We return to the lodge room, turning the lights off as we go.

Everyone settles into position, sitting on the carpet for the vigil. Suddenly, Vlad receives a phone alert. "There's a geomagnetic storm happening as we speak," he reports. "It's been active all night." Not a physical storm, he explains, rather an increase in fluctuations in the earth's magnetic field.

When Vlad had first described for me his academic background in neurophysiology, he had mentioned transcranial magnetic stimulation: the use of a magnetic field to impact brain neurons. This is one of his favorite areas. "It's used a lot for treating depression," he said. "The other beautiful thing it's used for is to interrupt sensory processing."

He told me about Michael Persinger's God Helmet. Persinger, a Canadian psychology professor, used very weak magnetic fields—in the order of the earth's magnetic field or slightly stronger—to stimulate certain parts of the brain. He found that by stimulating a specific location he could induce a sense of presence, that feeling of not being alone in a room. And that slight adjustments could evoke a positive or negative emotional state associated with this feeling.

"If you can explain all paranormal experience as brain activity modified by magnetic fields," Vlad had said, "then you don't need to have all the other explanations like consciousness outside the body—it's all explained by misperception. Problem is, not all of these experiences are purely psychological. Some of them are physical. Things moving, cameras stop, doors slam . . ."

It also cannot account for instances where multiple people report seeing the same thing, he said. "It's very unlikely that a magnetic field will affect everyone in exactly the same way because in theory everyone's brain activity will be different, so they shouldn't really see the same thing.

"There's a more exotic interpretation of this magnetic field thing," he continued, explaining that files had recently been obtained from the early penal settlement of Port Arthur— years of "haunt-type experiences" reported by the public. "We found that there are certain buildings that seem to have a similar type of activity reported by people over the years. You have a hundred people walking through that building and they will report the same type of activity. They don't know that it's been reported by other people.

"There's one building where they'll say, 'I saw a light coming from under the door,' but all the electricity is turned off in the building. Or they'll say, 'I saw a little girl in a dress in the yard.' But that wasn't publicized.

"That kind of data, to me, suggests another possible interpretation for this electromagnetic theory—and it's a more exotic one: that the electromagnetic activity somehow modifies the environment itself. And the people are just there at the right time to experience something. But that's a little bit harder to justify."

Vlad squints into his phone, reading about the current electro-magnetic storm.

"Who's got the time?" Evelyn asks.

"The time is 9:27," Vlad replies.

The forensic scientist snaps the lights off.

16

THE DEATH DOULA
ANNIE & KATRINA

"It feels, Annie, like you're going to be an important person on this journey," says Carol on the couch, her hand resting on Katrina's outstretched legs as Peter hands his wife a barley sugar.

Though she is enormously unwell, Katrina doesn't look it. Her hair is full and sleek, her skin is vibrant, her lips are a deep natural pink. I don't yet know how tall Katrina is because I haven't seen her vertical; it will turn out that she is not so tall. But I am already acutely aware that her intense energy has little to do with physical factors, because even in her diminished state she is radiant, strong. Which is to say that although she is being assaulted by a wave of nausea at this moment and needs to close her eyes and concentrate on breathing, she is still very much the woman who "always power-dressed" for work in red lipstick and stilettos that she wielded like a ceremonial knife. Still the same woman who balanced four school schedules with work and friends and family. Still the same woman who ate right and meditated and read *Psychotherapy Magazine* and took the spin classes that gave her the deep satisfaction of observing how, even in extremis, her resting heart rate of seventy beats per minute only went up to a nonchalant one-twenty—a sign of just how healthy, and in control, she was.

On Katrina's lap is a book that Annie lent her a few weeks ago when she first visited the house: *What to Do When I'm Gone.* She explains to Annie, perched on an armchair close by, that she's been using it to guide an ongoing discussion with Lachlan, her sixteen-year-old son.

"Good on you," Annie says with deep emotion. Then, at Carol's invitation, she goes into a detailed explanation of the role—more accurately, the roles—of a death doula. Her tone is frank but soft as she explains what she cannot do (palliative action) and what she can do (almost everything else). She sets out her professional bona fides, which are also her personal bona fides, explaining her Buddhist practice and her own personal experiences with "end-of-life," a phrase that, while gentle, is acceptably accurate.

There are words and phrases that Annie neither uses herself nor plays along with when used by others because they mislead or obscure. These include: client, patient, to fight, to battle, don't give up, anger and love. If you drop one of the verboten words into conversation Annie will interject and ask you to explain to her what you mean by that. Love, she has said to me, what does that mean? Tell me the components. What makes up love?

Sometime around 1881, from a house over the Danube, a woman named Elise Brock leaves her three-year-old son, whom she will not see again until he has children of his own. For the rest of his life, the philosopher Martin Buber would remember how, after some time had passed, he stood on the balcony of his grandparents' house with an older child who told him his mother was never coming back.

"I suspect," Buber later stated, "that all I have learnt in the course of my life about genuine meeting had its first origin in that hour on the balcony."

Though he would see his mother again—after decades had passed—it is true that she never came back.

"When . . . I again saw my mother, who had come from a distance to visit me, my wife and my children, I could not gaze into her still astonishingly beautiful eyes without hearing from somewhere the word *Vergegnung* ["mismeeting"] as a word spoken to me."

The idea of "mismeetings" explains—by way of counterpoint—his emotional, spiritual and intellectual preoccupation with the true encounters that are possible between the "I" of the self and the equal "I" of the other. That place where pain becomes purpose, where dialogue conquers subjectivity; where we are greater than our parts and where holiness resides.

"The words 'She will never come back' remained with him," his biographer wrote, "and over the passing years they became indelibly fixed . . . [H]e began to perceive that what had happened to him—unusual though it was—concerned not only him but everyone."

"We—the community, society—think that we are all entitled to live to a ripe old age with no hiccups in the middle," Annie says to Katrina, who is nodding. "Well, that's not reality. In my own experience, I know that. Truly."

The room fills with the scratching sound of Peter taking notes. Satisfied, Katrina stops Annie there.

"If I'm short, please forgive me," Katrina says. "Can't always say please and that. Haven't got the energy."

Annie is delighted by her straightforwardness.

"Okay, let's cut to the chase," Katrina continues, struggling to take a full breath. "Advance care directives."

Annie is off and running, with gentle authority. "When you are unable to speak for yourself, and only then, the advance care directive comes into play. What things are important to you, in your own life, for you to live in comfort and in peace . . ."

Paging through a copy of her own plan, which she's brought along as an example, she continues, "For me, it's important to verbally communicate, the ability to care for myself physically and intellectually, my family, my animals, quality of life, nature, walking, my Buddhist teachings, to live an independent life." She pauses, looks into the faces staring intently at her from the couch. "*At this stage.* But I review this. *Because it changes.*"

Annie continues, outlining which treatments she refuses and in what circumstances. "So that's me," she folds the pages neatly behind their staple.

Carol asks whether Katrina should follow a similar process with specifying her wishes.

"Yes." Annie nods vigorously. "Because when it moves towards the pointy end, I understand that Katrina wishes to die at home. My role is to make that as smooth as possible. Which is why it's so important to put everything in place. Then myself, loved ones—we're all here so that Katrina can have her wish and Pete will be supported, and the children will also be supported."

Carol asks where Annie will get that authority from. Before Annie answers, Katrina interjects and explains briskly how Annie works in concert with the council and the hospital. "So it'll be a combo of the three supported by a legal document," she says in a businesslike tone.

"If I get down to the point of not being able to talk—you know, I'm down to forty kilos," she continues, pausing briefly to cough and spit, "then I would assume I'd be starting to have a bit of pain. They'd have an infusion here, a pump, and I wouldn't think it'd be too many days after that. My kidneys would've shut down, everything'll shut down . . ."

"Yes," Annie nods. "That's when the body starts to take over."

"I don't want to be in pain too long, I really don't," Katrina says, her tone frank. "As you can see, I've given it a really good shot." She smiles, gives a small laugh. "Hopefully, I might be alive for another six months, but if I'm not . . ." She pauses, conscious of Peter beside her, and that these words, because they are true, are so many razors. "Or whatever it is, anyway, doesn't matter what it is, six months, six years, sixty years—towards that end, yeah, of course, I wouldn't want resuscitation. But you've gotta put it all in there." She gestures towards a booklet about advance care directives which Annie has placed on the coffee table, *Take Control* written in red on its cover. This is said in the tone one might use when handing over files to a co-worker before a holiday. It is this tone that makes this room, where I sit on a soft ottoman, the fire warming the left side of my face, terrifying to me.

Katrina's illness might have focused her, but I get the sense that she has always been this way. Unlike me, Katrina would not have allowed a friend to waste years of their life on a partner she considered an irrevocable asshole. Unlike me, Katrina would not have reflexively nodded and smiled for the comfort of a person cutting her deeply. You would not wonder where you stood with Katrina. And this is the tone she is now extracting from herself for herself and for Peter, who stands to add a log to the fire.

"If I can't talk," Katrina says, pausing briefly to consider the scenario, "I'd probably want to make sure that my mouth's moist and that I've got some oxygen. Okay, next?"

"Well, that's basically it," Annie laughs, and everyone joins in.

Advance care directives comprise two parts: an instructional directive, which is legally binding, and a values section, which is not, but which functions as a guide. In Annie's experience, those who could benefit most from such a document either do not know it exists or do not know how it works, so she is always keen to talk to community groups about it.

This is what she is doing today, alongside a bearded representative from the Public Advocate's office and a Buddhist monk, at the Springvale Neighborhood House. The attendees sitting in rows have each received one mandarin and a stack of reading material, including the *Take Control* booklet. You would not know from looking at her—glowing and swathed in black-and-red fabric—that Annie saw the doctor two days ago for the dull pain that is still radiating around her kidney.

The representative from the Public Advocate's office answers a question about how binding the document is. Individuals who are competent, the man replies, are considered autonomous beings that can create their own destiny. This oracular wisdom is what I'll remember later as I look at Annie's advance care directive—which she keeps at the ready on a hook by her front door in a clearly labeled plastic pocket.

Because it is a masterclass in the level of detail and consideration that should go into such documents, she shows it to clients. Because it is a masterclass in Annie, here is what she has written, in her neat and funky all-caps handwriting, under the values section:

What matters most in my life:

To be able to verbally communicate. The ability to care for myself, physically and intellectually. My family. My animals. Quality of life—nature, walking. My Buddhist (Tibetan) teachings. To live an independent life.

What worries me most about my future:

That I need to be fed, washed and moved when I cannot do them myself. That I won't be able to continue my Tibetan Buddhist practice. Dying in emergency or among strangers. Not be allowed to refuse fluid and food.

For me, unacceptable outcomes of medical treatment after illness or injury are:

Loss of independence. High-level care and inability to recognize and communicate with people. Being dependent on others for washing, feeding and dressing.

Other things I would like known are:

I don't like to sleep on a pillow. I am vegetarian. I don't like milk. I am a Tibetan Buddhist practitioner.

I am a body donor. I am comfortable about death conversations. I need certain times for meditation practice with no interruptions. I am allergic to broccoli. I love my animals. I love massage.

Other people I would like involved in discussions about my care:
[Blank]

If I am nearing death the following things would be important to me:
Natural light if possible. Nature. Quiet. Tibetan monk/s chanting. No crying out loud. Readings from the Kalachakra, teachings. Harp music.

Here is what it says in the instructional directive, the legally binding part:

I consent to the following medical treatment:
Pain control. Sedation only if pain not controlled. Palliative care: ASAP if required. Honest, clear medical communication at all times, even if I am unconscious. Life prolonging treatment if outcome considered highly possible with good outcome that matches my values statement.

I refuse the following medical treatment:
If not expected to live for up to a year, I refuse peg feedings, dialysis, any life-prolonging treatment, CPR, intubation (unless for organ harvesting). If I

have been diagnosed with Alzheimer's, dementia, or neurological disease do no life-prolonging, colostomy, artificial respiration.

Elevated train tracks bisect the window through which light pours and pools in Annie's glasses as she explains that when we are reasonably healthy, it's hard to imagine and plan for when we are not. Still, it's important to do so and to revisit that plan every couple of years. This is a situation where one would benefit from strong convictions, lightly held. She's seen enough cases of people suddenly revising what they had previously considered unimaginable erosions of their quality of life once confronted with the alternative. The Jehovah's Witness at the last moment accepting treatment though it meant excommunication. The athlete accepting a colostomy bag. Knowing yourself is important, she says, but so too is flexibility. We are dynamic creatures, changing with time. Her voice is briefly muffled by a train passing, then another. For one moment, as they barrel down their tracks in opposite directions, they look like one train, expanding. Annie exhorts everyone to have these difficult conversations, not leave them too late: no one expects to be the forty-year-old with brain cancer.

I have trouble writing this in my notebook, trouble typing it now. I open the *Take Control* booklet, consider the questions for myself, something I should have done—I now realize—much sooner, given my immersion in Annie's story, her work. I make myself breathe as the woman beside me eats her mandarin, making a pile of peel and pith. Talking about death hasn't killed anyone yet, Annie smiles. The next morning, she will be loaded into the back of an ambulance, gripping Khedup's hand, crying with pain.

17

PARANORMAL

ROB

At first, it surprised me to learn that Rob can clear a haunted house without physically being there. That, if needed, he could clear my house in Melbourne from his house in Sydney.

"There's no boundary in time or space if you're psychic," he explains to the workshop. "It's just as easy to see what's going on in the house next door as it is to see something five thousand kilometers away."

Here's how it works: first, Rob psychically locates the client by remembering their voice. The bad spooks, eager to be seen, then pop into view. He calls on the good spooks, directing them to the location, often by way of passing on the street address. The ideal time for doing this is in the wee hours, since Rob finds that the psychokinetic energy used for psychic healing is quite high between midnight and about four in the morning.

Someone asks if Rob ever feels scared. The answer is no. The closest he has come to feeling frightened was one time on a possess-ion job for a nice young man. "There's not much literature on possession cases," he mentions, as an aside. "Dr. Edith Fiore and Dr. Adam Crabtree have written books on it—both say that the possessing entity is invariably a deceased blood relative." Holding eye contact with the man, Rob saw his eyes change. "Suddenly someone else was in his body looking at me, and I thought, 'Whoa, this is bad. Is this young Dan or is this the spook?'" Still, the fear was at arm's length. "I always feel really well protected at all times," he explains.

For instance, one day in 1972, Rob was in his lounge room in Bondi when he was informed by a spook that he would have a very bad car accident in two days' time but not to worry because he would be completely unharmed. He considered not getting in a car for the duration of the relevant period, but he was twenty-two years old, which meant that he ended up getting in his crazy mate's Mini Cooper and driving down to Adelaide for a wine festival. His friend fell asleep at the wheel, drifted onto the wrong side of the road and rolled the car into a sandbank. Rob emerged to find that the car no longer had wheels or windows, their luggage had been scattered all over the road and the glass from the shattered windscreen had left his mate bleeding. Not a scratch on Rob.

"I've had this sort of charmed life," he laughs, wheezily.

One aspect of this protection is that sometimes the spooks won't let him do a job. If it's not for him, no matter how keen he is to get amongst it, they simply won't respond. He understands this silence as them saying, "Nah, Robbo, you're wasting your time, mate. Wasting your time."

"It can get pretty complicated and a bit frightening, so if this stuff scares you, don't get involved, all right? 'Cause if you show fear, that's what the bad spooks want. Once you're frightened, you're easy to manipulate."

For the purposes of qualitatively evaluating his efficacy, Rob has distributed to clients over the past year a ten-page questionnaire headed *AIPR Survey—Haunt and Poltergeist Clearing in Australian Residences*, to be filled out when the job is done. The questions relate to the clients' personal circumstances, as well as their assessment of his labors.

"Have you seen any mystical beings such as angels or demons?" Rob reads out to the group from the survey after putting on his glasses. "Have you seen elves, fairies or other types of little people? Have you seen objects floating in the air? Apparitions of deceased entities you *do not* know? Apparitions of deceased entities that you *do* know?"

Also: objects being moved or thrown; opening and closing of doors and/or drawers; lights switching on and off by their own volition; animals shying away from specific areas; unpleasant smell of body odor or tobacco; unusual tastes; a mysterious sense of a cold spot.

"What else we got here?" he says, perusing the document. "Knocking? Tapping? Scratching sounds? Doorbell ringing— that's a very common one. Music? Anybody here have a case of music being played?"

One of the women says, "Yup," and explains that she's had radios come on. Another says she frequently hears faint music. Lee says that when they have the SB-11 going (a "spirit box" that sweeps AM/FM radio stations), he's heard "very old music" on that.

Rob explains that this survey was formulated with a fellow AIPR member who works in the psychology department of a university and has certain psychological tests embedded in the questions. I bear this in mind as I answer the true or false section in my head. Certain propositions I wholly disagree with (e.g., *Horoscopes are right too often for it to be a coincidence*). Some I greatly wish I found true (e.g., *My thoughts have sometimes come so quickly that I couldn't write them all down fast enough*). And there are many propositions with which I wholly agree (e.g., *I am fascinated by new ideas, whether or not they have a practical value; It is sometimes possible for me to be completely immersed in nature or in art and to feel as if my whole state of consciousness has somehow been temporarily altered; At times I somehow feel the presence of someone who is not physically there*).

Most interesting, to me at least, are the four questions in the final section:

Thinking about your own life and personal circumstances, how satisfied are you with your life as a whole?

How satisfied are you with your standard of living?

How satisfied are you with your health?

How satisfied are you with what you are achieving in life?

Rob continues reading aloud: "Experience of my physical body floating in the air . . . Nobody's been levitated?" he asks, looking around the circle over his glasses. "Nobody's been possessed?"

One of the women, a medium, mentions that as part of her practice she occasionally allows spirits into her body so that they can communicate with their family.

Rob advises her against such trance-mediumship. "I wouldn't do it," he says. "There's only one person who can be in this body and it's me!" He gives a chuckle but the instant return of his face, the set of his eyes, shows he is dead serious.

He continues. "Do you normally have psychic experiences? They all tick that box. We know from this survey that everybody that reports haunted houses is psychic," he says. If you're not psychic, Rob explains, you can walk into a haunted house and find it completely unremarkable. Anyone, however, can improve their psychic abilities, open up at least a little bit more. "The people that are having psychic experiences have access to the spiritual dimensions of consciousness, they have an extrasensory perception, get more information," he says.

"But how do you get that way?" Lee asks, plaintively.

"By being curious about it," Rob replies. "Psychic people are endlessly curious. They're always thinking, 'How does that work?,' 'Is God real?,' 'What happens when we die?' If you're thinking about that all the time, then that curiosity will get you there. It's about the evolution of consciousness. In the same way that intelligence is a potential—there's no limit to how intelligent we can become."

•

The second, and only other, time my phone has refused to work was the day after I left the conference at the Convent. I was again in my car, and chatting hands-free with my friend Kris. Immediately after I told her I was at a ghostbusting demonstration on Friday night, the call cut out. I called back and we laughed about it.

Before I got out of the car, I turned my phone off to reboot it. When I switched it back on a moment later, a song from my iTunes library that I had not chosen, from an album I had not played recently or indeed ever, flooded through the speakers. Fleetwood Mac's "My Little Demon."

"Sounds like you might've picked something up on Friday night," Rob said when I rang him later that week, mentioning the incident. He said he'd take care of it from where he was. This comforted me. It genuinely comforted me.

18

THE DEATH DOULA
ANNIE & KATRINA

The morning after her advance care directive talk, Annie lay on a stretcher in her driveway, Khedup squeezing her hand before paramedics wheeled her into an ambulance. He looked into her eyes and reminded her to open up, to not go small but to think of her own pain as connected with all the suffering of the world. This helped somewhat, she reports; the morphine helped mostly.

She stayed overnight in the hospital where the doctor told her that the pain—which would later require the removal of her gallbladder—was merely muscular. Though she felt this to be wrong, the doctor had her discharged. Of the nurses and doctors standing around outside her room, no one offered to help carry her bag. No one directed her where to go. They simply stood there looking at her as she left. Her voice was very fast and very small as she told me these things.

Katrina is coming off her last round of chemotherapy. She's been in treatment for five years. It's enough now, she's given it her best, she says, but it was eroding the quality of the time she has left with no discernible benefit. It is true that her illness has magnified the importance of every remaining moment, but it strikes me, again, that the directness with which Katrina speaks is not new. It feels not just as if she is comfortable in this straightforward mode, but that it is one she has long chosen as a matter of principle. She speaks with the directness of someone who at one time needed to find, then claim, her voice and will not be returning to her former state.

On our first meeting, I have only one question for her: she seems stronger than most people in good health. How is that?

"Because I've worked with people all my life," she replies immediately. It will not be until after she dies that I understand what she meant by this.

Not exactly that "shit happens," nor that escorting others through the fire gives you a muscle memory you can use later for yourself. It's more that one goes into the devastating work to which Katrina devoted her life for highly specific reasons, and that if this work is genuinely done with "excruciating vulnerability," one is also inexorably tending to the old wounds in oneself. In a culture where the only socially palatable coping mechanisms are to look on the bright side or drink something or buy something or hit refresh forevermore, this type of strength—perhaps the only true strength—is often mistaken for its opposite.

For twenty years, Katrina worked as a sexual assault counselor at the Women's Hospital. She completed a masters in social policy on sexual assault in the Catholic Church, knocking on doors, collecting stories, listening. She advocated for women in the workplace, worked with victims of crime. She has listened to those raped in church, those nearly murdered at home, and those whose loved ones were simply walking in the city when they were mown down and killed by twenty-nine-year-old James Gargasoulas, driving a stolen car. She is an encyclopedia of human trust—in parents, priests, the universe—betrayed.

"The heart of all that is, when you do face-to-face work with people, you have to be authentic," she says. "You're looking at them in the eye, they're looking at you, telling you—often for the first time—their *horrendous* trauma and their *horrendous* childhood." She starts to tear up.

"Most women—and men—aren't just abused once, most are abused multiple times. Indigenous victims you could multiply that by four. But the one gift I could give them was authenticity." She is weeping now.

"So I would go to therapy. I would climb mountains. I would keep fit. I would eat well. I would not come in hungover, okay occasionally I would, but not much," she smiles. "And I'd be able to just sit with them and see what happens."

Across from her, Annie nods. I can see her breathing deliberately, expanding her abdomen, her rib cage, her back into the space behind her.

Some people would come to see Katrina only once, tell their story in vague outline and say fuck it. But a lot of them came back. A police officer who had investigated a pedophile ring, crippled with rage. Victims pouring themselves into statements for cases that never made it through the system.

Katrina's uncle was Father Kevin O'Donnell of Oakleigh Parish, one of Australia's most notorious child sexual abusers, a man who offended prolifically and whose repeat victims included a preschooler. She breaks down remembering the faces of his victims, many of whom she worked with. It is as though her face has cracked open, so violent is her sobbing. She mentions survivor guilt, her hatred of the Catholic Church, her shame at being related to "this bastard." They are here, now, in the room—the betrayal and shame and rage, the great teachers one is forced to share the world with.

"Does that answer your question?" Katrina asks me. "What was it again?"

"It was how you became this strong," I say.

"I've done a lot of therapy," she smiles. Meditation, breath work for the "knots in the tummy," retreats, journaling, a dream group with a Jungian analyst—weekly meetings for fifteen years.

"Had to deal with a bit of adversity too," Peter adds, from his chair next to the couch. "Well, that's how you get your strength. By not quitting, pushing through it."

Peter is referring to her personal history, but she is still thinking about her work.

"I had a lot of wins," Katrina nods. "Sometimes you don't know they're wins. I saw them over the years get better, have healthy relationships with their partners, just be able to sleep at night, have less trauma. That was very rewarding."

Katrina's father was a Christian Brother from the age of fifteen until the age of thirty-nine. Her mother, an opera singer with a master's in music, was deeply religious; Katrina cries remembering the set of her "blank face." But she is close with her siblings, still has the friendships she formed after being kicked out of home as a teenager for attending Satsang—a form of communal meditation and reflection.

If you continue to go to that and not to church, her parents said, you can't live here. So she asked for a suitcase for her birthday and used it to move into a share house two kilometers away. Her mother never visited.

"Best thing I ever did," she says, sitting up on the couch to take small sips of water and glycogen. "That's one of the things that gave me the courage—meditation. So when I can't sleep at night, I use my breath."

She's had three dreams in a row about death. "But anyway I woke up and I'm not dead," she laughs, and Carol joins in, stroking the brown furry blanket as she re-tucks it around Katrina's feet. Katrina is breathless. Closes her eyes; it hurts to turn them towards the periphery. She apologizes for not looking directly at me or at Annie.

"It's not surprising that you're dreaming about death," Carol says. "Your psyche is processing stuff all the time now. There are aspects of yourself that are dying. You're losing capacity to do things that you've done in the past. So your death dreams are probably about those things that are dying."

Peter stares out the front window, his eyes like tunnels.

At this point, I thank Katrina for her time, turn my recorder off and close my notebook. She asks me to turn it back on. She wants to talk about another aspect of her life, wants it documented. It surprises me at first, what she wants to talk about.

She says: "I'm really proud of working with Victoria Police when they changed the family violence legislation to have a wider, broader context. I was still at South Eastern Center Against Sexual Assault, they gave me a secondment. So I helped change the definition of family violence. It was difficult being in that office, with all the men and that."

She continues. She is also deeply proud of her role at the Australian Football League, working at the MCG sports stadium to implement cultural change around gender equality and raising awareness about violence against women and children. "It was very intimidating," she explains, "but a very exciting place to be. I could see the place was changing . . .

"I was very proud of working at the MCG," she says. "I knew I was going to die—I don't know why, I just always knew—and I wanted the boys, every time they passed it on the train or went to a game there, to think of me and be proud of what I'd done."

What surprises me about why Katrina wanted me to turn the recorder back on is not her pride in her professional roles— the worldly wins that we are told (women, especially) are "not what matters." What surprises me is that Katrina's rightful pride—her strong sense of self—is not in conflict with how reconciled she is to its imminent extinction.

It shows a dexterity that feels less like dissonance, more like dancing. It is probably the same dexterity that allowed her to steep herself in grief while remaining open enough to maintain thick, rich connections with herself and others. Doesn't mean she's not terrified. You can see that in the thoughts that ripple the muscles of her face like fish under water. But without fear there is no bravery.

"When I got those positions," Katrina continues, "I was so proud of myself. That was all I'd talk about, because I was so proud of how I'd got there, I'd had a lot of failure, a lot of sadness." For one minute the room lifts, is lighter.

"But it's cost me." She pauses.

This is when I feel it, the thought fluttering from her to me like a dark bird changing branches.

"Oh, this might've happened anyway . . ."

And what can someone whose work is also to listen, to collect stories; to remain authentic, to not look away; someone who has read hundreds of sexual assault cases; someone with her own sadness, her own knots in the tummy and memories of her own mother's blank face; someone who does the therapy and the trauma counseling, the meditation and the breath work, who does the spin classes and eats right and loves her family and her friends; someone who is also proud of what she's done, in spite of—

What, in the end, might someone do with that?

19

IN THE BEGINNING
TIM

"If evolution is real," a woman is saying to her husband and young son, "why don't mothers have five arms?" They laugh heartily as they pass by.

Cruising the exhibits inside the Ark Encounter, I am currently watching a man who is watching, with enormous concentration, an interactive screen demonstrating how "solid waste removal" from the ark may have worked. It's taken an hour to make my way up from the bottom deck, through exhibits of animal cargo and the antediluvian world represented by detailed dioramas of people sinning extravagantly. Illustrated panels depicted man's descent into darkness which involved: Violence, Music, Polygamy, Metalworking and Giants. The last panel, in which women drown as Noah sails off towards the horizon, asked: *The pre-flood world was exceedingly wicked and deserved to be judged . . . Does our sin-filled world deserve any less?*

Tim Chaffey, "content manager" for the Ark Encounter, writes the copy for these exhibits. Tim—who describes himself as "a husband, father, author, apologist, and theologian"—is a tall man with a stellar smile and a bald head as pleasingly shiny as a peeled egg. He seems younger than his mid-forties on account of the still-packaged Hot Wheels displayed on his office bookshelf, the chill way he leans back at his desk and the fact that he's the kind of guy comfortable using the phrase "pretty neat."

As an author, Tim has a varied oeuvre, though his tone is fairly consistent. Aside from numerous blog posts, he has written articles (for *Answers Magazine*), "In-Depth" articles (for *Answers in Depth*), movie reviews (for the Answers in Genesis website) and book chapters (see, for example, *Demolishing Supposed Bible Contradictions* volume two). In addition, he has co-authored a graphic novel (*Searching for Truth*), a youth fiction series ("to teach young people how to defend the faith"), book-length nonfiction (a "comprehensive biblical, theological and scientific critique of old-earth creationism" with "Jason Lisle, PhD in Astrophysics") and historical fiction (a trilogy that takes an "imaginative and respectful look" at the "perilous situations" Noah finds himself in before and after the flood, at least one of which involves confronting a T. rex in front of an audience). Tim is also a cancer survivor. He was diagnosed with leukemia in July 2006 and has been in full remission since September of that year.

In a building down the road from the Creation Museum, I follow Tim through a vast and sparsely populated open-plan office. It could be any open-plan office, except that the cartoons tacked to the partitions are less likely to be jokes about office politics and more likely to mock the idea that the behemoth wasn't real. A very young woman walks past in a sweatshirt featuring a cross and the statement *This is illegal in some countries*. In his small windowless office, Tim's computer screen is open to an online Bible.

Surviving the cancer that was diagnosed the summer he stopped being a high school science teacher and started being a Bible teacher strengthened Tim's faith. "I'd already believed what this ministry teaches about why there is death and suffering and disease. And that's because God created a perfect world, and yet man ruined it through sin.

"I remember when I was being wheeled into the ICU thinking, 'Okay, I've told my students time and time again that when things are good we praise God, and when things are tough we praise Him, and the reason things like this happen is because we're sinful. Can I walk the walk?'

"I spent a month in the hospital. I was in very bad shape by the time I checked in. Who thinks the reason you're anemic is, 'Oh, you've got leukemia when you're thirty-two?' That wasn't on my mind." He laughs with a shrug. "When I googled it, it was, 'Oh, it might be a heat rash.'

"But anyways," he continues, "going through that process not only reinforced what I already believed to be true, but I guess every day you don't take for granted anymore. I've been given a second chance. Lately, I've been forgetting that. I need to remember it. You know, it's silly, but we get so focused on ourselves and what we're doing. I could be six feet under. And so let me be thankful."

Something clinks inside me at this, no greater than ice in a glass but just as clear. Finally, a bridge over the distance. Common ground. From this place, I think to myself, I will surely understand.

So I ask him to explain how we can be truly confident about what is meant literally in the Bible and what is meant figuratively and, in the end, why should that matter?

"Sure," he says. "Well, you're a writer. So, if you were to write something poetic, you would use different verb tenses—you know, if you were describing something, a lot of times you may write in present tense, you're going to use a lot of metaphors, you're going to describe things in similes, you know, 'this is like a flower'.

"And Hebrew poetry is similar—lines are repeated. It's not based on rhyme like it is in English. So we can recognize, generally speaking, what is poetic in Hebrew and what is narrative."

I consider, for a moment, a world where narrative is always the opposite of poetry. Where you can say something or you can sing something but never both. While I now know where such a world can be found, I do not agree it is the one on which Tim and I were born, perpetually turning in a brightness in the darkness.

The distinction matters, Tim continues, not only for accuracy but for what it says about God's character. God wouldn't have called millions of years of death "very good," would he?

"So, God calls death and suffering and diseases like cancer—because we find cancer as a tumor in dinosaur bones— 'very good'?" he asks. "When I'm on the hospital bed, not knowing if I'm going to get out of there, is God 'very good'? Because the thing that's killing me. He *said* it's very good. He likes it? It's just the way He made it? Or is death an enemy as the New Testament talks about? In First Corinthians 15:26, is God the God of life, and death is an intrusion into this world? Something that is a result of what *we've* done in our rebellion?"

In 1973, Hannah Arendt became the first woman to deliver the Gifford Lectures, a series established in 1888 to promote the study of a strain of natural theology that strives to integrate science, history, philosophy and the arts into a particular vision of the place of humanity in the universe. These lectures formed the basis for her book *The Life of the Mind*, in which she explored the powers and limitations of our cognitive function. One of Arendt's most powerful insights is a warning against mistaking knowledge for thought, and truth for meaning.

"Truth" refers to fact knowable through scientific methods of reasoning and error-correction. Truth is the what. Meaning is the why, and the nature of its questions are that they are "all unanswerable by common sense and the refinement of it we call science." Meaning, however, is no less important than truth and may be more so, given the immensity of what remains unknown to us.

"[T]o lose the appetite for meaning we call thinking and cease to ask unanswerable questions would [be to] lose not only the ability to produce those thought-things that we call works of art but also the capacity to ask all the answerable questions upon which every civilization is founded," Arendt wrote. In other words, our social survival—even our physical survival—is bound up with our spiritual survival and it might rely, as a matter of first principles, more on the aspirations underlying our questions and our ability to tolerate uncertainty than on our proficiency at defending solutions just for the sake of having them.

There was a strangely silent line of toddlers and kindergartners in front of me the other day when I watched Georgia Purdom lecture, listened to her deliver—almost verbatim—the sermon Tim has just given me in lieu of conversation.

"We know the world is not the way it's supposed to be, right?" she had said. "We know that it's wrong." The popularly accepted explanation of death is that it's always been here and always will be, she said, because it's integral to the process of evolution. "You can't get progress over millions of years from some sort of single-celled organism to mankind today without millions of years of death, disease and suffering. There's no such thing as 'nice evolution.' It's a *death-based mechanism,* okay? Now here's the problem for Christians in believing that God used evolution—the only conclusion you can draw from Scripture is that God saw death and suffering as 'very good,'"

She allowed a triumphant silence to hang. "One time I asked an individual who is a Christian but believes that God used evolution and millions of years, I just point-blank asked him one day: 'So what's the punishment for sin? Just curious, because if you've got death before that, then what is the punishment for sin?' And you know what his *amazing* answer was?

"'I. Don't. Know.'"

•

The solution to death and suffering and sin. Answers in Genesis. "Want more ANSWERS?" "Find More Answers . . ." "Get more Answers on Answers News." Answers for Women. Answers Magazine. Answers Radio. Answers Research Journal. The Ultimate Answers Pack. Kids Answers Mini-Magazine.

I am ten, eleven. Yom HaShoah, Holocaust Memorial Day. We are sitting on the gray floor of the school gymnasium. That great room is dark, lit only by candles held by older students taking turns at a podium reading out the names of our dead. They will read names all day, though the list is so long that to read for a day is to not even make a start. I can tell you what the Luftwaffe is, what the Einsatzgruppen is, what the Kindertransport is. I can tell you where in my house I will hide when the war happens again, what I will take with me into that crawl space, how quiet I will be there. I have already considered which of my non-Jewish neighbors are most likely to hide my family. I have read *The Diary of Anne Frank* and, after her, I call my own diary Kitty. I write in it to keep a record of myself. In the flickering dark we watch grainy footage of a layer of bodies as white and thin as paper being bulldozed into a pit. I am looking in the mirror of their faces for my reflection, searching for a sign of the family my grandparents refuse to talk about, for a face like theirs, like mine, on the flesh being concertinaed into the hole in the earth. I could be related to any of those bodies, and so I feel myself related to each of them. We sing in Yiddish. We sing in Hebrew:

> My God, My God
> I pray that these things never end,
> The sand and the sea, the wash of the waters,
> The crash of the heavens,
> The prayer of man.

For Hannah Szenes, the young poet and paratrooper who wrote these words before she, too, was killed by the Nazis, their atrocities were not inconsistent with the beauty of the world and a God ruling over all of it.

I have been mesmerized by this poem since I sat in that gym, thirty years now. Have tried to grasp the meaning of her words only to slide down the side of them with horror or cynicism. And here I am, returning to them again, still perplexed. Can I get closer, if only barely, to that astonishing tenderness which is the source of all fear and its only true antidote?

Szenes, too, kept a diary until she was executed. She wrote: *I loved the warm sunlight.* Refused a blindfold in front of the firing squad.

I was not a young father, feeling unreasonably exhausted, covertly typing my symptoms into Google after everyone had gone to bed. I will never be Tim. But I imagine that, while it would be excruciating to confront your own mortality at the age of thirty-two, it might be infinitely harder to think you were doing so for no good reason at all. That you had been abandoned—not just suddenly, but all along—by the loving protector you'd thought you knew. I can see how situating human terror and confusion and pain within a causal chain that is, somehow, the result of one's own unworthiness would be deeply comforting. Because it would be explicable, and in that sense, controllable. I am not Tim. But I am intimately familiar with this logic.

There are no solutions to this problem of death and suffering and injustice. There is, after all, no problem. Only the knowledge in the bones that nothing is perfect: there are no unmixed blessings. What, after all, is the Tree of the Knowledge of Good and Evil if not that? This can be the blade that we throw ourselves on, or the gravity that keeps us together. The universe doesn't care. We decide, and we must keep deciding. And that is very good.

20

PARANORMAL

VLAD

Because of the snacks and the banter, I vastly underestimated how unsettling this would be. We are now sitting in darkness as thick as a mattress, silence on all sides. It is cold from the air leaking through the high, covered windows, and I am too aware of the void at my back and at the edges of my vision. My eyes don't adjust to the dark, which is mitigated insufficiently by pinpricks of light on the various devices.

Tonight's session is apparently more relaxed than some previous vigils, which followed a strict formula: timed fifteen-minute blocks each of silence, formal questioning and quiet conversation. The quiet conversation block is not a break. "Curiously, a lot of the time when we got a response wasn't actually under formal questioning," Vlad explains, "it was while we were just having a chat." He asks Jessica if she has or can get any more intel about the gentleman who might be here.

"So, when I was in the corner, I connected with a man who was about eighty-three and he had a message for his daughter," she says to no one, in the tone of someone returning a missed call. "Not quite sure what the message was about but it was something about something that was misinterpreted? He didn't mean to do it, it was just an accident? So if there's any more information to come through . . ."

"Or," Vlad says, clearing his throat, "if you want to leave a message on one of our voice recorders or you want to kick the little ball we've got on the ground—just anything you can do to show us that you're here with us."

There ensues only silence, eventually broken by a car alarm in the distance.

Earlier in the year, I attended Vlad's workshop at the Ghost-busting conference which was called "A Short Course in the Principles of Ghost Research." One of his slides outlined three general "explanations of ghosts":

· Misperceptions—Distortions of perception, emotional exaggerations, pareidolia etc.

· Imagery or Hallucination hypothesis—Data from the outside world is not necessary, Autosuggestion (being primed to expect something).

· Survival hypothesis—Spirit or soul remains at the locality after death, Potentially nonhuman "entity" inhabiting location.

Pareidolia is interesting. It refers to the tendency of our minds to organize random visual stimuli into recognizable objects or patterns: the man in the moon, pictures in clouds, constellations, an image once brought to Vlad of a ghostly owl, which turned out to be an assemblage of branch and shadow.

Apophenia, similarly, is the tendency to perceive illusory meaningful connections between unrelated events or ideas. For example, that ghost owl being interpreted as a sign from a dead relative. Coined in 1958 by the German neurologist Klaus Conrad, apophenia was originally understood to be a psychotic thought process but it is now viewed as ubiquitous human tendency. We are wired to seek coherence; will reflexively choose certainty over accuracy. From the absurdity of our deepest paranoias to the radical coherency of our highest art, we are compulsive converters of fact into meaning. This human impulse to make something out of nothing is what once kept us alive. And it continues to serve that function, spiritually at least, for the vast majority of us who are unwilling to deem nothing its own something. It allows us to resolve our cognitive dissonance around what Haruki Murakami tidily referred to as the existential reality of nonexistence.

Pattern perception—accurate and illusory—functions as a type of banister, allowing individuals to feel as though they are making sense of past events and have a grip on the future. I once read about a study in *Science* magazine that's stayed with me. The title was "Lacking Control Increases Illusory Pattern Perception." The authors wrote that the desire to combat uncertainty and maintain control "has long been considered a primary and fundamental motivating force in human life and one of the most important variables governing psychological wellbeing and physical health." Lacking control, they explained, is an unsettling and aversive state that activates the amygdala—a fear response. "It is not surprising, then, that individuals actively try to reestablish control when it disappears or is taken away." They proposed that when we are unable to gain a sense of control objectively, we will try to gain it perceptually. Also—that our current needs can influence our perceptual processes.

To test that proposition, they conducted six experiments to see if lacking control increases illusory pattern perception, which they defined as a coherent and meaningful interrelationship among a set of unrelated stimuli. Participants who lacked control were more likely to perceive illusory patterns. This included "seeing images in noise, forming illusory correlations in stock market information, perceiving conspiracies, and developing superstitions." So although these different forms of pattern perception are usually discussed as separate phenomena, these results suggested there was a common motive underlying them. The authors concluded that the need to be and feel in control is so strong that "individuals will produce a pattern from noise to return the world to a predictable state." This tendency towards illusory pattern perception was, however, reduced "by affirming the self."

This last part—about the impact of being made to feel psychologically secure, equipped to deal with whatever may come—struck me. And so did the authors' own pattern-seeking behavior. Could the key to seeing clearly, I wondered, lie less in calling each other out on our magical thinking, and more in focusing on why we are all compelled to do it from time to time?

In the dark, it is hard to find a ledge on which to rest my eyes.

"I still want to buy a haunted house," Vlad is saying, and there is an exchange about various haunted premises before the room dips back into silence.

"So if there is somebody here, could you please let yourself be known to us?" Vlad asks. "Somehow tell us that you're here, in whatever way you can."

Silence.

"Were you part of the Masons?" he continues. Suddenly, a disembodied male voice rises up from behind me, faint but unmistakable.

"What was that?" Vlad asks, evenly.

"Outside," Paul says.

A dog barks down the street.

"But *why is the dog barking*?" Vlad deadpans. Everyone chuckles. The room quiets again, but it doesn't hold for long. Vlad baits Evelyn gently about climate change for a few minutes.

"My issue isn't with global warming, whether it's happening or not, that's one thing," he says. "I became very disgusted at the way the science was corrupted by politics very early on."

"It goes both ways," Evelyn says. "We have to look at the evidence."

"Yes, but the problem is that I don't trust the evidence now because I don't trust the people doing the research," he says.

They both hold strong views on the topic but this discussion is intended to serve a different function, because they agree on one thing: a watched pot never boils.

"You said we have to get into renewables," Evelyn says.

"We do," Vlad replies, "you can't rely on fossil fuel, oil and coal, it's moronic."

Then he stops to point out how, as they've been speaking, the lights on the EMF meters in the center of our circle have started going off.

"Good," Evelyn says, pleased but unsurprised. "When we talk, they are listening."

"I started zoning out when you were talking about climate change," Jessica explains with a giggle, "and I started doing this exercise about drawing in all the energy and that's when the second light started going on." She asks Vlad if someone died in this room.

"Not that I'm—Oh, go on, look at that!" he exclaims, all three lights on the meter suddenly illuminating.

"'Cause the guy that I was connecting with before, I think he died in here," Jessica continues, "and I think that's what the accident thing was about. I don't know if it was over there where that piano-y thing is or it was here. But I had this thing of him coming through and I think he was a bit drunk or something but whatever it was, wasn't meant to happen. And that's what he wanted his daughter to know—he didn't do it on purpose."

Vlad asks Luke for the readings on his meter, which has a digital display instead of lights.

"It's gone up, one-point-eight . . . two," Luke reports. This is the highest it's been so far and, while it is interesting that it reflects what was happening on the other EMF meter, Vlad is quick to point out that amplitude alone is not enough to prove anything. "Because there could be wiring underneath the floor . . . But at the same time it did seem to be responding to what Jessica was saying."

"I think he might have hit his head on something," Jessica says. "'Cause I saw that there was a stain, it's not there now."

I exhale deeply.

"Please tell me someone did that sigh then," someone pleads.

"It was me," I say.

"Thank god."

"There was one where we thought we heard a little girl's voice and it turned out it was someone's stomach rumbling," Vlad laughs.

"If someone has died," Luke says, "could they make the lights on that meter go up to confirm?"

"Ask them questions, Vlad," Evelyn directs.

"Um, why don't you ever respond to me?" Vlad asks with a sad laugh. "Look, we just want to know if you're here and if there's something we can help you with. It seems like you have some unfinished business here. If you just give us a sign?"

Nothing.

"If you can talk to us that'll be great, leave us some information. Walk past the lights, try and make them flicker?" he suggests.

Nothing.

Jessica summarizes again what she thinks happened, and Vlad chuckles. He explains that he hasn't been laughing at her but rather is reacting to what the rest of us have been observing; whenever she speaks, the lights on the EMF meter illuminate.

"Jessica," Vlad asks, "have you had weird stuff going on around you? Like phones not working properly or anything?"

"No," she replies breezily, "but there's this exercise I had to do at a workshop where it's like drawing energy through the earth and then up through spiritual realms into your body and then you release it? I've done that before and my phone has glitched."

"Perhaps it's your energy that's interfering with it," Vlad wonders. "All right. Let's give it a break."

Someone goes to put the kettle on.

"11:40. 28 September. Masonic Hall, Yarraville," Vlad says into his audio recorder.

Paul, Bridget and Luke have gone home. Vlad's EMF meter lacks the light display Luke's and Paul's had, but its oscillating squeal slices through the dark. He explains that's what happens when something magnetic moves over it.

Chuckling, he recounts being on an overnight vigil where he picked something up with this device. He and his colleague started asking questions, and the meter would remain silent or respond: *reeeerrrrr*. "So we eventually determined it was a female, fifty years old, a nurse. And then we thought, 'Hang on, let's just not say anything,' and the thing kept going. So we came up with all this information about this lady and it was just the meter going off by itself." The laughter diffuses into silence.

"Could you please give us a sign if there is someone in the room with us?" Jessica pleads.

Marina, stretched out full-length on the carpet, yawns.

"All right, Mister Man," Vlad says. "Whoever is here, can you please make yourself known. Are you angry about the way that you died?"

Nothing.

"Well, hopefully we get something on the recorders," Evelyn says. "I'll need some time to analyze the audio."

"Is there anything you know about this place that could direct some questions?" Marina asks Vlad.

"Not particularly, no," Vlad replies. "Lots of people have just reported feeling something in the room with them, like a sense of presence. Or feeling uncomfortable, like they're being watched. Even Nick, the guy who turned up, was saying that sometimes late at night it feels a bit weird being here."

Jessica says she doesn't think there's anything too major in the lodge room. "I thought there had been more things happening in the other room," she says, referring to the hall.

"If you're here with us," Evelyn says, "would you please give us a sign? Make this instrument here have a loud noise because Vlad needs to have some evidence."

"It's all about me," Vlad says with what sounds like a smile. "You know what would convince me the most? Having one of the little toys light up. Because if you know how they get triggered, it's physically impossible to fake it."

"If there's anyone in this room who wants to communicate with us, come into the middle of the circle, make the little machine make a noise," Jessica commands.

"Or this little ball glow," Evelyn adds. And then, "They probably don't like us directing them . . ."

"Sometimes it could be a block," Vlad says. "Someone in the room stopping the activity. I get that feeling whenever I walk into the room . . ." he starts, and everyone laughs.

"Like at parties." Marina laughs.

"Yes. I am the dissipater of fun."

"Because you're a skeptic, right?" Evelyn asks.

"If I was a skeptic I wouldn't be here. I want to believe, but . . ."

Evelyn, explaining how she underwent hypnosis to uncover a childhood experience of alien abduction, says she doesn't blame people for not believing. "Unless you experience it, it's almost impossible to say 'I believe.'"

I leave just after midnight, before they move into the hall. It happens while I am still driving home.

•

VLAD: It's 12:44 AM

In the open space of the hall, a slight echo haloes around the words as he sits. A laugh—probably Marina's. Metal scraping wood as chairs are set up. The sonic wail of Vlad's meter.

JESSICA: See, I feel like this room's a lot worse than the other one. Where the other room didn't feel scary at all—it just felt like there were one or two spirits there—this room feels very busy and very negative.

And there was something here on my leg just now as well.

VLAD *(calmly)*: Well, that's positive. If there's someone here could you let us know?

That incense smell is quite strong.

Murmur of agreement from the other three.

JESSICA: If there's any spirits here with us in the room can you please give us a sign?

A long silence.

JESSICA: It feels like where the other room had an older man in it, this room feels like it has a group of younger people?

VLAD *(mimicking a bored child)*: Come on, do something!

The others crack up.

JESSICA *(speaking about Vlad's trigger objects on the floor)*: Can you roll the ball back to us?

General chatter about how much energy that would take and where the entity would draw it from.

VLAD: The problem, from a skeptic's point of view, is always you just don't know how much of what people are saying is true. It'd be good to have an objective test for psychics—if they all come up with the same information . . .

Marina begins to talk about an experience she had at a venue in the city.

MARINA: I sent you an email about it—

Jessica gasps, a short and strangulated sound.

VLAD *(militantly calm)*: Wait, what was that?

JESSICA: Don't know. I didn't touch it.

VLAD *(marveling at one of the trigger objects at his feet)*: That's interesting. The light's just gone off by itself.

It is only the second time in nearly a decade of ghost hunting that Vlad has witnessed a trigger object illuminating on its own during an investigation.

VLAD: What time is it? 1:11. Eleven past one. One one one.

A series of stomps on the floor fails to elicit the same reaction from the ball.

EVELYN: Well, four witnesses here. *(Resigned)* It's a shame we didn't capture it on film.

21

THE DEATH DOULA
KATRINA

Katrina sits with the sun on her legs neatly crossed in perfect white capris. With her pristine ponytail and the linen sleeves of her pink shirt rolled up crisply, Katrina looks like she is waiting on a skinny latte extra hot with the other moms after Pilates. In fact she is about to eat pureed minestrone in a palliative hospice, which is as pleasant as possible on this bright afternoon, given its twenty-two rooms are full of people who are dying.

Katrina, however, is fielding phone calls, making lists. Leaves a message for her counselor, says she's feeling a bit better. She certainly looks it. "I'm doing well," she says, "because I'm in control of everything—medical, social, spiritual."

She is planning her living wake, an event she refers to as "the Do," which will be held at the beach club where she and Peter married a decade ago. We've just paged through their wedding album, Katrina explaining who's who, the sunny locale melding the occasions in her mind. She points to a photo of some particularly close friends. "You'll meet them at the wedding. I mean the funeral . . ."

"It's actually insane not to be at your own funeral," she says, examining a dish of mashed potato. The concept of a living wake is only momentarily startling, only superficially contradictory before it immediately makes perfect sense. Living. Wake.

Recently, her close friends and family have been talking to her in a different way. "I didn't realize people loved me so much. It's a shame it took this terminal illness, though." Then she adds, with some sadness, "I was always a bit of a present-buyer . . ." Only now does she realize how she belonged, that she needn't have felt she had to sing for her supper.

"These are the parts of cancer that bring me so much joy," she explains. "When we're well we don't give each other much feedback. We pick on each other. We're so judgmental. We're like the walking dead—consuming, being mean to others. But when death comes knocking on our door, we put it aside . . .

"I'm having these one-on-ones with people—it's a miracle. People are telling me things they've never told anyone because I'm safe. They can trust me. To be in the company of speaking truth is transformative."

Katrina's first thought when she received her diagnosis was that it didn't make sense. *But I've been such a good person!* Then it felt like a nightmare. She is one in eight million, has an extremely rare form of cancer, one most often seen in Holocaust survivors. "Now I'm looking at this like a miracle," she says. "A chance to have intimacy."

All going well, Katrina will be home in a few days. All going extremely well, she is looking forward to the possibility of enjoying one or two sips of a very good wine she has at home, ideally in the hot tub with Peter under the night sky. The minestrone is okay, she reports, blowing on a spoonful before she takes a minuscule sip. But what she would love, what she is really craving, is the deep-fried ice cream you get in Chinese restaurants. Maybe she could make it when she gets home and just have one mouthful, with a bit of banana, surely that would be manageable for her stomach? She is silent for one beat, losing herself in the imagined sensory joy and there is a crunch in my stomach like a key in a lock.

A doctor knocks on the door of Katrina's small room, comes in smiling.

"How are you going today?"

"To be honest," Katrina says, looking up from her chair, "very good."

In her sunny room, she directs me to refill her water bottle. To turn my recorder off, to turn it on again. To tell her why I have suddenly teared up: *what's going on for you?* To get her a blanket. To wheel her red walker out from next to the table. I maneuver it around awkwardly like I'm holding on to someone else's dog and steady it for her while she slowly stands, gets behind it, and threads her way through the room out towards the kitchen to gently confirm an order for French fries she put in earlier today for Lachlan, who will be visiting with Peter after school.

This manner of speaking she has with me, the bluntness of her requests that makes them into commands, makes me feel not just useful but included. It is the same tone she uses with Annie, with Peter, with Carol, with the doctor. It is a tone that I registered initially as tension, but which I am coming to understand is the sound of walking a wire, reflexively reaching outward for balance. It appears, at first, like she needs those she is addressing to steady her, as though it is their support that keeps her from falling. And I will believe this for exactly six weeks, during which, living in increasing pain, she will attend her own wake and then go downhill with more acceleration than anyone expected. Eventually, though, I will come to suspect that it wasn't just the requested support that was helping to sustain her. It was what lay beneath the request itself: the grinding desire to grip tight for just a little while longer. The dwindling energy, as strong as it was invisible, that she somehow spun out of herself like spider's silk and clung to while she swung herself into the future until she was there.

•

I am standing in a cemetery in the rain, watching Annie help Lady out of the car, her fur the glossy brown of a highly polished shoe. The dog stretches her front legs and drags herself to sniff a nearby tree, the rain falling lightly on her diaper as Annie keeps an attentive eye on an approaching car.

Annie has spent the last half-hour weaving down rows of gravestones looking for the one that belongs to her great-grandmother, Lucy. On and on she walked until the distance reduced her to just the orange dome of her umbrella. After much perplexity with the cemetery's directions, we finally found the right grave and she stood there with her bright blue shoes in the mud, moved at the thought of this forebear whom she never met. Like Annie, Lucy never practised the religion into which she had been born. In the end, however, Lucy insisted on being buried in a Jewish cemetery, even though it meant physical separation from the husband she loved.

This reminds me of a couple I am acquainted with. Jewish; not religiously observant, except it was important to the woman to be buried in a Jewish ceremony. So her partner converted solely for that reason. Couldn't bear the thought of being physically separated for eternity.

Annie has children, grandchildren, great-grandchildren. She is very proud of them all, though I know she wishes she were closer with her sons, one of whom is religious to a degree that has resulted in some emotional and physical distance. In response to a question I once asked, Annie replied that she is uninterested in romantic love, will not be partnering again. "I used to think, 'Ah, love . . .' I really wanted to have love in my life, and I realized that it's so conditional. So, yeah. That was a good teacher."

On the drive from my house to Annie's, I always pass a cluster of buildings, long and low, completely interchangeable except for their signage: Bunnings, PetBarn, Repco, Officeworks and a church, Revival Centres International. Its frontage bears an image of a trumpeter on a bucking horse and three Sphinx-like phrases of unequal intelligibility: Personal salvation, Divine healing, World events.

The world is full of different gods, its website says, but the God of the Bible is the one who answers.

It used to be a battery factory, explains the small group of older congregants that flock around me after I attend their Sunday service. "We're trying to convert you, if you haven't already guessed," a bald man says, with a smile. A woman hands me a small booklet, *Your Personal Invitation* typed on the front.

Inside, a numbered list of things they believe. Number seven: *the Bible instructs the Spirit-filled believer on how to live an overcomer's life.*

They inquire whether I have experienced "the infilling of the Holy Spirit."

I have felt filled with spirit, I reply, but I don't believe we would be talking about the same thing. When I ask the man what it felt like the first time he received the Holy Spirit, he dismisses the question by saying it was not a human emotion.

"It's a pure language," he explains.

During the service the pastor spoke at length, an elderly man behind me interjecting a well-oiled "halle-loool-yah" at regular intervals. Truth needs no adjudication, the pastor said, because it is absolute. And with God's law written in your hearts you have the beginnings of perfection. Then he closed his eyes. "Hallelujah praise his name, hallelujah praise his name," he intoned into his microphone, eliciting a rippling response from the congregation like water rushing over rock, and then, like a fish breaking surface, someone would suddenly speak.

In 2006, researchers at the University of Pennsylvania School of Medicine demonstrated changes in cerebral activity during glossolalia, speaking in tongues. Though suffering from the limitations of a small pool of subjects, "since it is difficult to find experienced practitioners willing to perform glossolalia in a laboratory setting," the neuroimaging during this practice found decreased activity in the frontal lobes—the area of the brain associated with thinking, language and self-control. It also showed changes in the oldest areas of the brain, those involved in emotions and establishing our sense of self. Interestingly, these findings contrasted with brain imaging taken during meditation, a highly focused practice, in which the frontal lobes are activated and engaged.

The principal investigator stated that the finding of decreased frontal-lobe activity was fascinating "because these subjects truly believe that the spirit of God is moving through them and controlling them to speak."

I heard a few people speak in tongues during Sunday services at RCI. They fell into two groups. Those in the first group spoke in English using the first person. They addressed their fellow congregants as "My children," exhorting them towards strength and bravery: "For I am with you."

The second group was smaller, did not use formally representative language. They spoke in a register slightly higher than normal speech. It sounded like someone heard Gaelic or Hebrew or Arabic one time and fell in love, going home to replay the syllables in the mouth. What it felt like, though, was another matter. It felt like a lament, a surrender. At once completely alien and instantly familiar. And though I knew that any dream of a common language would evaporate the moment English resumed, for a time, in that old battery factory, I felt I was hearing a true sentence.

Reclining in a lawn chair on her back deck, Katrina is home from the hospice and sucking the sun into herself, stunned with warmth like a lizard on a rock. The newspaper lies, unopened, at her side. Her red walker is nearby. As I approach her, the only sound is a plane passing overhead. Then she sits up and feels for her sandals, her toenails a bright pink, painted by Peter. She directs her cavoodle, Ricky, inside and pops on a straw hat and I am struck, again, by how healthy she looks, how vital she is, how very easy to talk to, to feel comfortable with.

She says that if she has the luck or the grace to be here for another six months she wants to love the people in her life. She wants to feel the sun. She wants to spend Christmas with her family and with Pete's family, attending Lachlan's school Christmas party. She wants Pete to know how much he means to her. She doesn't want to fight about anything. She wants music on all the time. She wants to listen only to uplifting songs, to Celine Dion's "My Heart Will Go On" . . . oh, also "Ave Maria"—she wants me to write that down in my notebook so I can remind her about it later. She wants to go to the forest, up to the low mountains of the Dandenong Ranges. She wants to not be bothered by the little things that are still, yes, even now, rankling—the calls that haven't come, the slights remembered, the rug that's long needed to be replaced in the front room that should've been done earlier before all these visitors were coming through. She wants people to leave her feeling better than when they arrived. She wants to slow her mind down. She does not want to be a burden on others. She wants to speak to the neighbors, to the school, to family and friends to make sure that people are keeping an eye on Pete and the boys, make sure they're coping all right after she's gone. She wants to meditate. She wants to be at peace.

When Peter says to her, "How am I going to cope without you?" she replies, "But I'm everywhere in this house."

She believes that after this, there lies some kind of life. "I'll be in the stars," she says. Next month she will die.

22

IN THE BEGINNING
GEORGIA

Though Georgia Purdom and I are both holders of doctorates, readers of the *New York Times* and the *Proceedings of the National Academy of the Sciences*, type-A personalities, teachers, writers, mothers, women with two hundred and six bones in our bodies and twenty-four hours in a day and twenty-six letters to describe our time here on earth, I know any fleeting intimacy between us is about to drift off like an unmoored boat.

"Is death always a 'bad' thing?" I ask. "I know it's a *sad* thing, but why wouldn't that just be part of us not being gods ourselves?" Occasionally, I look at my hands—on the keyboard, holding a coffee, folding a tiny pair of pants—and it strikes me that they have become a mother's hands. The same impression applies to my voice—words, intonation, approach. I have just, I realize in the doing, used the mother's voice.

"Again, it just comes down to *what He said He did*," Purdom enunciates from behind her desk. "When people want to question what the Bible says about these things, my question always is: '*Why* do you want it to be another way, why do you want it to be different than what He says?'"

I smooth nonexistent wrinkles out of the page open on my lap. Look down at my mother's hands. If only truth were a matter of what we wanted, what made sense, what we wished for.

Purdom continues, her voice entirely uninflected by doubt and getting louder as she goes, "To me, God creating ex nihilo, *that's* an extremely powerful God that can do that just by His word alone. *That's* ultimate power. And so I could say the reverse: to me, a God using trial and error and struggle, and all of that, isn't a very good God. You know, I could say *that*.

"But again"—she calms, a pot removed from the boil—"we try to put our sense of justice, our sense of ideas of things on God instead of letting God just be who *He* is and speak for Himself."

The transactional understanding of suffering is not one befitting an adult; it is reminiscent of an earlier developmental stage. But there is something about it that feels familiar—the nonsensical insistence on *sense*, the stamp of the foot: *but it's not fair!* It's in me too, has never gone away. Julia Kristeva said that the adolescent is not a researcher in a laboratory, he is a believer. That we are all adolescents when we are passionate about the absolute. And what is more absolute than death?

"There's a doctrine of perspicuity," Purdom says, "that Scripture is clear, it's not meant to be challenging or difficult. God wants us to understand Him, so He hasn't written it in a way that's supposed to be like, 'Oh we don't really know what that means ...'"

I feel I can see it, what lies shaking under the quilt of Purdom's words: just the heart's refusal to accept the world as it is. While this particular flavor of high insistence is monumentally strange to me, the impulse to push against a great locked door is not. And though it feels silly at times, this conversation is, in form if not in content, a representative exchange between very different adults. We are no longer in the throes of first struggle, no longer destabilized by the disjunct between what we want and what we get. The wet plaster of adolescence—when anything seemed possible—has long dried and left behind the masks we wear over the fractures that lie beneath: those places where pain has ossified into blame of self and of other.

So I stop thinking and start breathing, which is something I am working on. And in the space this clears, there are just two people in a small room on a speck spinning in infinity. What is space anyway, Joseph Brodsky wrote, if not the body's absence at every given point? So in light of that vast absence, despite the distance between Purdom and me, each being unreached by the other, our proximity at this moment is not nothing. And if you really listen to her, and not her words, there is something so nakedly vulnerable in this room that it feels like a baby is crawling underfoot.

The writers Cheryl Strayed and Steve Almond had a podcast called *Dear Sugar*s. On one episode, a woman had written in seeking their advice, asking if her reaction to a painful situation had been wrong. Almond did not respond directly. Instead he said: *reading the letters we receive, I'm always struck by how much, and how quickly, people convert their pain into self-loathing.* This stopped me cold.

I hadn't previously thought of anxiety as an autoimmune disease. But of course it is.

I have a sticky brain. Intrusive thoughts get stuck there, connect themselves like toy trains running long loops of self-loathing rumination, carving neurological tracks deep as canyons. Before my mother left, my brain felt like a playground. After: the canyons. If I was someone that not even a mother could love, so it went, better force everyone else's hand. Get it over with so next time I would not take the bullet from behind.

In my efforts to cull myself from the herd, I would confess anything about myself that might remotely cause the people who loved me to reconsider. I would speak at speed until I could not breathe. If no one was there to listen, I would write these thoughts in my diary until I ran out of pages and then I would write in the margins, the lines scraping over each other, breaking like branches on an overgrown tree. I would think until my vision whited out. And then I would sleep. A decade passed like this.

Stress along that fault line can send me hurtling back. Still, I am getting better at catching the old wound at work.

In hindsight, the fact that I had found the right therapist was evidenced by my conviction that I had found the wrong one. At our first appointment, I took out notes and quickly ran through the relevant history before explaining that I needed to understand how to fix this in order to claw my life back from the devouring drain of my days. In response he sat very still. Then he apologized for not thinking in as ordered a way as I did. But that it seemed to him that if this was a problem that could be satisfactorily solved by thinking, I would have done so by now. Perhaps it was time to come to someplace below the neck—I remember how he placed one hand on his abdomen, so tenderly, as though he needed it too—and just breathe.

My focus was not on breathing. My focus was on how I had wasted my lunch break and now would need to fish the list of psychologists out of the bin and resume my search for help while my work piled up around me and my mind ate itself alive. I had no idea what he was trying to tell me and no interest in what sounded absurd. What problems could possibly be immune to thought?

But seeing as I was there anyway, I gave it a little go. I breathed exactly enough to begin to reverse the direction of one speck of frantic discomfort inside me.

It would save me, his seemingly secret knowledge that the homes we build in our heads are no safer than the ones we build in the world. And that the only solution to this is no solution at all, but rather one breath, and the next one.

•

"You know, I always say you have to develop a very thick skin, you do," Purdom reflects when I ask her whether her work takes a personal toll. "Initially, it was hard but the more that I've worked here, the less difficult it's gotten. Because I really try to see it as: the people that oppose me or say bad things about me, it's not me that they have a problem with, it's God. That's who they're really fighting against, I just happen to be the outlet for it. So I just learned not to take it personally."

I thank her for her time. She tells me that my questions were really, really good. And then she walks me out past the office cubicles where our feet make no noise on the carpet. It's like we're not even there until we say goodbye.

23

THE DEATH DOULA
KATRINA

Katrina is eating duck à l'orange at her funeral. By "eating," I mean savoring a few microscopic morsels of the solid food she has been unable to digest for the past five months, before elegantly retiring her cutlery to her plate, which is positioned in front of a wine glass of coffee-flavored Sustagen. By "funeral," I mean her living wake, the Do, the event currently in full swing around us at the Beaumaris Motor Yacht Squadron where 113 of her friends, family and former colleagues have been invited, most of them now loudly chatting and laughing while eating either the duck or the salmon. If that seems odd, I direct you to what Annie—who first explained the concept of a living wake to Katrina and to me—said about such occasions: there are no rules here, apart from the aim that it best reflect the person being honored.

The white envelope that arrived in my mailbox was sealed with a single gold star. The invitation it contained was printed on a small sheet of rose-colored paper that I thought, initially, was a bar mitzvah invitation on account of the Star of David at the top, which Katrina later explained was there to symbolize unity, balance and wholeness. It said:

Celebration for life achievements of
KATRINA

Saturday May 11th 5:00–10:00 PM
(Arrive 4:45 PM to allow for parking)
Dress code: Semi Formal with a Touch of Gold

At 5:00 PM the gathering in this room, with its walls of glass facing the water, felt like a work function—awkwardly yet determinedly social. Katrina sat this part out, rationing her strength for the rest of the night. Carol, the MC, wove between knots of guests having drinks in their touches of gold, checking last-minute items off her clipboard with the venue staff.

Over the playlist of Katrina's favorite songs was a burbling soundtrack comprising chatter and laughter, too-loud HI-HOW-ARE-YOU-DOINGs and parabolic replies of "Good, good!" which flew, initially, with reflexive enthusiasm towards a high register before descending just as sharply under the influence of gravity. The youngest guest was a baby, parked in a pram near a table bearing family photos and a heart-shaped cake dusted in gold with a wooden topper that read *Love*. More family photos were projected on a screen at the front of the room: holidays and dinners with friends, selfies in groups and in pairs, Lachlan in front of Uluru, and all the Katrinas—brunette and blonde, larger and slimmer, curlier and straighter, glam and natural. And in none of them, strangely, did she look as young as when she entered the room on Peter's arm to spontaneous applause, appearing like the just-married couple they were when they celebrated in this room ten years ago and nothing like they will be later this year when Peter returns to scatter her ashes in the water that is now turning black beyond these walls.

As she walked to her table, her guests said, "Darling, how are you sweetie?" and "I don't know if you feel it, but you look a million bucks." And it's true. It's not simply that you wouldn't know Katrina is sick, or that she is dying. It's that she is gorgeous. Solar in a gold gown with gauzy arms. You wouldn't even notice the soft plastic tube connecting her to a syringe driver nestled discreetly in the little black bag that dangles casually from her shoulder. After settling into her seat at the front table between Peter and Meg, an honorary auntie who was once Lachlan's babysitter and is now part of the family, Katrina looked over to check on the boys sitting nearby with their mates. Annie, next to Meg, smiled at Katrina, who took a long, slow breath as the waiters began to serve the food.

A syringe driver is a small battery-powered pump that delivers medication at a constant rate through a continuous subcutaneous infusion—a very thin line running under the skin. Katrina says softly to Annie that she hopes she doesn't vomit during the evening, but it is what it is. Annie nods, her shaved head as soft and gold as a billy button.

Katrina recently had to go into the hospital, stay overnight. She sounded upbeat on the phone when she returned home, telling me how she'd had a heart-to-heart with one of the nurses, a young man who was once a Buddhist monk. How compassionate he had been, how reassuring, how much strength talking to him had given her. Also, that sharing a room with heavily sedated patients had only confirmed her resolve to meet whatever lies ahead unmedicated. A woman was so out of it she managed to get her hand stuck down the toilet, she said; don't ask. It's not the path for me.

"Can you please make your way to your seat, we've got a big program to get through . . ." Carol says from the low stage at the front of the room, where she stands under the projected photos, speaking into a mic. "I'm just going to have to interrupt so we can get this shindig on the road." The crowd disperses no faster than it would at any other function, the small talk continuing for too long as people settle in front of name cards at tables with white linen and pink floral centerpieces in gold vases. There are bread rolls and bottles of San Pellegrino, red wines and white, candy jars with chocolate freckles and jellybeans, pens and paper, little packets of tissues. Everything has been anticipated by Katrina with the same determined energy with which she is now dinging her glass with a knife to direct attention to Carol. It is the same determined energy that shows it is possible to be both knowingly gathered for the last time with the people you love and also pissed off about the extra salt on the saganaki. It is a holding on, a clinging to; a very thin line running under the skin.

Finally, silence. After an Acknowledgment of Country, Carol says, "This is a unique occasion. I've never MC-ed at a live wake before. Katrina has spent much of her life nurturing and developing with integrity her contribution to the way we live in our communities. So I'm delighted to be MC-ing for her, Katrina, in this sixtieth year of your life." Sixty speaks to a slightly fairer fullness that fifty-nine lacks. It is an age she will not live to see.

"It is an honor for all of us to be invited to share this celebration with you, Katrina. And there are many here tonight who will have the privilege to offer our reflections on a life well lived . . ."

The tone is elegant, the words jarring. We aren't used to them, they clog the throat, disturb the ear—phrases about the present that refer to the past but not the future. I watch the room, the family watching its photos. And I do not feel I can stand it. I look past Katrina. Past Peter, wiping his nose with a white hanky he pulls from his pocket, past Lachlan in his suit, to the glass wall that is now a dark mirror reflecting the fairy lights strung over the dance floor, dangling—like our faces— over the void.

Carol invites Annie to the lectern. She strides across the stage softly in orange boots, her long orange top billowing around her. Introduces herself as Katrina's end-of-life advo-cate, "death doula" being considered too confronting for the audience tonight.

"Perhaps you've never experienced a living wake before," Annie says gently into the mic. "I'm sure that many of you have been to a funeral. Perhaps to many of them. At the funeral you would've heard shared stories and memories of that person. Per-haps you may have considered, 'Wouldn't it be nice if the person whose funeral it was was here to listen to these words.' I've heard many people say, 'I wish I could be at my own funeral. I wish I could hear what they say.' So that's the purpose of a living wake. Together we get to manifest the intention for Katrina's living wake, and together we get to help create a sacred space.

"Tonight each of you have entered here carrying gems. The gems of your shared experiences. These gems will multiply as you begin to remember your stories, your interactions with

Katrina. None of us stands alone. We are who we are today because of countless other beings."

The baby starts to wail and is taken out into the hallway.

"Bishop Desmond Tutu said, 'You can't exist as a human being in isolation. My humanity is inextricably bound up in yours. We belong in a bundle of life.'" Annie asks the guests to write to Katrina and her family using the paper and pens provided on the tables. They can write messages, or memories, and together the letters will form a golden record of her time here with us. "They're very powerful. They will be kept and later they will be made into a book for Peter and the boys and for future generations."

A young friend of the family starts singing Nick Cave's "Into My Arms" while the projector continues the slideshow of family photos behind him. Lachlan kicking a football. Katrina and Lachlan boarding a train. Katrina and Peter at a café in Paris. Lachlan on the beach . . . There they are, I think, unburdened, most themselves, most alive.

I am trying not to watch Peter. But I am watching him. I am watching him in his black suit and white shirt and gold bowtie as he keeps removing his glasses to swipe his cheeks with the heels of his hands. I am watching until those hands are my hands and those photos were downloaded off my phone, I am watching as it presses on my chest through the fabric of my black suit and my white shirt and my gold tie until I stand up and screech that I can't do it, I will not do it, I cannot leave or be left, I cannot, I cannot, I cannot . . . And it takes everything I have not to excuse myself from this table, where I am sitting next to Annie, and run home to my husband and our child for

I cannot conceive now of wasting a single second I might have with them. Instead, I sit as silently as I can and wrest one tissue out of the leopard-print packet that has been placed in front of my name card.

"Stressful," Meg nods, her eyes welling up too, one hand placed gently on her chest. Only then, the realization: this, now, is when they are most themselves, most alive.

I'm scheduled to visit Katrina ten days after the Do. When I text the night before to confirm she's still up for it she responds that she's fatigued, feeling like she's had enough, that it may be our last chat. Annie drops in some books to her and reports that Katrina is going deeper inside herself. *The Forerunner. The Glance. Spirit Walker. Sacred Fire. Preparing to Die.* "I have to go within," Katrina explained, "because I cannot control what is happening outside."

When I text Katrina the following morning, a friend replies on her behalf, saying she's feeling slightly better today but not up to speaking, perhaps next week. Next week she is worse, pretty much bedridden according to Peter, who is now up nights administering her medication. This is the pointy end, Annie says, coming back from the house, where a whiteboard sets out the visiting schedule. Katrina's lost more weight. Has double vision, can't read, can't watch TV, can't meditate. She asked for a mandarin, which she couldn't eat. Annie peeled it so she could suck on the segments for flavor.

Katrina said she no longer had any quality of life, was considering stronger medication. Annie asked Katrina why she could not meditate. Katrina has forty years of meditation practice, alone and in groups, at home and on retreats, would do it daily before her feet touched the ground, could go so far inside herself that she heard music on a few occasions—so why not now? Katrina replied that she could no longer physically sit, as she had for decades, for her practice. And that she had lost the attention span anyway. She did not sound like herself.

In Tibetan, Annie told her, the word for meditate simply means "to familiarize." You can always, in any situation, make a decision to get a bit closer with wherever you are, with whatever is there, she reminded Katrina.

Fear might be its own dark meditation, I think when I hear this. How deceptively it focuses the mind, blocks out all distractions. I am not surprised by Katrina's state of mind and do not think she has been defeated. I'm in awe of how long she lasted in her aspiration to meet her death unblinking, and confirmed in my sneaking belief, all along, that in the end no such thing is possible.

"Katrina died around 2:30 AM, and it sounded perfect," Annie tells me a few days later. By "perfect" she means that Katrina was at home next to Peter, in a bed that had been placed in the front room among the life of their house, with a view of her garden. That she was lucid—no medication. That when it came, her death was sufficiently gentle that Peter woke up to find it as fact. But most of all she means: "In the words of Frank Sinatra," Annie smiles down the phone, sniffing, "she did it her way!"

Katrina had felt the fear, had faltered in the face of it, but she did not let it stop her. Her last words: I want the light on.

24

PARANORMAL
ROB

"Go on, you lot! You can go. Have a nice day," Rob says in a mild tone from the armchair where he sits in the formal lounge room of an elderly man named Gene, who has hired him to clear his house. With a clipboard on his lap and his spectacles poised at the tip of his nose, Rob is less thrilling to watch at work than I had anticipated. Less like *Ghostbusters* and more like being stuck in a doctor's waiting room with a person having a too-loud conversation on their phone.

"Yeah . . ." Rob nods, staring into the middle distance while Gene, leaning forward in his chair and gripping the handlebars of his rolling walker, watches him intently. "There's nothing for you here gang, this life is over . . . Bye-bye."

Two hours ago, I was watching a lizard scramble in the sun-bleached weeds growing around a fridge that had been deposited in the front yard of Rob's apartment building in Sydney. The sky was opaque white, closed as an eyelid. Bush fires were burning towards each other on the outskirts of the city and not so far away, ash studded with thousands of dead ladybugs was washing up on the sand of the North Shore. I heard it before I saw it, Rob's black car with the fifties fins growling down the empty street.

On the way to Gene's he explained that the survey results are in: he is eighty-eight percent effective at clearing houses, data which pleases him greatly though not in regards to his efficacy per se. It's more because he feels it vindicates his thirty-year insistence that the causes of these disturbances are not (contrary to an entrenched school of thought) resolutely psychodynamic, existing only in the mind.

"There's nothing mentally wrong with the people," he told me, recounting some of what he said when he presented the data at a recent conference. At the other end of the spectrum, he derided the idea that psychic clearing is a religious matter. "At best exorcism is not very effective and at worst it makes matters worse. People die, people get killed," he said. "The whole idea is based on a Christian logic which is not matched to reality. When I did philosophy of religion at University of Sydney, we were taught there's no proof that Jesus Christ ever existed, that God is an idea borrowed from the Jews, and Satan is a creation of the Church to add symmetry to theology." He explained that the people who taught him how to clear houses all learned their skills in spiritualist churches which they eventually left, finding the institutions too limiting. "They still psychically clear haunts and poltergeists without any reference to religion at all and it's just as effective. So it does rather suggest that the religious thing is just a nonsense."

Returning to his survey results, he said those who had filled out the questionnaires self-reported high psychic ability and no mental illness. Otherwise, his clientele is pretty diverse—many ethnicities, many religions, many ages. "Social status means nothing," he said, with a wheezy chuckle.

"They rationalize it for a while," he said about haunting activity—but clients seek him out when it reaches crisis point. He's got one puzzling case at the moment in Bondi, an elderly Jewish woman from Europe. "Very strange stuff happening there," he said, perplexed. "I cleared the place of all the bad spooks—that was easy enough—but there's this other stuff going on and from her descriptions I can't quite make out what it is."

I inquired whether she might have Holocaust-related trauma.

"She doesn't seem to have psychic scars, seems to have missed out on all that," he mused. "But of course, being Jewish, there's no escaping it." And then we arrived at Gene's.

I had imagined the house in Gothic strokes: if not towers and turrets, there would certainly be something to hint at the horror within. Instead we pulled up in front of a tidy brick home on a busy road across from a golf course. Rob unfolded himself from the car holding a honey-colored wooden briefcase. Stood in the driveway, tipping his white-crowned head back to take it all in.

"*Phroar*, you can feel it from the street!" he said with gusto. "This house is haunted."

I did not—and would not—have that impression, but it only grew stronger for Rob after Gene, bowed like a candy cane over his walker, welcomed us from the darkness of his garage and led us down a narrow hallway hung with family photos and degrees from one of the best universities in the world, into the lounge of the home he built two decades ago. It is where he lived with his wife, who died ten years back, and their daughter, who returns weekly to check on him.

It all started about three months ago when an electrical cord went missing and then turned up later, inexplicably, in a suitcase. Soon after, Gene felt a touch on his back when no one else was home. The lights in his garage wouldn't work, though an electrician could find nothing wrong. And then he walked into his kitchen one afternoon to find himself confronted by an apparition of a "morose-faced woman."

The fact that these occurrences started only recently told Rob that this spook is a blow-in, passing through like bad weather or bad feelings. "It's not somebody who used to live here," he explained as we settled into armchairs on either side of Gene. "The spooks move around the suburbs looking for somebody who is psychic and then they latch on to you and become a nuisance and they—Ah, hang on," he interrupted himself, looking over my head. "Okay," he nodded. "Usually what they want is attention and they want help. So you've done the right thing by getting help." And then he added, "She's listening to what we're saying now."

He extracted his spectacles and a clipboard from his brief-case, perused his notes. "Tell me about when she touched you, was it a friendly gesture?"

"It was a nuisance," Gene replied.

"The morose-looking female," Rob continued, "describe her to me."

It was a blur, a flash, Gene said.

"She's here," Rob said, looking up with a dry sniff. "A kind of rotund woman, in her fifties. She's got an apron on. Gray hair. She's angry. Not happy at all." Then, projecting his voice across the room, he said, "We're here to do you a kindness, okay?"

After a moment of close listening, he observed that there were other spirits in the house as well. Then he waved them on, bidding them good day and bye-bye.

Now Rob returns to his notes. "Voices. You hear voices but can't make out what they're saying?" Gene nods. "Yeah, that's very common in haunted houses. Okay. Have you been psychic all your life?" The assumption startles me, Gene's psychic abilities had not been mentioned thus far.

"Yes," Gene confirms. "Yes, I have." It's something he developed twenty-five years ago, he explains. He subsequently wrote a book on parapsychology, getting both the desire to write and the content directly from a spirit guide.

"Okay, right—well you know what we're talking about!" Rob says, delighted.

The room is densely populated with the decorative scheme of another time: chandeliers, lamps, ornately scrolled tables and glass cases displaying dolls and souvenir spoons and porcelain figurines, every surface coated with a thick stubble of dust. There are photos from Gene's university days, his career, his parents, his wedding.

"Let me see what's going on in the house," Rob says, returning to the task at hand and closing his eyes. The only sound in this room with furniture for ten to sit comfortably is the purr of cars down the road outside.

"Okay. There's a couple on the couch. One's in that chair. They're all listening to us talk. That's normal. It's very rare that a haunted house has only one spook—very rare, in my experience. There's always a group of them."

I follow Rob's gaze but find only empty corners where cob-webs dangle like strands of gray hair.

Rob says that there are usually between fifteen and twenty spirits in this house, information Gene receives dispassionately. Currently, Rob continues, there is a crowd of such spirits banked up in the hallway and filing into this room to observe the pro-ceedings. For a time, Gene watches Rob studying the doorway.

The morose-faced woman is the leader. She is stubborn but the others actually want to go to the light. "We'll wait till they all get here," Rob says, "and they can go together, all right?"

Gene solemnly agrees.

"Usually at this point, we invite the good spooks to come into your home," Rob says. "Is that okay with you?"

Gene nods.

"Can you say that?"

"I invite the good spirits to come into my home," Gene says formally.

"Thank you," Rob says. "And all the lost spirits that are here—what would you want for them?"

"To go where they belong, to go to the light," Gene replies.

"Okay, I'm happy with that," Rob says, looking around. "They're all chattering away now," he reports.

Gene inquires about the good spirits to which Rob has referred.

"I've been working with them for over twenty-five years, done over five hundred and fifty jobs like this," Rob explains. "It's not always the same crew but somebody always turns up. All the communication is emotional. The bad spooks are just kind of frightened and lost, they don't realize they're dead."

Rob says he's had out-of-body experiences since he was a boy. It's a state in which he can think clearly and see and hear everything that's going on. That's what happens to us when we die, he explains. "And if you're not sure what's going on—say, for instance, if you're Christian and what you're experiencing doesn't match what the church told you—then you're confused. Or if you have a science degree and what you're experiencing is not oblivion, then you get confused," he says.

"Yes," Gene says, nodding slowly. "These are the spirits that should have gone up to the spirit world." Gene explains that he's always understood that the dead are met and escorted there by a deceased loved one; this is what he was told when he was younger.

"This one woman, she's really grieving because she's leaving what she knows for an uncertain future," Rob says. "Go on, it's okay. Yeah, bye-bye. You're safe. This life is over. When people have been to the light they don't want to come back 'cause it's much nicer, a better place to be."

"You ever heard about Dr. Elisabeth Kübler-Ross?" Gene asks Rob.

"She was a champion," Rob smiles.

Gene says that he knew her personally, the author of *On Death and Dying* (which first introduced her five-stage grief model) who later became interested in out-of-body experiences. That she arranged a free ticket for him to see her speak, at a point in his life when he was going through a rough patch. "She was telling me that when she started doing this, people thought that she was crazy and they nearly locked her up in a psychiatric hospital."

"When she was doing that the hostility towards spirituality, particularly in medical circles and in psychology as well, was huge, so she impressed me enormously," Rob says. While they chat about how parapsychology has long sat outside the bounds of academia, I look at how the room narrows at one end into a small vestibule which, I now realize, contains the front door. The door has been sealed shut, a long black bar bolted across its frame.

Rob suddenly interrupts himself with a lively, "What's happening?!" before checking in with the good spooks. "Yeah . . . Oh . . . Okay, got it." He scans the room. "We're just about done, I think, Gene. They've got to change the energy in the room, that's the last thing they do—so that this place won't be attractive to depressed, sad people, okay?"

After a beat during which he is perfectly still, Gene nods.

"You know psychometry?" Rob asks. "How you can walk into places and they don't feel good?"

Another nod.

"So you don't want that, because that attracts the bad spooks. But if you walk into a place that feels light and friendly and open, that attracts the good spooks and the bad spooks are repelled by that. We're nearly there, Gene. Okay, I'm getting a message here now."

Rob slips back into one-sided conversation like he's just taking a quick call. "All right . . . So what do you want me to do with this fella? Oh. Okay. Well, you take care of him 'cause you know what you're doing. All right. Good. No, I'm not getting involved in that one, you do it. We'll talk about that later."

Apparently, he explains, there's one character here who's a bit of a troublemaker and the good spooks have found it necessary to trap him in a bubble. "He's next to you, Sarah," Rob chuckles. I look over my shoulder but all I see is the collection of porcelain boxes.

"This is your lucky day," Rob says sternly to the space above the porcelain. "You've been a bloody nuisance up to now but it's all over. You can't win in this situation, pal, so go to the light with everybody else and become a decent human being, all right?" He sighs deeply. "There's no point hanging around me. I've got no time for you." And then, to Gene, "Very stubborn, this one."

"A man?" Gene asks.

Rob nods. "Not a very big fellow. About five foot two. Very belligerent. Both angry and frightened. Kind of a psychopath—stunning lack of empathy . . ." His gaze shifts into the air. "You've been a bully all your life, pal. Didn't get you anywhere, did it? That's the good spook next to you, just do what he tells ya."

He turns back to Gene. "He's getting wound up now, starting to cry, here we go. He's in the middle of emotional turmoil at the moment, so we'll leave him alone. Let the spooks work on him, manipulate his emotions, get him to feel things he's never felt before, like love and kindness and peace and compassion." He looks over at the empty couch. "There's a row of old ladies sitting there now. Not a lot of smarts."

"Are there any relations of mine?" Gene inquires hopefully. Rob says he doesn't know, but can't see a resemblance.

Rob now reports feeling the emotion rising in the room. "The good spooks flood the room with emotion, calming people down, making them feel that everything's going to be okay. So we have to wait for that to happen. But the process has started now and once the emotions come down, they'll be ready to go to the light."

He does a walk-through of the house to check that the bad energy has dissipated. The walls of the dim hallway open out into a bright living space. While that area is relatively tidy, the bathroom needs a clean and the bedroom is a migraine. The sheets have been wrenched from the mattress, sit atop it in a swirl of weary fabric; the curtains entirely reject the day. The bedside lamp lies like a fallen tree over packets of medication pinned beneath it.

Of the various discarnate presences Gene has recently encountered in his home, none has belonged to his deceased wife. He does not feel her around him, has never felt that since she died a decade ago and is glad of it considering she had some mental-health issues. He has, however, felt strongly the spirit of a dog he once loved and, as he shows Rob that good boy's photo, I think about what it means to grow old with a partner you would not miss. To live, still, among the mementos of the world you had been trained for, the rational world you had once been welcomed into like a warm home, only to find yourself locked out late in life.

To find, then, another place—more expansive, more open—a realm that was there all along like a habitable planet waiting to be discovered—only to be cast out from there, too, disempowered in your ninetieth decade before forces you could neither recognize nor control. Strangers swirling randomly around your home where you sat waiting for the faces of your family who had told you they would return for you, taking your hand as though walking you home from school.

How satisfied are you with your standard of living?

Twice, listening back to this day on my voice recorder, I hear a strange sound: a sustained *whoosh* at a volume much louder than my memory of the vehicles passing out front, much louder than I can reasonably account for. Perhaps I was primed for this by my discussions about EVP with Evelyn. But there it is, a sound both disorienting and displacing, which I can easily imagine to be the roar of the accumulated past through the narrow portal of the present.

How satisfied are you with your health? How satisfied are you with what you are achieving in life?

Rob makes sure Gene knows how to call on the good spooks by himself next time. It is not so different from what I do in my mind a second after I wake from the dream of treading gray water, my toe scraping something beneath the surface of the deep.

Certain now that the energy has come up, Rob folds his glasses and returns his clipboard to his briefcase. While I feel no change, I also know that nothing can be more terrifying than something.

Thinking about your own life and personal circumstances, how satisfied are you with your life as a whole?

Rob is shaking Gene's hand in the dark garage, taking his leave and walking out towards the light, which, for one moment, is the difference between feeling fear and being defeated by it. Before the house disappears behind us, it provides that clue, that Gothic hint. It is its total banality, the fact that it could be any house at all.

25

THE DEATH DOULA
KATRINA

Peter's truck is parked in the same spot outside. The lawn is the same radiant green. The potted yellow flower still sits on the table by the front door.

Inside, trackies and socks are drying on the clothes rack in front of the back door, through which I can see Katrina's lounge chair on the rain-splattered deck. Ricky the cavoodle weaves under a stool on which Katrina's sister is balanced, and between pairs of legs that belong to the school principal, in a dark suit holding a cup of tea, and Katrina's brother, leaning on the kitchen bench speaking with him and with her husband who is now a widower.

When Peter opened the door I was painfully aware that his wife died thirty-six hours ago, yet I still defaulted to a reflexive "Hi, how are ya?" And my ensuing chagrin did nothing to keep me from rolling it out again when I said hello to the family gathered in the kitchen. Then again, they welcomed me the same way before we moved on to speak about the traffic. Who has the words for this?

Annie. But she's home with pneumonia and I am here looking at Katrina's fruit bowl and her fridge with its photos of her sons as their laundry goes round in the machine.

Peter asks if I'd like to spend some time with Katrina. And I say yes, of course, yes. So we walk down the hallway to the closed door of the front room. He ducks in first, explaining that the undertaker advised keeping her face covered between visits. Alone in the hallway, I rest my eyes on Katrina's red walker parked near a table by the front door, which displays a gold-framed wedding photo next to a black-and-white photo of three little children. Pete and his sisters, I think. An antique clock, stopped, and the ornate key with which to wind it. A plastic folder containing Katrina's advance care directive— *Take Control* on its cover in bold red. The tableau is a memento mori more powerful than any Flemish still-life festooned with skulls and smoke.

Reappearing, Peter ushers me into the room. And then I am alone with Katrina, who is lying on a cooling plate on a hospital bed in candlelight, a single flower wilting on the white sheet pulled up to her chin. Annie—who made these arrangements so that Katrina could stay at home for the next week—will say tomorrow that the flower "works beautifully" in Buddhist terms as impermanence in action. But that thought does not occur to me now, so shocked am I standing there because it is nothing like I thought it would be.

I am ashamed to tell you that I remember walking into a darkened room, dimly lit by two flickering candles, Katrina supine in a sort of sepulchre. However, when I later looked at the photo Annie requested, and which Peter allowed me to take for her, the room is perfectly bright—a hospital bed in a home office, blinds open on green garden in early afternoon. Katrina appears nothing like a figure on a tomb—more like she just nodded off while reading. I am also ashamed to tell you, because it does not feel generous of me, contrasting so starkly with Peter's gently domestic manner, that my first impulse the moment he shut the door behind him was to immediately wrench it open and flee.

I was not aware of myself as scared, I only *was* scared: an ice-cold tingling shooting from the top of my head down the sides of my body. I had expected an open casket, with a degree of artifice closing the gap between the person as you thought of them and the body they had become. Instead there was just Katrina, looking both like herself and not like herself, her head angled precisely towards the spot where I stood.

And then I felt that I heard it. *You can always, in any situation, make a decision to get a bit closer with wherever you are, with whatever is there.* So I talked to Katrina, shaking in a light I felt to be dark, feeling extremely small. Still, though, I did not look away.

PART 2
ABOVE

Chord noun. Also **cord**.
[ORIGIN from accord]
Agreement, reconciliation; an agreement, a peace treaty.

MUSIC. A group of notes sounded usually together, combined according to some system.

ANATOMY. In spinal cord, vocal cord.

A straight line joining the extremities of an arc.

AERONAUTICS. The width of an airfoil from leading to trailing edge.

The string of a harp or other instrument. Chiefly poet. or fig. strike a chord evoke some reaction in a person. touch the right chord appeal skilfully to emotion, evoke sympathy.

ENGINEERING. Either of the two principal members of the truss of a bridge.

Chord verb.
Form a chord (with); harmonize.

From the *Shorter Oxford English Dictionary*, 6th edition

26

HALFWAY HOME
LYNN

Sometimes the lie is linearity. The necessity of beginning somewhere: privileging that one initial detail so that it sticks in the mind like corn in the teeth. This first fact, this slim and stubborn fiber, undermining—simply by virtue of primacy—all others.

So I will start this way. One month and twelve days after they married, by her count, Ray broke Lynn's cheekbone. She iced it, the red skin turning hard under the cold towel. Patted foundation onto and around the high, broken plane beneath her green eye. Brushed her hair, changed her dress and sat beside him, smiling, at her birthday dinner with her parents.

"That was my first mistake," she tells me, there in the homeless shelter. "Well, my first mistake was stopping at the red light where I met him. I wish for all the life of me that I had run the red light."

All the life of her means, in purely quantitative terms, seventy years. Thirty-four and a half years old when she went to prison for murder. Thirty-four and a half years inside.

"Exactly half of my life out, half of my life in," she says, a certain wonder in her voice.

27
THEORIES OF FLIGHT
FRED & RHONDA

At 6:19 PM on Saturday, October 21, 1978, one year to the day before I was born, a twenty-year-old training pilot took off from Victoria's Moorabbin Airport in a rented blue-and-white single-engine Cessna 182 that still has not been found.

Frederick Valentich is remembered for disappearing, but he had a wonderful presence. He was a gentleman, according to his fiancée, Rhonda Rushton. Handsome in his Air Training Corps uniform, old-fashioned—would open doors for her, bring her flowers—and punctilious. He marked their anniversary every month, though they were together less than a year. If he was running five minutes late to pick her up he would stop at a pay phone on the thirty-minute drive from his place in Avondale Heights to hers in Preston and ring the four-digit phone number of her parents' house. She was sixteen when they met, he was still nineteen.

What did it mean to be turning twenty in 1978? It meant looking and acting like the man you very much wished to be. Keeping your car just so, your hair just so, having a two-drink maximum, and never after 9:00 PM the night before a flight. It meant keeping your own counsel, being respectful, being the sort of person who would go straight to the police if you knew of anyone who was on drugs. It meant peering with great attentiveness into the flying manuals you wished you could simply absorb osmotically to be worthy of your family's pride, your father's financial support for your training, your little brother's rapt attention when you tell him sagely that pilot error is at fault for most crashes. It also meant loving dirt bikes, disco dancing, the Bee Gees, your nonna, the hamburgers at McDonald's and UFOs. It meant being meticulous about your ambitions, but not your spelling. It meant having around one hundred and fifty hours of flying time and a class-four instrument rating that allowed you to fly at night but only in clear conditions. It meant receiving not one but two citations for deliberately flying blind into a cloud, the threat of prosecution still hanging over your head.

Fred had been a cadet and then an instructor in the Air Training Corps. Left school at the end of form four, having earned a D in science ("lacks understanding") and failed math ("difficulty in comprehension"). He applied for a radio tech position in the Royal Australian Air Force but was rejected because of his test scores, which were deemed indicative of "low IQ," an assessment rendering him "fit for unskilled labor only." But he was determined to become a pilot, relentless as gravity. Found another way in, the civilian route, obtaining his student pilot's license in 1977, and then his restricted private pilot's license. He was studying for the five exams required to obtain his commercial pilot's license. Had passed his subjects (Aircraft Performance and Operation on the fifth attempt) but failed all five exams twice.

Fred arranged for Sunday tutoring sessions in navigation and aircraft performance with an Air Force reservist. Was getting his flight hours up while tidying up and selling tents at a camping shop in Moonee Ponds. He failed another three of the commercial pilot's license exams in July 1978, did not sit the remaining two. Told everyone he was going good, going good, only one subject left before he could get his license.

"He wanted to be the youngest commercial pilot," Rhonda remembers. "He wanted to be there quickly. He had to learn to slow down."

Fred and Rhonda are introduced by a mutual friend in March. As they part after that brief encounter, each turns to look back at the other. He gets her number. She spends hours in the hallway of her parents' house on the phone to him. Next month he takes her home, where he's called Freddy and they speak Italian. He has his father Guido's face and his mother Alberta's birthday, which they also share with his four-year-old twin sisters. His brother is twelve that year. Guido regularly corrects Freddy's spoken Italian, which the son resents, and Freddy does not regularly attend Guido's Catholic church, which the father resents— love, even at its deepest, rarely taking the form we'd prefer it to.

She is short beside him but strong, fearless; a speed skater and diver as well as a sprinter and thrower who would reliably win every athletics event except for long-distance running. Like Fred, Rhonda wasn't great at school. Left at fifteen to earn eighty dollars a week at the Night Owl pharmacy, returning home to the whine of the tram, her elderly parents, her distant older brother. *The Don Lane Show*. A roast, a puddle of peas, potatoes and pumpkin on a plate. Bonnie Tyler on the radio, nothing but a heartache. And this looked to be her life until something different landed in her hands.

Now she thinks to herself each day: *How lucky am I? I've got a man in uniform going to marry me.* Sixteen—the age when one can be only mildly shocked at the thought that dreams really do come true, the feel of it like one of her javelins landing beyond where she expected.

In October, Fred will ascend from the runway and never be seen again. Four decades later—having lived so much more of her life without him than she ever spent with him—Rhonda will still think of him every day.

Fred spends weeknights studying for his exams, has lectures on Saturdays, tutoring sessions on Sundays. But Saturday nights the two of them are dancing at the Chevron nightclub to "Stayin' Alive" and "Rivers of Babylon" and "You're the One That I Want." And whenever their work shifts allow, they go for a fly. He is so confident in everything he does, she always feels safe with him though their feet are on a floor of sky. They talk about the children they will have, a big family, what life will look like when he's a commercial pilot and she's a mom.

They take short trips over Melbourne. A relaxed run beneath clouds, roofs tented below like books on their bellies. A line over the bay. And, one time, acrobatic arcs in a little yellow plane. That was her favorite time: the clouds looked like a blanket that day; she wanted to just jump out and walk across them, they looked so solid. She loves sitting beside him in their private world where chemicals combine into flight and they can gaze at the clear logic of life from above, the infinity of their future on the horizon.

Their longest flight together is a visit to Rhonda's uncle in Newcastle where they lose track of time and have to stay the night. On their way to Bankstown to submit the flight plan for the return trip to Moorabbin, Fred flies into restricted air space, has difficulty landing, makes several attempts while sweating so profusely that she has to mop his brow to prevent it from blurring his vision. Still, he manages.

She goes along to a few of his tutoring sessions. Air Force reservist Captain Edwin Robert Barnes took on the role reluctantly, as a favor for a colleague whom Fred had impressed during his cadetship, but he has come, it seems, to enjoy helping the dogged young man prepare to retake the exams he's failed. In July, Fred tells Barnes that he thinks he's passed. Shows up with Rhonda and two bottles of wine to celebrate. Barnes declines the drink saying he's on reserve but they'll celebrate when the marks make it official. He returns from holidays in mid-September to a call from Fred, ringing to tell him he's passed both exams, thanking him for all his help.

1978 means Space Invaders—the first video arcade game, the first female astronauts, the first test-tube baby, the first Sydney Gay and Lesbian Mardi Gras, the unsolved disappearance of Sydney couple Michelle Pope and Stephen Lapthorne in his lime-green van. Fred clips articles of UFO interest from newspapers and magazines. He's teaching Rhonda to drive. They are learning how to dance: four weeks of lessons to prepare, eventually, for their bridal waltz. They win a disco competition, the bass line to "Night Fever" pulsing around them. He takes her to a restaurant in Moorabbin called Troika where the waiter places the napkin in her lap with a flourish and a violinist bends like a stem by their table. Each month on their anniversary there is a present: two stuffed monkeys embracing, roses, a hairdryer.

Close Encounters of the Third Kind is playing at the cinema. Sitting in his car one day, looking out over the Dandenong Ranges, they chat about spaceships, what would happen if one landed. I'd love to go in and have a look, Fred says, but I wouldn't go without you.

Rhonda and Guido will both say Fred was no fanatic but Guido will describe him as "a firm believer in UFOs," an interest that started around fourteen. He will share how, earlier in the year, Fred's mother called him to come see a light in the sky, ten times larger than a star, stationary for a time before moving off at speed. How Fred said he'd been allowed to see the Air Force's confidential files on UFOs at East Sale and Laverton, but didn't discuss the content with his family. And how Fred had once mentioned that he was troubled about the possibility of attack by UFOs. There's nothing that could be done about it, Guido had replied, so there's no point in worrying.

One night, Fred returns home earlier than planned from a night flight. When his mother asks him why, he tells her that he had the feeling he was being followed.

On Friday, October 13, 1978—one week before their five-month anniversary—Fred drives Rhonda to their spot in the Dandenongs. He pulls a ring from his pocket, silver with three sapphires in a line, and asks her to marry him. Yes, she replies, yes! Beneath her excitement, though, a quiet drip of misgivings—the inauspicious date, her confusion about why they are suddenly celebrating a week early, the way he slips the silver circle on her ring finger though it is only a placeholder, a friendship ring. The real engagement ring is on lay-by at a jeweler's in Moonee Ponds, he explains. He will pay it off by Christmas and propose again, in front of the family. Until then, it will be their secret. Then a year-long engagement will follow so she will be eighteen at the wedding. Punctilious.

Fred has told a flying instructor that he intends to fly to King Island on Tuesday, October 17. The instructor will later report that the flight was canceled due to the weather.

Saturday, October 21. Fred wakes up around six on his last morning and eats breakfast with his family: cereal, orange juice, coffee. Showers, shaves, gets dressed. He's probably wearing his flying clothes. Brown-and-white jumper, brown pants, a short blue raincoat—similar to those worn by Air Force personnel— his good-luck coat. Drives to work and spends the morning at the shop. A colleague notices that he seems preoccupied. Fred explains he's mentally reviewing his flight plan for his first night flight across deep water that evening.

When his shift ends at midday, he drives down the Nepean Highway to Moorabbin Airport, probably arriving early for his 1:30 PM class. Maybe uses the time to study. Maybe he just stares through the windscreen running through the list of problems without solutions that he keeps tucked in the back of his mind. When his class ends at 4:30 PM, he prepares the plane and lodges his flight plan with the office. And then there is a gap during which the Fred everyone knew would have driven to McDonald's and taken his order of two Big Macs, two cheeseburgers, a Filet-O-Fish and some chips down the road that leads to the bay to eat slowly by the water, drinking a Coke and practicing his flight in his head like a dance book-ended by silence and triumph. Maybe, though, he's not hungry. Maybe he simply returns to his car, his list, a conversation with himself that feels like a furnace.

He returns to the airport too late for his 5:40 PM scheduled take-off. No change is made to the flight plan. According to that plan, he will be heading towards Cape Otway to fly over Bass Strait for King Island. The plane is fueled at 6:10 PM. He takes off at 6:19 PM. He's told Rhonda and his family that he's flying there to bring back crayfish. He's told flight officials that he's flying there to pick up passengers, took four life jackets in the plane with him. There are no crayfish, no passengers waiting at King Island Airport. He hasn't informed King Island Airport of his intention to land, has made no arrangements for lighting on his arrival.

Just before midnight, an eleven-year-old boy staring out a car window will be the only one in his family to see a greenish-white flash moving quickly across the sky as his father drives them near the coast at Barwon Heads. But at 7:00 PM the sky is just darkening over Cape Otway. Calm water, light winds, almost limitless visibility. The end of daylight is eighteen minutes away. Fred's last transmission is twelve minutes away. If her co-worker at the pharmacy hadn't called in to say she was running late for her shift, Rhonda would have been in the seat beside him, she says to me forty years later.

It is Fred's habit to release the seat and push it rearward to accommodate his long legs. Also, to wipe the microphone on his shirt before using it. And he tends to rest it in his lap instead of returning it to the hook. He picks it up at 7:06 PM.

"Melbourne, this is Delta Sierra Juliet," Fred says, identifying the Cessna's registration in a businesslike tone. "Is there any known traffic below five thousand?" At that altitude his plane will not show up on Melbourne Air Traffic's radar. So, while Fred's location over water or land will never be confirmed, the fact that he is communicating on this frequency is proof that he is in the Cape Otway area.

"Delta Sierra Juliet, no known traffic," replies air traffic controller Steve Robey, who is working five other frequencies, a normal shift at the Melbourne Flight Service.

"Delta Sierra Juliet, I am—Seems to be a large aircraft below five thousand," Fred says.

After a pause Steve inquires, "Delta Sierra Juliet, Melbourne. What type of aircraft is it?"

"Delta Sierra Juliet. I cannot affirm. It is . . . four bright, it seems to me, like, landing lights," Fred says, sounding more alert than alarmed before lapsing into a prolonged pause.

"Delta Sierra Juliet," Steve says briskly, holding space for the rest of Fred's reply.

"Melbourne, this is Delta Sierra Juliet. The aircraft has just passed over me at least a thousand feet above . . ." Fred says. His voice is tight.

"Delta Sierra Juliet, roger, and it is a large aircraft? Confirm."

"Er, unknown due to the speed it's traveling. Is there any air force aircraft in the vicinity?" Fred asks, the businesslike tone dropping away slightly.

"Delta Sierra Juliet, no known aircraft in the vicinity," Steve confirms.

"Melbourne, it's approaching right now from due east to-wards me . . ." Fred says, before another extended pause.

"Delta Sierra Juliet," says Steve, waiting.

"Delta Sierra Juliet," Fred replies, sounding confused. "It seems to me that he's playing some sort of game? He's fly-ing over me two, three times at a time at speeds I could not identify."

"Delta Sierra Juliet, roger. What is your actual level?"

"My level is four and a half thousand. Four five zero zero."

"Delta Sierra Juliet. And confirm you cannot identify the aircraft?"

"Affirmative."

"Delta Sierra Juliet, roger. Stand by," Robey replies, with the composed rapidity of a man whose job it is to receive and respond to distress signals. He has been on the line with pilots shouting mayday, men falling from the sky.

"Melbourne, Delta Sierra Juliet, it's not an aircraft," Fred says, his voice rising in pitch and emotion. "It is . . ."

(In the background, another air controller's voice momen-tarily rises up as the control room kicks into action. "G'day mate, we got a . . .")

"Delta Sierra Juliet, Melbourne," Steve says to Fred. "Can you describe, the, er, aircraft?"

(From the control room: ". . . identified . . . Cape Otway . . .")

"Delta Sierra Juliet. As it's flying past, it's a long shape. [Cannot] identify more than that . . . [It is] before me right now, Melbourne."

"Delta Sierra Juliet, roger. And how large would the, er, object be?"

("... King Island ... Four five zero zero ... nothing at all, no ...")

"Delta Sierra Juliet, Melbourne," Fred says, confusing the call signs. "It seems like it's stationary. What I'm doing right now is orbiting, and the thing is just orbiting on top of me also. It's also got a green light aaand sort of metallic light ... It's all shiny [on] the outside ..." He is not audibly panicked.

"Delta Sierra Juliet," Steve replies.

"It's just vanished," Fred reports.

"Delta Sierra Juliet," Steve says.

"Melbourne, would you know what kind of aircraft I've got?" Fred asks, grasping at an answer. "Is it a type of military aircraft?"

"Delta Sierra Juliet, confirm the, er, aircraft just vanished?"

"Say again."

"Delta Sierra Juliet, is the aircraft still with you?"

"[Now] approaching from the southwest ..." Fred replies before another long pause.

"Delta Sierra Juliet," Steve says.

"Delta Sierra Juliet. The engine is, is rough idling. I've got it set at twenty-three twenty-four, and the thing is coughing," Fred says.

"Delta Sierra Juliet, roger. What are your intentions?" Steve asks, with a small but significant amount of solemnity. It is the first time he uses this tone and I understand it to mean: *I will not desert you, but there are no answers, you must deal with this now and alone.*

"My intentions are, ah, to go to King Island," Fred says, sounding, now, very young. "Ah, Melbourne, that strange aircraft is hovering on top of me again ..." And then, at his most confident, "It *is* hovering, and *it's not an aircraft.*"

"Delta Sierra Juliet," Steve says.

"Delta Sierra Juliet, Melbourne," Fred says.

[Silence for seventeen seconds, open microphone, with a distinct unidentified noise.]

"Delta Sierra Juliet, Melbourne," Steve says.

This is where the transmission ends on the copy of the tape that I have heard, and which I believe to be authentic and complete.

"I am very happy to give you a taped copy of your son's voice to have as a keepsake," replies the acting director of the Department of Transport to Guido's request for a copy of Fred's last radio communication. "I would ask you, however, in view of the department's firm policy of confidentiality, to confine the hearing of the tape to your family for the specific purpose stated in your letter."

One of the handwritten transcriptions in the official file describes the distinctive unidentified noise as a long metallic "clanging." It will be routinely described, in certain stories that become accepted over time, as metal scraping on metal.

Forty years later, Steve Robey will tell me something different but equally unnerving. "To me," he says, "it sounded like he had his finger on the push to talk [button] but something was impacting the carrier wave."

28

THE KINGDOM OF HEAVEN
SUNDAY SERVICE

They are singing hymns in four-part harmony, down in the basement of a building in the Bronx that used to be a synagogue, a place now called The Light of Truth Mennonite Church. Women and young children on the right, men on the left; occasionally one of the fathers will soothe a baby there as well.

The rows face a low platform where an extremely tall blond man stands at a lectern before a red velvet backdrop and under a sign that says: *Miranda con esperanza hacia una nueva vision.* Look with hope towards a new vision. Under his black blazer he wears a round-collared white shirt. His pleasant face is stretched in an expression of concern as he speaks about God's command to Moses to remove his sandals when he approached the burning bush for he walked on holy ground. His theme this morning is the importance of knowing whose house we are in. Obedience. Respect.

This is a missionary church and I was invited to attend today. So it is easy enough for me to walk in, however I do feel the consideration of every pair of eyes upon me. Not that many pairs, though, the congregation being relatively small. Its members appear as if they could belong to the same family and they are mostly from Myerstown, Pennsylvania, not the Bronx.

Mennonites are named after Menno Simons, a Dutch Catholic priest who aligned himself with the Anabaptists in the 1530s. Unlike Catholics, who baptize babies, Anabaptists believe that the decision to be baptized can only be made consciously. Persecuted for their differences, Mennonites began arriving in America in the late 1600s and the majority settled in Pennsylvania. There has been a certain amount of theological ferment since then and these days it is easy to get lost in what they laughingly call "the Mennonite maze"—the many differences between churches and between the conferences under which groups of churches are united. But to simplify: Old Order Mennonites physically resemble, but are not, Amish. (The Amish are in fact an eighteenth-century breakaway sect.) Liberal Mennonites look like anyone else walking down the street. The Conservative Mennonites at The Light of Truth are not in-between; they are closer to Old Order Mennonites, and even to the Amish, in significant ways.

Though they drive cars and, generally, use cell phones and filtered internet, Conservative Mennonites separate themselves from mainstream society in many areas of their lives, the most visible being their preference for "plain dress" that to outsiders resembles that worn by the Amish. As a general rule: no TV, no movies, no radio, no secular music. They operate their own schools or rely on homeschooling. They believe in a binary reality. First, there is the earthly kingdom where "a heathen culture" predominates and in which they have little interest and minimal involvement. (For example, they do not vote or take disputes "to law.") Then there is the kingdom of Heaven, where they hope to eventually go and which is ruled by "a holy, just God who you're going to have to answer to some day for your actions."

I sit beside Becky Kreider, who has a preschooler beside her and a toddler on her lap—two of her six sons. She wears a pink dress, a pink cardigan, pink glasses and black Nikes. Her little boy hands me a hymnal. Her toddler stays quiet for the next hour and a half. For an astonishing length of time, he looks attentively at a worn board book about tractors while she softly points things out in the pictures.

The sermon continues, and a different sound hums around us as another tall blond man—Pastor Tim Kreider, Becky's husband—simultaneously translates the service for two elderly Latina women, his Spanish like the bassline to another song. Rachel, a white woman who looks very thin and very tired, sits next to the women, stroking the shoulder of the one closest. When the sermon ends a young man steps up to the lectern. Becky extracts a notebook and a pen from a worn leather case, poised to take notes.

It was explained to me earlier that their preachers do not have formal training, that there's been "a very strong backlash reaction to higher education to train them." The young man at the lectern looks to be in his early twenties. His blond hair is cut short, Caesar-style. His beard, still coming in over his acne, is in the shape worn by the other men: squarish; no mustache. Stumbling on the name, he begins with a quote on environmental destruction from David Attenborough, with whose work he is proudly unfamiliar.

"Is man behind the problems on earth?" he asks, one side of his mouth lifting into a knowing smile.

Heads shake. Someone calls out, "No, Satan is."

"Satan of course was the one who created the whole mess," he continues. "We have to understand that's the doctrine of the Devil, to think of man as a type of pestilence."

I ponder the likelihood that Sir David ever spread the doctrine of the Devil, intentionally or otherwise, as the sermon abruptly ends and the Sunday school portion of the service begins. A few teenagers lead the children into a room off the hallway behind us and the adults take out, or are handed, booklets consisting of three photocopied pages. The young man at the lectern launches into a lesson on "The Creation of Man" while I page through the booklet:

- *Man's Creation:* God gave man moral understanding and the ability to discern . . .

- *Man's Commission:* efforts of population control stand in opposition to God's design . . .

- *Man's Companion:* the marriage union is between only one man and one woman, for life. When individuals and nations disregard God's design, chaos and confusion result . . .

From the lectern, the young man quizzes the congregation on the booklet's study questions and I try to keep a record of the dialogue that follows but there is a disjunction between the questions and answers; like an awkward high-five, they never quite match up. I swiftly lose the thread of the discussion.

When the time allocated for adult Sunday school ends, we have not got through most of the questions.

The children file back in and recite memorized verses. Then everyone sings one last hymn, this time in Spanish, and the service concludes with some housekeeping announcements. A man in the hospital has requested to hear some hymns; they'll be running a van up there. People volunteer to go sing. I am invited to stay for lunch, which is being laid out on card tables at the back of the room. There are roast chickens, wide bowls of salad, jumbo bottles of ranch dressing and platters heavy with pineapple and watermelon. The kids descend on the food as Becky and I wander over to the tables. We are joined by a woman who made the three-hour drive from Myerstown with her own six children for today's service. She has bright pink cheeks and intensely blue eyes.

"Are you a Christian?" she asks.

"No," I say. "I am Jewish."

"What do you think about Jesus?" she asks.

"I don't usually think about Jesus," I reply. "But to the extent that I do think about Jesus, I think about him as a historical figure."

She nods. Becky says, with perplexity, that she is sometimes mistaken for an Orthodox Jew. So I explain to them the similarities in modest dress and then about the upcoming Jewish New Year and Day of Atonement and how I will be required to fast although I always think that I could concentrate better on my sins if I was allowed a little snack of pizza, and this makes them laugh loudly. And when they laugh my heart surges for one moment and I want to read aloud the last line in today's booklet, which I circled: *Marvellous are thy works; and that my soul knoweth right well.* I want to tell them how the lines of scripture in this booklet made me think, yes, we are actually "formed from the earth" given the borrowed nature of our corporeal atoms, once star stuff, now holding forks loaded with iceberg lettuce and ranch dressing. I want to marvel with them at that intuitive sense of Oneness. And how artificial the distance is between us, given our like atoms and the fact that we are each women, each mothers, tiny and enormous, fleeting and enduring, on this grain briefly populated in time everlasting.

But such a conversation will not be possible. Because they believe I am going to Hell and I believe they may already be living in one, and it is 1:00 PM, which means it is time for us to return to our homes.

29

THEORIES OF FLIGHT
FRED & RHONDA

If Fred had left on time he would have returned around dusk for his date with Rhonda. But he didn't turn up and he didn't call. So she waited by the phone, smoothing down her blow-dried hair as it got later and later, and then went to bed in her clothes. Lay looking through her window until 6:00 AM when her father snapped on the radio in his bedroom like always, the opening music to ABC news marching down the hallway ahead of the announcer's voice reporting that a pilot had gone missing over Bass Strait.

She rings Moorabbin Airport, says she thinks she knows who the pilot is, her boyfriend, Frederick Valentich.

Hold the line, comes the reply.

Mounds of dead moths are washing up on the shore from an inundation in the area as the first morning of the air, land and sea search begins around Cape Otway, the margin of the mainland. It goes for four days; finds no trace of Fred.

The Air Safety Incident Report states that no wreckage was sighted. But also: "Two major problems were found during the course of the search: (a) much search time was lost by the optimum aircraft, the Orion, in directing a surface vessel to the position of possible oil slick and debris for retrieval. (b) When light aircraft, without internal navigation systems, found possible debris when out of sight of land they had to climb to fix position and in doing so lost sight of debris."

Three and a half years later, the Bureau of Air Safety Investigation will release its finding that, while the reason for the disappearance of the aircraft has not been determined, it was presumed fatal.

Like its subject, the government's accident investigation file also went missing. It was found in 2012 by researcher Keith Basterfield while searching an online National Archives index on a different subject. Shortly after, Basterfield stated that he didn't believe the file was deliberately covered up. "Put simply," he stated, "many people within a department will have no idea how their filing system works and where files end up." Frequently, the most astounding discovery of all is that it's more mundane, more banal than we ever would have thought.

The parallel narratives of the Valentich story all converge at a vanishing point—Fred in his airplane over Cape Otway. They share little else. As with any perspective sketch, the character of Frederick Valentich is scaled relative to the viewer. What seems accurate to some appears grossly foreshortened to others.

In the idiom of air crash investigation, "human factors" refers to explanations related to the pilot and not the plane. Three days after Fred disappears, Rhonda attends the Department of Transport's Melbourne office where she is interviewed by three men, bright lights shining in her eyes. She can only vaguely see the faces of her interlocutors. One of them is air safety inspector Jim Sandercock, a former Royal Australian Air Force squadron leader from South Australia who, twenty years prior, commanded Antarctic rescue and expeditionary flights.

Jim Sandercock's been busy lately, his work difficult. Three months ago he was investigating an incident near Essendon Airport where a plane crashed into a house, killing the family inside—a thirty-year-old woman, her four children aged twelve years to four weeks, and her mother. That was in July, a four-week stretch in which twenty people died in light aircraft crashes around the country.

Jim is a man who grew plants in a beam of Antarctic sunshine. Earned his OBE flying into a blizzard. This is a person who is not just undeterred by uncertainty but who is capable of ascending in a void, landing on ice. "Occasionally a little pedantic with regard to detail," one of his early promotion summaries stated. I imagine such a person imagining Fred. What does he think as he pieces through his piles of undifferentiated information, now all that is left of a passionate young man whose aspirations appear to have swiftly outpaced his abilities? How does Sandercock speak with—and listen to—Rhonda?

"They asked the most *personal* questions," Rhonda remembers. "And other questions. But very, very personal questions as well. So it was—horrifying."

Sandercock's report states that Rhonda last saw Fred on Friday night, after he finished work. That she said he hadn't been himself. Usually he is cheerful, and outwardly very happy, but that night he was not quite in the spirit of things. Quiet, a bit down. Perhaps a bad day at work. The job wasn't quite what he expected; instead of being trained to be manager he's made to clean the shop. It could have been the upcoming flight—he told her he was scared of the water. Mentioned how he was not a strong swimmer. Sandercock reports that it became clear to Rhonda that Fred had forgotten they'd made plans for Saturday night. But that they planned to keep their date anyway, Fred saying he would pick Rhonda up when he returned from King Island, would take his good clothes along in the car so he could go straight to her place. Sandercock notes that she was aware that no good clothes had been found in the car, still parked at Moorabbin Airport. No mention is made of a plan for her to have accompanied Fred.

She tells the investigators that Fred always thought before he acted, never acted intuitively. That he becomes nervous dealing with the unexpected. That he held problems in the back of his mind, and that he held them as a list, mentally crossing them off when he had worked out a solution. That he had lied to her very soon after their first meeting, about passing his meteorology subject for his commercial license. But that he'd admitted to it four months later and told her he was repeating the subject.

In his report on the interview, days after Fred's disappearance, Sandercock finds Rhonda honest, dependable, "a stable person for her years."

Writing from the superficially impressive altitude of the third person, he states: "The investigator gained the impression that Valentich had chosen Miss Rushton carefully, as someone to discuss his problems with, she being receptive, perhaps more so than a girl of 18–20 years, who might have rejected his problems and ideas and pushed him aside.

"The impression was gained that Miss Rushton was becoming aware that Valentich was 'different' from her other male acquaintances and that she was being used as a 'prop,' based on the odd phrase used and the time of some of her comments."

"They made up stuff," Rhonda will say when I ask her about this report. She wouldn't have told Fred to remember good clothes, they weren't going anywhere fancy. She has no idea about the "prop" comment; does not remember saying it, nor that he was different from other men, and does not believe she ever would have. It was upsetting to read, she says. "We were truly in love."

They write in from the Melbourne suburbs, from down the coast, from South Australia. From Penguin, Tasmania and San Diego, California and J. Allen Hynek's Center for UFO Studies in Chicago, Illinois. They write on behalf of their children and their wives and themselves. They describe a bright white light with colored rays. An oval object, gray-silver in color, encircled by a ring of light and traveling very slowly out to sea. A green-white flash moving extremely quickly across the sky. Metallic scintillations, thirty bright centers, at an angle of forty-five degrees from the horizon. A large triangular yellow-white light surrounded by colored lights. They preface their information with the fact that they are a responsible person, do not want to create the opinion that they are a nut. They write to help or to be helped; Fred's story, in some strange way, is now their story.

At the investigator's request, Fred's tutor, Air Force reservist Barnes, provides his impressions of his pupil in a two-page letter written nine days after the plane disappears. Blue pen on unlined white paper. Barnes is thorough, frank. Exacting with what he knows and what he doesn't about the "sober" young man, in a record that is meticulous and humane. (I imagine him finishing this letter, removing a single sheet of lined paper from beneath its painstaking pages. Switching off the desk lamp with a click: the only sound in the house where his wife lies above him, sleeping. He pads into the dining room where he sat on Sundays with the tall young man in whom he saw not himself, but someone familiar, passionate about the things he, too, loved. Stands motionless before the front window, one dry hand extended behind him resting on the chair where Fred used to sit. The air is cold through the clean pane as he looks up at the blackness he knows conceals the new moon but tonight makes him feel only that everything is moving and that nothing he has known can be relied upon for the useful ordering of a human life.)

"In summary," Barnes wrote, "I would say that he was impressionable, a 'battler', and that he had the determination and stability to achieve his goal of commercial pilot." He admitted his extreme disappointment on learning from investigators that Fred had not, in fact, passed his exams the second time around, noted that Fred's apparent dishonesty on that account was completely out of character. "I now wonder," he continued, "if he was ashamed for not having passed the exams, possibly realizing that he would never get his [commercial pilot's license]. Because everyone had forged the same high opinion of him, was he a good actor? Did he have a split personality? Could he have really been unstable?"

"The balancing of a flyer may seem, at first thought, to be a very simple matter," Orville and Wilbur Wright wrote in the September 1908 edition of *Century Magazine*, "yet almost every experimenter had found in this the one point which he could not satisfactorily master."

It makes no sense; his towel is still hanging in his bathroom at home. There's no plane, no message. Rhonda doesn't know what to feel. No one knows what to say to her. She tells the reporters that she thinks he's alive somewhere, hopes he is alive. She goes to stay with a friend for a few days to avoid the reporters swarming her street. They are still there when she returns home; they are parked outside all day, all night, one pulling up with a toot to relieve the other. When she tries to return to work at the chemist, the reporters hound her so badly her boss lets her go. She is constantly crying. No friends come to visit as she lies long in her room. As she sits blinking on the couch.

Gravity causing all bodies to fall at the same rate, two weeks after Fred goes missing Rhonda swallows seventy-five of the pills that were given to help her sleep after she heard the news. "I obviously didn't want to go," she tells me, "because I could've gone to my room and that would've been it. But I went and sat with Mom and Dad, and I don't remember much after that." She had her stomach pumped. No one at the hospital asked how she was going, or mentioned what had happened, though her name and face were in all the newspapers.

"And I admit it, many times in my life I still sometimes want to do that because it never ends."

•

When he fails to come home that night, his parents think he's had an accident, that he fell from the sky.

"But then as the people came along from various news-papers," Guido explained later to a reporter, ." . . some jour-nalist, I think it was from Channel Nine, he mentioned to me that he'd heard about—it was to do with some strange object surrounding . . . That was the first hint that we have about a UFO. And as they tell us, myself and my wife, we felt much more relieved because we knew that Freddy was always mentioning about UFO[s], that he would like to meet one, and our heart really opened up with a great big hope."

"When I heard that," Alberta added, "I was, more or less, put it this way, don't get me wrong, I was happy, because at least he's *somewhere* . . ."

She will make the point that an unidentified flying object doesn't necessarily have to be from another planet. Guido will say that most people believe we're not alone in the universe, there's got to be another civilization somewhere, that a lemon tree doesn't only have one lemon.

Mount Stromlo Observatory, in Canberra, will advise that the night of October 21st was the peak of a meteor storm.

Six months after Fred disappears, the *Australian* newspaper reports on a clairvoyant's claims that he had a conversation with the pilot during a séance at his home, in which Fred told him that sixty seconds of the radio transcript had been suppressed before it was released. "The allegation is in line with highly publicized claims by friends and family after its release," the article says. "Valentich is supposed to have said he was safe but no longer had a physical body. He is claimed to have said: 'I am in light. I can move to wherever I need to be.' Fred reportedly told the clairvoyant, Colin Amery, that extraterrestrials needed his skills.

"Mr Guido Valentich said yesterday he still believed his son was alive but was skeptical about Mr. Amery's claims. Mr. Valentich said it was just possible Mr. Amery might be trying to publicize his book, *New Atlantis*, which predicts severe upheavals and great changes to the earth in about a year."

When asked what he believes happened to his son, Guido tells reporters that he believes Fred must have been struck by some unidentified flying object. That he hopes a UFO is involved; he'd prefer that option over the others. He will attend meetings of the UFO research societies where he will be welcomed, remembered with near-reverence twenty years after his death and with a wince for his pain. Spoken of with total respect for the fact that he insisted on looking up rather than down for the body of his child, and that he never stopped looking.

The investigators find that Fred presented a façade of his ability, achievement and future to his acquaintances, close friends and family. That he was running out of time on that front. They note Rhonda's statement that "he perspired profusely and his voice changed in any unexpected or out of the ordinary situation." How this sits uncomfortably with the evidence that "his voice remained 'matter of fact' and completely normal" on the transmission. They note that had the vehicle crashed into the sea, wreckage would probably have been sighted. "It therefore is not possible to determine the cause of the disappearance but it seems likely that the aircraft did not crash in the sea . . ."

On May 15, 1983, about four and a half years after Fred disappeared, a piece of an aircraft washed up on the beach on the west coast of Flinders Island in Tasmania, opposite the northern end of the Flinders Island Aerodrome. It was identified as an engine cowl flap from a Cessna 182, used to control airflow over the engine. The aluminum fragment had once been painted white and it bore a steel operating bolt which, while heavily corroded, appeared to have failed on impact or in flight. It is not unknown for a cowl flap to separate from an aircraft in flight, but there had been no recent instances in the area, no aircraft wreckage dumped at sea, no missing Cessna aircraft besides that flown by Fred Valentich. Jim Sandercock wrote to the Royal Australian Navy Research Laboratory for assistance, noting that the serial number of Valentich's Cessna "falls within the range of serial numbers applicable to the part found."

He asked about the likelihood of this particular item traveling under the influence of ocean currents, over a period of close to five years, from a spot somewhere between Cape Otway and the northern tip of King Island to the Tasmanian beach where it was found. It would be, he writes, a step towards solving the mystery of the disappearance and its sole occupant.

It happened that unusually large currents had been seen on two occasions earlier in the year. They were of sufficient magnitude to constitute an unusual event, Ian Jones, of the Ocean Sciences Division, explained in his reply. Thus it would seem reasonable to speculate, Jones wrote, "that the storm induced large bottom currents over much of eastern Bass Strait and moved your aircraft parts towards Flinders Island."

In the photos on file, the three pieces that constitute this scrap of current-carried metal are not so much. They are the color of bleached bones, have the clean lines and jagged irregularities of pottery shards. The single certainty is that they were not built to exist in isolation. A meager and forensic accounting of something broken, somewhere.

30

HALFWAY HOME
LYNN

Lynn has her own room on the fourth floor of the shelter, which is where the only individual rooms are located. The beds there are mostly reserved for women with full-time jobs. Lynn's room doesn't have a door, but she has hung a purple curtain, behind which there is a bed and a locker, a window ledge to put things on. It is the most privacy she has had for thirty-five years, and she's grateful for it though the girls keep her up with their smoking and fighting and, if they happen to have credit, talking at volume on their phones at 3:00 AM. It's August, stiflingly hot and the air conditioner is broken. It doesn't bother her. The only problem is the stairs, which she takes slowly on account of her knee. She ascends carefully, sending her purple aluminum cane—a parole present—scouting out ahead. *Thud, step, step.*

Lynn was raised in a small town in upstate New York in a house so close to her grandparents it was like having two homes. Born with a bad appendix, she couldn't jump rope or climb trees, but her mother taught her to read early and she could go inside her closet and build a cottage, a castle, a world of her own making. Her family was Episcopalian, Sundays spent in the church her grandfather helped build, where her parents met after her father saw her mother singing in the choir. Lynn added her voice there too, growing taller each year in front of the pews that would turn to ash one freezing January day after the best efforts of her father and the other volunteer fire fighters failed to contain the flames lit by a troubled teenager.

She did well at school. Studied abroad for a year, navigated her way around a Spanish high school, found a place for herself there in a different country, a different language. In 1963, when she was sixteen, she made her own way down from New York to join the March on Washington. Became seasick on the Staten Island ferry before she'd even left the state.

It's all moving. Anywhere she rests her eyes. The dirty floor. The gray waves of New York Harbor. The gulls veering above. A voice offers her a drink, something fizzy to settle the lurching inside. She looks up and everything disappears.

This was how she met AJ, first when they were on the same boat and decades later when they found themselves in the same prison. Both times it felt like a miracle.

They make the rest of the trip together, ignoring the looks they receive as an interracial couple, Lynn white, AJ Black. Leaning against each other in the crowd, they listen to Dr. King's speech. *Now is the time to make justice a reality for all of God's children . . .*

They elope using AJ's fake ID which identifies him as male. Back home, she introduces AJ as her boyfriend. They are together for the next few years as Lynn finishes high school, then college. AJ comes up from the city to spend long nights at her small apartment which contains the world—her books, a Siamese cat, a Murphy bed that folds down from the wall and a Chevy Impala convertible parked outside. Lynn sometimes drives down to Manhattan, and they go out in the Village where they can be among friends. They're there in the early hours of June 28, 1969, running down Christopher Street, holding hands, the noise flaring out from the Stonewall Inn at their heels.

•

They broke up eventually because Lynn wanted children.

"If I had stayed with him, I think we both would've stayed out of jail," Lynn says of her first and last love. She thinks she could have persuaded AJ "to stop doing what he was doing." She is referring to the fact that AJ worked, from a young age, with an uncle as a "paid mercenary": a hitman. "Righting wrongs and settling scores," as Lynn describes it wryly. You wouldn't catch him standing up and sitting down in a church, but AJ was extremely religious, would pray every night on his knees.

Lynn graduates. Takes a job as a substitute teacher. Signs the mortgage on the old corner grocery store, remodeling it on her own line of credit. Opens Bailey's Deli, which she names for a lover she will one day wish she had stayed with and with whom she will seek respite when things start to get worse with her husband. She'll wonder later whether it was Bailey who in fact fathered her son.

She meets Ray at that red light in his fast car when he asks her for directions he already knows. Marries this older man who is so proud of her, who shows her off to his friends, *I'm dating a girl who speaks three languages!* Ray stops selling cars and starts selling strollers, purchases a baby-supplies shop in the next town over. She will have children, she will live near her parents, she will work hard, go to graduate school, and that will be her life. All its ingredients perfectly proportioned like the salads she stands on the wooden floor of her own deli confidently making and handing over, with a smile, to her regulars.

In the beginning is the aberration.

What happened at his work to cause this? This isn't Ray. Of course she accepts his apologies, his gifts, his compliments. His remorse rights the world. Though his pride in her accomplishments (*She's studying her master's in clinical psychology!*) has long curdled into resentment (*You think you're so smart . . .*) she keeps thinking things will return to how they were. When they don't, she starts to feel a burning shame: her bruises, her black eyes; her judgment in selecting this person as her person. The marriage crumbles, she starts seeing Bailey again in secret, she resolves to leave Ray for good and start over. And then she is pregnant, which stops nothing. His rage and her shame a double helix spiraling out of control.

She doesn't tell her parents what is happening, though they live on the same street. They could have heard her from their porch had she shouted for help after he pushed her down the front stairs, separating her from her front teeth. Her father—former Canadian special ops—would have charged across the intervening driveways to extract her in a heartbeat. But Lynn remains silent, this small woman who thinks of herself as so

self-reliant that hours before she goes into labor she is still lifting bags of potatoes and crates of celery around the deli to fill
the orders for Fourth of July parties.

July is raspberry month, as the article above the birth an-
nouncement for Lynn and Ray's son informs readers of the
local paper. Ray beats her while she is nursing through the
night, running the deli, checking in on her mother, who is
getting increasingly ill. He shows no particular attachment
to the child. He says, "Now who does he look like?" in a tone
that makes her skin crawl.

She stops going to the church she grew up in. Drives a few
towns over instead, where she can sit unrecognized, her tongue
probing the spot where tooth is now air as she strives to reach
some accord with the world as it is.

Eventually she reels it up from the trench of herself like
some luminescent deep-sea creature, files for a divorce and
changes the locks. When she returns home from work to find
he is in the house, she calls the police and reports a break-in.
They attend, then leave in annoyance. A nonissue, a domestic. "When I called they would be like, 'Oh, it's Lynn *again.*' I
could hear them. They were pretty tired of being called to the
house," she says, explaining that it would enrage Ray further,
that he would return and rape her.

From then on, she comes home to find windows broken,
things missing: her silverware, her jewelery, the relief she had
felt after she told him it was over. She packs suitcases into her
car, straps her son into his car seat, drives towards Canada,
planning on finding somewhere to stay when she arrives, has

enough savings to support them both while she finds work. She is pulled over before the border, forced back home by a man Ray hired to follow her and threaten her. The police respond by saying only that there is nothing they can do. Nobody saw him do anything. Her word against his.

In the world of legal proof, the expression "word-on-word" refers to the conflicting versions of an event that took place between two people in private. He said/she said. There is a danger in framing contested facts in this way. Too often it falsely gives "the impression of even odds, as though each side is as likely as a coin flip."

Ray shows up at the deli. Punches Lynn in the face, her jawbone breaking under his fist in front of customers, a man and his daughter standing at the counter. The presence of witnesses results in his first arrest. Though the Family Court will issue an order of protection against him, he is released the same day.

"Remember," Lynn says, "this was 1980, upstate." She is referring to the small communities, the conservative attitudes, the endless accumulation of snow over long winters of short days when nothing thawed or melted away.

31

THE KINGDOM OF HEAVEN
LOISANN

I am sitting in the home of Loisann and Anthony Witmar, where I've come to learn about their church and their lives and what snapped me like a magnet to the sight of them singing in the subway. In some ways this home would feel the same regardless of whether it was located in Myerstown, Pennsylvania—where they are from—or the South Bronx. Their children, Eliana, three, and Antoine, two, would wake up each morning and eat their cereal, play with their toys. The Bible verses printed across their plastic shower curtain would be the same, the drone of the washing machine, the taste of the molasses-infused shoofly pie Loisann just baked and the smell from the scented candles she lights would all be the same.

However, in Myerstown the Witmars lived in a farmhouse on five pleasingly green acres. On the way to their two-bedroom apartment today, I passed through the most dangerous police precinct in New York City and stepped around a dead dog wrapped in a garbage bag to reach their front door. In Myerstown, they were embowered by family and friends. Here, hardly anyone speaks to them. In Myerstown, the clothes they wore served to deflect attention from their appearance. Here, they have the opposite effect. It is true that both neighborhoods have been quiet, but the quiets have not been the same.

All going well, their children will probably never attend a school; Loisann will start homeschooling in a few years. In the meantime, she settles next to Eliana on their squishy sofa each day, holding Antoine against the great orb of her pregnant belly, her feet not quite reaching the ground as she opens their Bible study book. In a sing-song voice, she keeps her children's attention as she reads about Joshua and the thief who, against God's command, looted items from the town after the Battle of Jericho, hiding them for himself before being discovered and stoned to death. At the end of this story, there are a few discussion points which Loisann runs through while Antoine squirms. When Eliana is stumped by a question about the fate of the thief, Loisann gently instructs her that, because the man disobeyed God, he and his family had to die. Then it is coloring time.

Loisann is thirty-one. She has sparkling eyes, brown hair and something in her smile that reminds me of the actress Katie Holmes. The Pennsylvania Dutch inflection of her speech means that her *O*s and *L*s are lilting, slightly elfin creatures: sweet surprises hiding like Easter eggs in the garden of her words. And those words are, sometimes, old words that entrance me with their strangeness: courting, youngsters, seamstress. When she says "the Bronx" her inflection contains the Dutch of the ships whose stone ballast was used to pave the streets on Lenape land they called New Amsterdam. It stops my heart every time.

Loisann speaks firmly and fast. The thoughts that she shares with me come out well formed and in monochrome. I can't even tell you how lovely is her laugh. She radiates a particular type of strong energy I think of as "high-density" and reminds me of a toy koala I had when I was a child: she is adorable and just below the soft surface she is as hard as rock.

"While Dad *called* himself a Christian, his life did not show it, at least at home," Loisann tells me, the last word rhyming with poem. "He could look good at church but at home—some people would use the word dysfunctional. Now compared to general America, we had a very good home. Anthony had more of a typical Mennonite upbringing."

One of eight children, Loisann grew up on a veal farm in Pennsylvania. There were lots of good memories, she says, in spite of how things were. There was a time there when her father went through a kind of rehabilitation program. He wasn't an alcoholic, wasn't on drugs. It was just to help him be more Christlike, she explains. But his heart wasn't really in it.

As the children play on the carpet between us, Loisann explains that she loved school. Remembers being sixteen at Myerstown Mennonite School, starting the new school year, thinking sadly, "Okay, that's tenth grade already." Her friends were leaving, starting jobs. "We opened our biology books," she remembers, "and I was like, 'Ahhh, I love it.' This was secure. This was my world. This was what I loved. I was like, 'I just can't imagine getting out yet. I'm not ready to quit.'"

But a call came from a cousin in Ohio with five preschoolers, a herniated disk and a sick husband. So Loisann did quit and went to help around the house. Looking back, she feels like it probably did as much for her as having stayed in school, since she was going to grow up and be a mother anyway. The next year she got the chance to teach at a summer Bible school in

Mississippi. Borrowed a car with her sister and took turns driving down highways in bright heat. Remembers the incredible feeling of sitting in a motel room, realizing that no one in the world knew where she was. They stopped at a beach where she swam, wrote a poem on the sand. And then they were back in the car, driving through the night, drinking coffee and Mountain Dew, playing music at full volume to stay awake. As she describes this to me, I can summon the rushing wonder of first adult consciousness. Then she emits a jolt of high-frequency laughter and the channel is changed. We are back in this room, back in our thirties, together, separately, again. She could've just had a very easy life, she says.

When Loisann turned eighteen, her school asked her to return as a teacher, although she had no formal training. A few years later, her church sent her to teach at a home for disadvantaged children in Honduras. She found it challenging: the language barrier, the children. "It was only five students but one boy was legally deaf, one girl was FAS, fetal alcohol syndrome," she whispers. "And then twins that were just *teeeeeerribly* disrespectful, just say whatever they thought in your face. So my hands were very full."

Loisann ended up moving back to Ohio to help another sister, who had thirteen children, and her brother, a trucker, whose wife had left him seven children.

"Antoine's fighting me," Eliana complains.

"You be a peacemaker, okay?" Loisann soothes her.

"I would go over and make breakfast, and then I would go to school and teach, and come back and make supper," she laughs bleakly. "Sometimes be there for the evening. Just do cleaning. But God knew what I would be needing that year and the same week I moved to Ohio was the week Anthony phoned, wanting to start a courtship."

It had been a long wait. In Loisann's world, a young woman makes herself a new dress for her first date with a young man, and another for their first Sunday together. A friend had given her a piece of special fabric for this purpose, but Loisann was twenty-four, then twenty-five, then twenty-six and still it lay unused. Finally, on a hot summer day, Loisann snapped. That material would be so nice and cool, she thought recklessly. Why let it rot in my drawer? Her friend advised that she should wait a little longer. A week later, Anthony called Loisann's father. "Probably most young men would ask a father permission to court the girl," Loisann explains. "Just as a way of honoring him, that my authority now is going to switch from him to Anthony."

•

Mid-morning. Loisann pushes a gigantic gray stroller around the block to the playground, Eliana skipping by her side. While the neighborhood is infinitely better than it was, despite the talk of urban renewal this is still, by a number of measures, not a place many people would enthusiastically choose if they had better options. But those people are not the Witmars.

There are no other strollers on the sidewalks, no children at the playground, there is no one anywhere until someone stops to use the toilets near the chain-link fence at the park. Loisann allows Antoine to find his own balance on a ladder; Eliana points her toes up into the clouds as I push her on the swing.

We are under a flight path and planes pass low overhead, gray on gray, their roar muting our voices. A light rain falls and we head back. Her sneakers soft on the sidewalk, Loisann rolls the stroller over a condom wrapper and tells me that during her first pregnancy, back in Myerstown, she would take beautiful walks every morning.

Thinking generally of the homicide rate in this borough, and specifically of the mother who died three months ago shielding her children from stray bullets on a playground not far from here, I ask Loisann whether she ever feels unsafe. "No," she replies lightly. "I'm safe, I'm protected. And if I'm not, that's because God has a different plan for me."

Each time I visit Loisann at her home she pads around in her slippers, but I have never seen her without the white dome that covers the bun into which her long hair has been twirled. "It's called a covering or veiling," she explains, snapping an elastic at the end of Eliana's braid and letting her go play. "When a child comes to an age where they sense in themselves they're a sinner bound for Hell, they're not going to make it, they need Jesus to cleanse them and give their life to him, we call that the age of accountability. It's often around then that a girl will start covering her hair."

The sound of the children squabbling rises and boils over. "This is *my seat*, Antoine," Eliana tells her brother, over by their toy box.

"It's for a couple different reasons," Loisann continues. "For a woman to show that she is under God and also she's under her husband. Now that does *not* mean that we are, like, below or less than. We're equals. But when it comes to the final word, then the woman has to submit." She reaches for her Bible, opens to First Corinthians.

"But I would have you know," she reads, "that the head of every man is Christ; and the head of every woman is the man, and the head of Christ is God. Every man, praying or prophesying having his head *covered*, dishonors his head. But every woman that prays or prophesies, with her head *uncovered*, dishonors her head . . .

"So," she says, crisply closing the book, "I take that verse to mean that the angels see that our heads are covered and—because we are purposefully putting ourselves under our God-ordained authority—the angels acknowledge that and have a special protection for us."

There is another book in the house that is very special to Loisann. Part diary, part scrapbook, part photo album, Loisann made it when she was sixteen. She shows it to me and I stand very close to her, peering down at it. Pointing to a photo, she explains to Eliana, "This is when Mommy was a baby. Let's turn the page!" She shows us a colossal snowman. A snow cow. Her as a toddler, holding a plastic comb on her head and standing next to a rooster with a red comb of his own. Her wedding day, mugging with Anthony for the camera next to a car on which someone has graffitied in soap: 1 + 1 = 15.

Gesturing towards her belly, Loisann says, "My mom was really hoping that this baby would be twins, because that would've given her the fiftieth grandchild. But now my sister-in-law is expecting, so she's got her fifty."

I see her home, her school, her sisters, her best friend, her nieces and nephews. Her bubble letters, her teenage poetry, her lists, her goals, her questions to herself, so private and so like my own at that age that something is suddenly plucked in my stomach that feels like a guitar string sounding. She turns to another photo. A teenage slumber party. "All the girls got together after the last day of tenth grade. We all went to my friend's place overnight. In the spring, once a month the moms get together and bring in a hot lunch for the whole school." Tenses are getting mixed up; the past in the room with us now.

As I look at this book, which she opens to me like her rib cage, it all falls away—the bonnets and the tractors, the odes to her god—until there is just the fast-beating heart of the gabbing and laughing, book-loving, overly conscientious girl who thought perfection would protect her. Writing so diligently to herself, whoever that would turn out to be. And for one moment, I feel I can see myself on the doorstep of the world just before everything I thought I knew dissipated.

It didn't strike me as anything when she said it, but it feels like a gift now. When Loisann was teaching, she told me, they would make a point to do fun things to start the school year. Donuts and chocolate milk on the first day. A teacher leading all the students in a big game of follow-the-leader through the school and down a giant slide. And one year, everybody got a helium balloon. Tied a tag with the school's address to the string in case someone who later found it cared to write and let them know. Then all the students simultaneously let go of their balloons and watched them float up and into the sky.

"We got responses for the next couple of *months*. One was as far away as Delaware!" Loisann said enthusiastically, before directing Eliana towards her chores.

I looked out the window, ground level, at the heads passing by. I did not know it then, but I was looking in the direction of the apartment, three blocks over, where my great-grandmother—for whom I am named—grew up. I know nothing else about her so do not really feel myself to be from there, or—for that matter—anywhere. But since I've discovered this fact of her address, it's funny, she has become inextricably bound up with the Witmars in my mind. So that when I see those who are closer to what came before them, and feel that void at my own back, I reflexively think of the image Loisann described: a hundred hands letting go, releasing a hundred balloons into the clear sky. A colorful, collective surrender. The possibility that it might also be mine.

32

THEORIES OF FLIGHT
FRED & RHONDA

Eventually a neighbor helps Rhonda get a job at Coles Super-market and she steps back into her days, dragged into and out of the city for her shifts, looking through the train window at the world drained of its rightful color. She goes to see *Close En-counters* without Fred, her heart breaking in the dark. The final scene is a foothold, somewhere she can rest on the cliff face. She watches the screen as the long-missing, the never-found—pilots and sailors—are returned home, striding out of an enormous flying saucer, their faces untouched by time. Maybe that's what happened to Fred, she thinks. Maybe their life together is simply on pause.

Her father says he will pay the balance on the engagement ring at the jeweler's in Moonee Ponds so she can have it as a memento. When they go to collect it, however, the jeweler will not hand it over, won't even let her see it. Will never explain why.

She eventually gets her driver's license, an apartment, fur-niture of her own, makes friends who never knew Fred, wears clothes Fred never saw, accepts a certain bluntness, her real life unspooling the whole time inside her like a quiet road.

Rhonda is nearly sixty, her hair a short gray. She lives in Queensland and enjoys crocheting and painting. She is still, in certain ways, the girl she was. Goes ice skating every Monday with a friend, tries to get faster every time. Has jumped out of a plane—loved the falling that felt like flying. She shows me her paintings, holding each one up for the camera as we skype. They are dreamily rendered. A forest scene. A country cottage. The last one is my favorite: hot air balloons hovering between water and sky.

"It's like that movie *Sliding Doors*," she explains, about the span between ages sixteen and fifty-seven during which she has always seen double—both the life she wanted and the life she had. "I think of Fred every day." She never had children, though she's had other partners and has been in her current relationship for thirty years. Each relationship has been challenged by the strength of her feeling for Fred, his phantom presence and the absence of the parts of her that vanished with him.

Some partners wouldn't let her talk about him. This was how she learned to cry without making noise, locking herself away in the bathroom. Occasionally, while out grocery shopping, say, or paying for petrol, the Bee Gees' "Night Fever" will come on, reminding her of their dancing lessons, and she will dissolve.

"I don't know if we'll ever have an answer," Rhonda says.

"For a while there I believed that he was taken by a UFO— only because you could believe anything Fred said. He was so truthful. All his friends said the same: he wouldn't say that [about the UFO] if it wasn't happening." She pauses. "Also, you've gotta think too, that by saying that he's jeopardized his career, and his love for flying and for airplanes was so deep. But then, he's telling the truth, so . . ." She shrugs her shoulders.

"A lot of people have gone through the records and important people, like pilots, say it wasn't handled very good." She mentions the witnesses who saw the lights that night. A couple in Apollo Bay who said they saw Fred's Cessna flying towards land, the green light above it. "They reported it but they were criticized by everyone at the time, so the gentleman just shut up. Didn't say any more for all this time.

"By hearing that, I sometimes think now, 'Well, is he in the bush there at Apollo Bay, Cape Otway?'" She remembers how Fred's mates drove down to Apollo Bay to do their own land search. She went down too, with her parents, but the media was unrelenting and her father decided it was best for them to turn around and go home. A mate of Fred's told her that the police effectively stopped them from going into the bush. "It's so thick, so rugged," she explains. "The police said to them, 'If you're going in there, we're not going in after you.' So they made that decision themselves not to go in. Anything could happen in there. If Fred is in there, it'd be like finding a warplane hidden in the jungle.

"So," she says, the thin strokes of her eyebrows rising up and out like a drawbridge, "I don't really know, truthfully, whether he's in the bush there, whether a UFO took him, or whether he just flew off."

There is a part of Rhonda that is still in her parents' hallway holding the line. She has the registration of Fred's plane and the moment it disappeared tattooed on her arm. She's kept in touch with Fred's family. Tells me his grandmother is still alive. Rhonda sees the occasional clairvoyant, asks about Fred. "You want answers, that's the thing. And some don't know or some you can tell the answer's probably not right. I went to one earlier this year and she did a card reading and she said that he has not passed over. So, let's throw that in there as well," she says with a tired chuckle. "You really don't know. There's no answer. I've looked for the answer but there's none."

Every ten years, on the anniversary of his disappearance, Rhonda flies down to Victoria, drives to Cape Otway where there is a plaque to *The Unknown* commemorating her long-missing, her never-found Fred. And every year on their anniversary she opens a box, slips the ring on her finger. A placeholder, curved like the horizon itself, signifying objects eternally trapped in the distance and flattened to the impossible simplicity of a line.

There are many hypotheses about what happened to Valentich. Here is one of them.

Writing in the *Skeptical Inquirer*, James McGaha (a retired US Air Force pilot and astronomer) and Joe Nickell (a former stage magician, private investigator and "skeptical ufologist") emphasize Valentich's age and inexperience. How he was "enthralled with UFOs." "In brief, Valentich may have been an accident waiting to happen," they argue.

What could they have been, those four bright lights above him, hovering at height? Venus. Mars. Mercury. Antares, one of the brightest stars. A diamond-shaped constellation, McGaha and Nickell suggest, the interstitial darkness back-filled by the mind to suggest a presence.

What I'm doing right now is orbiting, and the thing is just orbiting on top of me.

And the green light he reported? Potentially another error in his perceptual shorthand. "Remember," they write,

"Valentich's first description of the UFO involved only four bright white lights; he made no mention at that time of a green one. It could actually have been nothing more than the Cessna's own navigation light on its right wing tip."

If the UFO was really just a constellation, then Valentich mistook the movement of his own plane in relation to stationary celestial light for the movement of a UFO in relation to his plane. "This points to what was really happening to the poor inexperienced pilot," McGaha and Nickell lament. "Distracted by the UFO, he may have then been deceived by the illusion of a tilted horizon." This effect occurs when the sun has gone down but still illuminates part of the horizon—the rest of the sky gets gradually darker and the resulting imbalance of light can cause the horizon to appear at an angle. If a pilot compensates by "leveling" the wings, the plane will start to spiral downward: "at first slowly, then with increasing acceleration."

It is their contention that the young pilot—"flying while excitedly focusing on, and talking about, a UFO"—entered such a graveyard spiral. Noting his statement, seconds before he cuts out, that his engine was "rough idling," they explain that the plane's tightening spiral would cause an increase in G-forces with a consequent decrease in fuel flow, resulting in that effect. Alternatively, if the Cessna was already inverted by that point, it would produce the same effect because it had a gravity-fed fuel system. In other words, Valentich thought he was flying when actually he was falling.

"It's called spatial disorientation," the air traffic controller Steve Robey said when this possibility was raised in an early interview. "You've lost control of the airplane, you fight to regain the orientation, and it is quite a strange feeling, really. There's no way you can talk on the radio like he was talking to me ..."

As a pilot himself, Steve had experienced that situation. "You've lost visual contact with the horizon and you're fighting like hell to fly the airplane by the instruments when your senses are telling you something different. You're doing everything you can to regain control of the plane."

"I have believed all this time that he was genuine in what he was seeing and saying," Steve tells me over the phone. His voice is mellifluous and kind, and there is a straight, even grain to it like ironwood. After that night, he says, he got letters from all around the world. "I was someone they could talk to."

He is deeply empathetic to Rhonda, "Frederick" and the Valentich family. Also, the investigators—"you're going to want to look for earthly reasons about why this was happening"—though he believes it is misguided, "shameful" even, to focus on Fred's academic performance.

"I have always felt he encountered something we can't explain," he says. The week after Fred disappeared, Steve was on the radio with a pilot reporting three unidentified very bright lights over East Sale. There was a genuine increase in atmospheric phenomena and UFO sightings in 1978, he says.

Things are freer today, he explains when I ask about the professional consequences of reporting a UFO. Back then it was different. This is another reason he's confident Fred wasn't fabricating anything. "With his career in mind—to be saying those things, you'd have to be genuine," he says. "He was wanting to be a professional pilot. No young man does these things if that is what he has in front of him."

It has become, to total strangers, their story. They saw the plane, they knew someone who flew in the plane, they heard the original transmission, heard a copy of the full tape, he disappeared a year to the day before they were born. This has something to do with the fact that in the final analysis, there is no final analysis. The Valentich story refuses to cohere, cannot be captured in the neat net of narrative. There is, simply, an expendable piece of an unidentified plane, and the transcript of a radio transmission. What came before and after Fred radioed for assistance remains formless and empty.

And while this circumstance came, with the invisible in-gredient of time, to have perhaps a worse effect on those who loved him than knowledge—for those who did not know Fred, it gives rise to something else entirely. In his eternal suspension between belief and knowledge, truth and meaning, life and death, the immortal Fred in the dark mirror of our stories has become enlightened. Carrying our life jackets, our hopes for Nirvana, with him as he flies into darkness over the surface of the deep.

33

HALFWAY HOME
LYNN

Ray died, in Lynn's mind, the moment he backhanded their two-year-old son down the red-brick steps that led to the front door, the same steps where he had knocked out her teeth. As she scooped up the child, the imperative immediately converted into historical fact: good as done. Their divorce was about to be finalized. Ray had come to the house, they had fought and he'd stormed out through the front door, Lynn behind him. This is when he threw the child down the stairs and ran off. "See," she explains, repositioning the ball of yarn on her lap, "he knew I'd stop to pick the baby up."

She calls the police, takes her son to the hospital, to a psychiatrist, to court. They all maintain that nothing can be concluded, no one saw him do it. "Do you think he called an audience?" Lynn replies.

She is awarded custody, but the judge approves Ray's overnight visitation rights, to begin on February 5. "That was a Friday," she explains. "I killed him on Thursday, February fourth. He wasn't getting that baby overnight." Her short, pristine, almond-shaped nails loop yarn around and into itself until there is sweater where there was once only string. "I killed him and I lied to the police. I did what I had to do to protect my son."

•

In the small towns of upstate New York and Massachusetts, her name will not become known for reasons connected to any of the dreams she had for herself. She won't be remembered for her work as a clinical psychologist or her contribution as a school guidance counselor or teacher; no one will talk about the macaroni salad at her deli, or identify her with the accomplishments of her child. But nearly four decades later, the local paper will still refer to her as a confessed killer who lured her husband to his violent death.

After the clothesline is unwound from Ray's neck in the basement of her home, his body is placed in his station wagon, driven across the Hudson River and brought to a stop behind the bus terminal where it rapidly freezes during the hours it takes for the police to discover it, believing, at first, that a robbery had gone wrong. When he is questioned, the twenty-three-year-old handyman whom Lynn paid to kill Ray will tell a too-neat narrative in exchange for a more lenient sentence on his own murder charge, including the improbable but cinematically satisfying detail that as Lynn held both of Ray's hands away from his neck, she soothed him that it would all be okay.

On October 30, 1982, the day before Halloween, Lynn is at the hospital, leaning down to secure her son's tiny Superman cape before lifting him up to the glass window so her mother can delight in his costume from her bed in intensive care. This is when the police arrive and handcuff her. On the way into the station, she is allowed to drop the child off with a friend at the deli; her father will pick him up after he receives the devastating phone call. And that was her last day of freedom for the next thirty-five years.

"Other than that, Mrs. Lincoln, how did you like the play?" her father asks gently, when he visits her at the county jail. It reminds her she is the daughter of a man who is both a member of the Royal Order of Jesters and a veteran of the Dieppe Raid. This is part of her stuffing: what holds her in shape as she sits, denied bail, awaiting trial. She won't see her mother again. Or her son, now in the care of her sister. She goes to the Episcopal service every Sunday, speaks quietly with the chaplain. Meets with her lawyers, does not plead guilty. She will deny involvement, say that Bob, the handyman, and Ray had a history of rancor. That Ray was enraged because Bob let his dog shit on their lawn. That Bob, who figured his only flaw was drinking too much, couldn't understand how he had been denied access to his kids while Ray, who beat his kid, had been granted visitation. And that Bob killed Ray in Ray's car, finding $1500 and some cocaine in Ray's pockets, which he later told her he sold.

She will testify about the sexual abuse. Also the physical abuse, of her and the boy; how her son had expressed fear about spending time with his father. She will testify that Ray had forced their child to watch as he and his new girlfriend engaged in sexual acts. All this will go towards her motive for the crime, not towards an understanding of its context that might have resulted in some mitigation of the penalty.

One day the battered-woman defense will enter New York courtrooms, and the actions of women who kill abusive partners will be granted some kind of contextual understanding—the same understanding the law has always offered, through the defenses of self-defense and provocation, to men confronted with violence.

That day is not today.

The jury deliberates on Lynn's murder charge for five hours before returning a guilty verdict. She is sentenced to twenty-five years to life. Bob gets seventeen to life and is released well before her.

In 1986 she appeals her conviction on a technicality, arguing that certain evidence—phone conversations Ray taped without her knowledge—should have been excluded.

The appeal is successful, but in the court's ruling Lynn's character and motives are eviscerated. She is portrayed as a woman cold-heartedly denying Ray access to his son. A woman so driven by rage that she would rather waive her claim to child support than give Ray access. A woman who tells him he will be afforded visitation over her dead body; that if he *is* awarded visitation she will move interstate with the child. That the boy is not his son anyway—something she's kept from him following advice from her attorney, who told her not to leave Ray until an (unrelated) arson charge against her was resolved. That if Ray presses forward she'll go to court and say whatever she has to say—doesn't everybody?

One line goes completely unremarked upon by the court: her contention that the child did not want to see Ray "because he had done 'something' to frighten the boy."

It may be true, of course, that all this is evidence of Lynn's "base character." I do not know the circumstances of her arson charge: Lynn has not gone into detail and I cannot find further information about it apart from the fact that it was ultimately dismissed. But it is possible to be charged with arson and to still hold the reasonable belief that your partner is a danger to your child. An offer to forgo the child support to which you are entitled is consistent with that belief. As are the anger, the threats, the willingness to perjure, to move, to make the statement (true or otherwise) that the child is not really the man's anyway.

The appeal court finds that the tapes were improperly admitted and a retrial is ordered. But the court's language points, straight as a papercut, only to Lynn's malice. And this is the clue that perhaps something is not right. Because the law—like memory, like books—deals not with life but with the story of life. So despite its granular concern with the numerous and conflicting details of which all events are composed, the law must ultimately pin its hopes on selectivity and approximation. This is why we must look again at anyone too perfectly characterized in its stories—too neatly one way, and never the other. They are not people, they are characters. Characters serve a function, but that function—as far as too much of the criminal law has been concerned—has not always been the production of justice.

At her retrial, Lynn is convicted a second time. She will serve nearly thirty-five years in prison for murder, her hair slowly turning white.

Every Sunday, Lynn goes to Trinity Church in lower Manhattan where she is now sitting in the fifth pew wearing a lavender sweater, her head angled towards a hymnal, singing: *Perverse and foolish oft I strayed but yet in love he sought me, and on his shoulder gently laid, and home, rejoicing, brought me.*

It is a newly new year, early January, ice on the rivers close on both sides here in the oldest part of New Amsterdam where the churchyard contains Alexander and Eliza Schuyler Hamilton, and lives abbreviated at thirty-four; twenty-three; six years, one month and eleven days. Lynn is just back from Chicago, a visit to AJ's sister over Christmas. Her first flight in nearly forty years. The travel pass granted by her parole officer is still folded in her wallet.

She will soon be an official member of Trinity, the three-hundred-year-old Episcopal church near Ground Zero which was the base for rescue operations when the Twin Towers were destroyed. They say the building didn't even shake. It will soon be getting needed renovations, work paid for by its six-billion-dollar portfolio. The leadership of the church is diverse, its congregation is diverse; all are welcome here. Its social justice efforts relate to, among other things, bail reform, LGBTQIA+ rights, advocacy for undocumented immigrants and homelessness.

The reading this morning is from Genesis. *Now the earth was formless and empty, darkness was over the surface of the deep, and the Spirit of God was hovering over the waters.* When he does the Old Testament, Reverend Philip Jackson explains, he likes to use the Jewish commentary and recently he came across a sentence he loved: *Reality itself is imbued with God's goodness.*

"Think about that," he says. "Things both great and small, majestic and tiny—in the fabric of reality. So you yourself are imbued with the goodness of God. Live with that. Amen."

They pray for those in prison, they pray for those without homes. They turn to one another, grasping hands and saying, "May peace be with you." They line up in the aisle for communion, which anyone may join and where everyone sips from the same cup.

Lynn stays after the service for the Sunday lecture series which this month is on Martin Luther King Jr's "Letter from Birmingham Jail":

> Any law that uplifts human personality is just. Any law that degrades personality is unjust. All segregation statutes are unjust because segregation distorts the soul and damages the personality. It gives the segregator a false sense of superiority and the segregated a false sense of inferiority. To use the words of Martin Buber, the great Jewish philosopher, segregation substitutes an "I–it" relationship for the "I–thou" relationship and ends up relegating persons to the status of things ...

In 1921, Buber embarked on a German vernacular translation of the Bible. He was still at it in the late 1930s, when the Nazis rose to power and he continued after the Holocaust had annihilated the world he grew up in, the people and institutions that formed him. Completed it, finally, in 1961. I stopped saying my religion's holiest prayer (*Hear, O Israel: the Lord is our God, the Lord is one*) around the age that I realized they were the words that died on the lips of my forebears as their bodies dropped in layers on damp leaf in Polish forest; on the cement floors of purpose-built shower blocks. Why would that god care about a mother who had grown increasingly distant until all that was left of her were the dints in the carpet where her piano once stood? Now, though, I watch Lynn listening to the words of Dr. King and it strikes me that there might be a different type of porousness between what is outside and what is in. That certain types of prayer are their own immediate answer and that this type of faith in open-heartedly reaching out is an act of basic sanity.

Lynn told me that she had been nervous, initially, about meeting Trinity's Reverend Jackson, who earned a law degree at Yale. She approached him after a service. His sermon had been about refuge, the story of Moses sheltering in the land of Midian after attacking and killing the Egyptian overseer he found beating a Hebrew slave. You never know, he had said, we may even have a murderer here with us now.

Introducing herself, Lynn explained that she was a survivor of domestic abuse and a convicted felon. Had recently been released from prison after serving thirty-five years for murdering her husband.

The instant reaction of this tall man in his long white robe was to fold her within the full wingspan of his arms and say, "Welcome home."

34

THEORIES OF FLIGHT
WESTALL

Australia's aerial defense is in their hands, says the RAAF recruitment ad that appeared in the *Age* newspaper on Wednesday, April 6, 1966. There is football news and soccer news and horseracing and golf. Updates on the Vietnam War. Reports on youths burning their national service registration cards, a mail strike and French border police patrolling for beatniks. On this cold and gusty day, tickets for Bob Dylan's Festival Hall show are $1.55, it is normal for a major newspaper to print a daily Bible text, no human has walked on the moon and young Colin Kelly is kicking a football on the field at Westall Secondary College during morning recess.

This is when he sees a metallic disk moving over his high school.

The older students on the grass tilt their heads skyward. The younger students in the primary school press up against the classroom windows to get a look. They see a domed, saucer-shaped object land near the school. A teacher grabs her camera, snaps as many photos as she can before it takes off. For a moment, the object appears still in the sky, and then it bolts off with a loud *whoosh*. Colin watches five light planes trail after it towards the pine trees in the Grange, the land nearby that the neighborhood kids treat as their collective backyard.

Inside, the younger students cower in small groups; at lunchtime they will refuse to go outside to play. On the football field some of the older students are crying but others shoal eagerly around Colin, ignoring the teachers' shouts to get inside as they leap the fence and run past the market gardens across the road to the Grange. Colin is dying to go, but he does what he's told and stays put. He's that kind of kid.

The police arrive, the journalists arrive. Some students are questioned in the headmaster's office by men in suits. The teacher who took the photos has not just her film but also her camera confiscated by these men; they do not return it. The headmaster calls an assembly. The children are told not to speak about what they've seen.

At the end of the school day, Colin's mother hears him calling to her from the end of their street as he races home. He stops in long enough to throw his bag down and tell her what he saw before running with great urgency down to the Grange, where the kids who chased after the object say it descended briefly before taking off again.

Trucks are parked there. Khaki uniforms and blue uniforms swarm the area. He sees the long scrub grass flattened in a swirling circle in the middle of the ring of tall pines.

The men are still there the next day. Then the grass is cut and the area where the circle had been seen is burnt. His mother will always say she wouldn't have believed it if it was his brother who told her the story, but that Colin wasn't the type of kid to make up lies.

Four days before the Westall sighting, a Melbourne man took a photo from his backyard of a saucer-type object that resembled the type seen above the school. Two days before the sighting, a construction contractor named Ron Sullivan was driving down a dark road in Central Victoria when he saw lights rising out of the trees. He saw the beams of his headlights bend, as if pulled towards that light. Feeling some of that suction, he reversed and drove away. Only reported it when he learned that a driver had been killed two days earlier, crashing into those same trees. According to Shane Ryan, a researcher interviewed in the documentary *Westall '66: A Suburban UFO Mystery*, there is no mention of these two incidents in the official record for 1966— the Summary of Unidentified Aerial Sightings Reported to Department of Air, Canberra—though the Air Force investigated both. When Ryan located the footage from the incident in the Channel Nine archives, he found the film cannisters— but no film. "And yet, this memory has survived," he says in the documentary, "and it only has to be slightly pricked and it's like the floodgates open and all the memories come rushing out."

George Simpson, Australian UFO investigator, is driving Don Schmitt, American UFO investigator, through Melbourne's southeastern suburbs to give him a personal tour of the Westall school area. Once there, Don will meet Colin Kelly, the boy on the school oval who is now a mustachioed man in his late sixties.

Don has extensive experience meeting UFO witnesses. He has spent decades tracking down and collecting the stories of those with direct experience of the 1947 Roswell incident, in which an airborne object—some say a UFO, others maintain it was a United States Army Air Forces balloon—crashed at a ranch near Roswell, New Mexico. Based on the hundreds of witness accounts he has collected over his career, Don is convinced it was the former.

He is in Australia to talk about Roswell—talking about Roswell being what Don does best, and what Don has done with Oprah, Larry King, Shirley MacLaine, Peter Jennings, Montel Williams, Fox Good Day LA, NPR, BBC, NBC, ABC News, CBS 48 Hours, CNN Investigates, Sci Fi Investigates, National Geographic Channel, Smithsonian Channel, the Travel Channel, Learning Channel, the Disney Channel and many more. But today he is going to tour the site of Australia's largest mass UFO sighting, and on the way there George (white goatee, blue wraparound sunglasses) is telling Don (black goatee, gold-rimmed aviators) one of the best stories I have ever heard.

On the evening of October 21, 1978, twenty-year-old George was outside his parents' house near Moorabbin Airport waiting for his girlfriend when he saw a white Cessna with blue trim flying overhead.

"I can't help it," George says to Don in the passenger seat. "I always have to look up and watch a plane go over. That's just me. I have to watch them."

"That's me too," Don agrees warmly.

"That's three hundred people going past having a cup of coffee!" George enthuses. "That's fascinating, you know?"

Young George stood watching as the Cessna flew towards the setting sun. Nothing unusual except for the thought that popped into his mind: *Don't take your eyes off that plane.* The girlfriend never showed up and he eventually went inside. Next day, he heard on the news that a search was underway for a plane that went missing over Bass Strait, the pilot believed to have run out of fuel. Soon the headlines changed: Pilot reported seeing a UFO before he vanished.

Years later, an acquaintance told George that he had a flying lesson the day Frederick Valentich disappeared. He entered the airport with his instructor to sign the plane back in—they walked in discussing the lesson and were told to shut up because a conversation was happening between Valentich and the air traffic adviser. "And everybody was listening," George says. "He said every time Fred spoke, you could hear an unusual noise over the radio, some sort of interference was coming through. He thought it had the Doppler effect, which meant that something was going past the plane. Now, I haven't been able to pick that up, and nobody else who's heard the tape has been able to pick up that sound . . .

"But there was definitely a continuous static and interference coming through his radio, which wasn't on any of the other planes communicating at the same time," George continues urgently.

"That would've been the classic EM," Don nods, staring ahead through the windscreen. "Electromagnetic effect."

"Electromagnetic radiation of some kind was interfering with the radio," George agrees. "But, of course, Fred said, 'I've got my engine running at twenty-three, twenty-four hundred RPM and the engine's coughing.' And at that point, the adviser says to him, 'Okay, what are your intentions?' Because the adviser knows he's six minutes out over the ocean in a single-engine plane, it's nearly dark and now he's reporting an engine problem. So the adviser asks, 'What are your intentions?'—meaning are you closer to come to the land or are you going to go to the island. I think Fred just misinterpreted the question, he said, 'Ah, my intentions are to go to King Island.' It was one of the last things he said. And he said almost immediately after that, 'Melbourne, that strange object is hovering on top of me again, it is hovering and it's not an aircraft.' And a couple of seconds after that, he said, 'Melbourne—' and was interrupted midsentence because there was a collision—an aerial collision."

"What about the scratching noise?" Don asks about the unidentified noise that filled the remaining seconds of the transmission. "The sound of the metal?"

"That came straight after," George replies, steering the car through a busy shopping strip. "He said, 'Melbourne' and then he was cut off and there was this *chich chich chich*—which I believe was the sound of the propeller cutting into the surface of something else."

"Striking the surface of something else," Don echoes.

George explains that his friend, UFO researcher Bill Chalker, has uncovered a potential explanation for that "something else."

"There was a lot of UFO activity happening in central New South Wales," he says. "A place called Coonabarabran. Did I miss the road I was going to take? Ah, no, I didn't, gotta keep going straight."

Coonabarabran is a small town near the Siding Spring Observatory, home to the largest optical telescope in Australia. It sits on the edge of an ancient volcanic mountain range located in Warrumbungle National Park, the first Dark Sky Park in Australia—land free from light pollution and possessing an "exceptional or distinguished quality of starry nights." It is a place, Bill Chalker will later tell me, where it seems everyone has a UFO story. On Thursday, November 17, 1994, the front page of the *Coonabarabran Times* reported that two days prior, six people had reported a UFO sighting to police after seeing bright lights above the road south of town. "It was described as a large diamond shape which made no noise," the article stated.

"It was a farming community up in the mountains," George says, steering past a Vietnamese bakery, a chemist. Chalker had gone up there with a mate in 1995 to investigate sightings. Everyone they talked to said, "Go talk to Laurie."

Laurie, a local character who made it into the papers for protesting restrictions on gun ownership, ran the hardware store. It was his habit to ask customers whether they'd had any unusual experiences, documenting anything he was told in a notebook or, if he was in a rush, on the backs of receipt copies.

"They went and tracked Laurie down, and Bill was recording the conversation and I've got a copy of this tape," George says, explaining that he's listened to it a hundred times.

Laurie said that the stories he'd collected were a real mixed bag but that the best one was from a South Australian farmer who had bought a property in the area and came into the shop one day. The farmer told Laurie that the day after Valentich disappeared, he was out on his South Australian property harvesting lucerne hay when he heard an unusual noise, a screaming-type sound, and figured a bearing had gone in his harvester. So he stopped and uncoupled the mechanical drive to have a look, but the noise kept going.

"'Well, hang on,' he goes, trying to work out how come he could still hear it," George continues. At this point, the farmer realized that he was in shadow. Looked up. Saw a huge circular object hovering over him. Going by the length of the tractor, he reckoned it was about thirty metres across.

"A lot of these farmers are pilots," George explains, "'cause they do their own crop dusting. And his understanding of aviation is you have to have a bit of forward movement just to stay aloft, but this thing wasn't moving fast enough. He thought, 'This thing's gonna crash down on me.' So he ran away from his tractor, to get clear of it."

Looking at the saucer from the side, he saw it had a dome on top with a black strip which he took to be a weather seal. "He said there was a doorway in it but no doorhandle. And he said it was like a church door—with an arch on top," George says. The farmer described the saucer as having two rows of rims spinning in opposite directions. One row spun so fast he had to blink to see that it was actually spinning, the other row moved slowly. And together they made the screaming noise which grabbed his attention in the first place.

"Then he said there was two large openings at one end which he thought was exhaust," George explains, peering up at the signs as the street opens out onto a wider road. "He could see shimmering heat coming out of one of them and spurts of flame coming out the other. And he thought, 'Yeah, this thing's in trouble.' But then he said, as this thing was turning around, there was an aircraft stuck to the other side of it."

It was a Cessna.

"And on the tape, Bill says, 'What? The whole aircraft?' And Laurie says, 'Yep, the whole aircraft.' The tail was hanging down, the wings were backed up against this thing like it's run into it and the wheels were sticking out. And he could see the registration number of the plane." The farmer hadn't heard that Valentich had gone missing at this point, George explains, but he scratched the registration number of the Cessna into the paint of his tractor with a nail before the object flew off over a ridge in the direction of a nearby army range.

"Well," Don asks calmly in his deep bass, "was it correct?"

"It was the number of the missing plane," George says, his voice wavering slightly.

"What are the chances?" Don says. "What are the chances? What. Are. The. Chances."

Chalker has called the account from the farmer an "extraordinarily bizarre and unbelievable claim." He tried for years to track down further information. "You can't *begin* an investigation when you don't have a name," George says, explaining that, because of the ridicule factor, the farmer told Laurie his story on the basis of anonymity and Laurie did not violate that accord when recounting it to Bill. "That's the trouble, that's what we're up against. We're racing against the undertaker and we're also racing against the ridicule factor."

I will find out later, from Bill Chalker's blog, that the mate he went to Coonabarabran with was Rob Tilley. When I ask Rob about this, he says that he remembers going up there with Chalky but doesn't remember that conversation specifically, which is implausible only if you don't know how many strange conversations Rob has actually had.

Apparently, Laurie is now dead and his notebook has been lost, although George would like to try, at least, to locate the tractor.

"Farmers are a tight group," Don says. "Somebody needs to go from farm to farm."

"I got on to the Lucerne Growers Association," George says. "We thought we might have had a name but we couldn't get anywhere. You know about reversing tapes and hidden messages?"

"Yes, yes," Don says with some enthusiasm. "Like the old Beatles—playing the record backwards . . ."

"I reversed it at the point where he's describing the guy getting off the motorbike and coming in to buy something, where he's skirting around not telling the name," George says as the low buildings of Westall Secondary and Primary School pop into view. "And in reverse it sounds like a name pops out. So I tried to investigate that. The name sounded like Ian. Anyway, I've got it. This is the Westall school."

35

HALFWAY HOME
LYNN

At seventy, Lynn is the oldest resident at the shelter where most of the staff and residents call her Ms. Evans, the honorific extended only to her and the director, a formerly incarcerated social worker whom Lynn knows "from inside." Lynn is usually the first to leave in the mornings, around 7:30 AM. At this early hour, she will ignore the rancid communal fridge and the dry cereal packets on a card table in the common room in favor of the smoothie blender she keeps at her office—an unbelievable luxury—and walk to the subway next to younger women and men holding juices that cost more than she earns in an hour.

Besides being a domestic violence counselor, a teacher, a writer, a cook, an artist and a skilled knitter of baby clothes, Lynn is also a paralegal. She works near Wall Street for one of the remaining sole practitioners in the area, whose office is over a café near the water. When she is not typing or filing, she is out serving documents around the city, handbag on one side, cane on the other. She is invigorated by the walking, by the city, by the interesting work and by the trust placed in her by her boss, who also has a felony conviction, having served time as a younger man for armed robbery before a nun encouraged him to enroll in college courses. Even if she did mind the walking, Lynn would do it anyway. Having arrived in the city four months ago as a seventy-year-old woman with no savings, no family and no home, she needs the job.

Lynn is never the last to return to the shelter. She gives herself a good buffer before the 9:00 PM curfew stipulated by the terms of her parole. She walks in around 6:00 PM and stops by the desk of the resident aide at the front door for a friendly chat while her bag is searched for contraband and her name is entered for the night's count, the shelter having its own curfew of 10:00 PM. There are days she gets in a bit later, depending on the train, the weather, how long it took her to walk the three blocks from the subway, past the stalls of T-shirts and bongs and cheap jewelery and sunglasses where the owners come out to greet her with a hug while she asks about their families.

She will sit for a while in the common room where the TV is always too loud and rarely plays the news, which she would prefer to watch. Where there is no fresh air on account of the leftover fast food on the tables and the dirty microwave and the stinking fridge and the cigarette smoke wafting in from the small courtyard. This is a place where women who would not choose to be in the same room sit close together avoiding eye contact, passing judgment, mostly containing the desire to hurt each other in order to use one of the three computers or watch the TV or sit anywhere beside the street during the hours when their bed is off limits. Lynn usually finds someone to talk to, something to talk about. If required she will hold her ground, speak strongly to someone and not look away, but usually she is smiling. She sits for a while among the life of the house, adding a row or two to the tiny sweaters with thoughtfully chosen buttons she knits for the children or grandchildren of people she knows. Counting stitches in her head, acutely aware of where each row ends and that the sum will be more than its endings.

•

Lynn broke bones in prison, lost more teeth, a lump from her breast, her gallbladder. She fell in love, went through menopause. She learned about the internet from movies. Saw a mobile phone for the first time on a guard in a prison transport van; she used one for the first time when she was released in mid-2017.

When you arrive in prison, Lynn explains, you are given a piece of paper called a time computation sheet that tells you how much time you have to serve before you are eligible for parole. In 1982, Lynn was given a time comp sheet informing her that her first parole board meeting would be on October 30, 2007, a date that felt like science fiction. This would be like someone telling you, in 2021, that you would not be able to go to a grocery store or visit your family or cook in your kitchen or read your own book on your own couch until—all things going well—2046.

She folded it up and never looked at it again.

"If I looked at that every day," she explains, "I would be doing twenty-five years every day.

"So, I decided right then and there, I was going to do today. Every morning I got up, and I said, 'Well, I gotta do today.' Every. Single. Morning. For thirty-five years."

When women learned she was doing twenty-five to life, they would say to her that they didn't know how she could do it, that they were struggling with lesser sentences. And she would reply, simply, "We have the same time."

What do you mean? We don't have the same time, they would say. I've got a two to six.

You have today, Lynn would say. Why are you worrying about two or six? You have today. Ask God or whoever you talk to for strength for today, and you can do today. You can do anything for a day. Tomorrow you can ask again. That means you and I have the exact same sentence. Twenty-four hours.

"I realized, right away, that if I was going to try to make something of my life, I couldn't do twenty-five years steaming out of the ears. People do, I saw them when I got there, and I was like, 'I'm not her and I won't be her.'"

Seeing twenty-four hours instead of twenty-five years meant that Lynn did not put her life on hold, did not give in to self-pity or rage. Instead, she found an intensely practical lifeline that utilized both her leadership skills and her intellect.

"The directives are a funny thing," she says, explaining how she set about learning the law that authorizes the Department of Corrections to set certain policies and procedures in prisons. "How to run the mail room, how to run the package room, how to run movement lines, how to inspect your fence every shift so that you know you don't have a breach. Everything. What was urgent, what was routine, what was required to give us, what was elective that we could petition for."

Policies and procedures had to comply with the directives but beyond that each prison superintendent was given a certain discretion. "They can give you slightly more than the directive allows, but not less," Lynn says.

Using this information, Lynn successfully lobbied for change. Approved sick days were better communicated to work managers to stop the frequency with which ill inmates were being unjustly penalized. A craft market was authorized at which inmates could sell greeting cards, blankets, clothes and jewelery ahead of Christmas, Mother's Day, Valentine's Day and the start of the school year. Correctional officers thought she was a troublemaker but Elaine Lord, the superintendent of Bedford Hills Correctional Institution, appreciated her efforts and hired Lynn as her secretary, a role she held for twenty years.

She tutored in the evenings. Helped initiate a domestic violence program. Joined the Long Termers' Committee, mentoring women who had nearly served their time, helped them prepare for release by teaching resumé writing, job-interview skills, advising on parole applications. She worked in the kitchen and law library, earned her qualification as a paralegal.

They say that you can get used to anything. This is not what I mean when I tell you that Lynn made for herself a life in prison. It never became her norm. What I mean is that she never surrendered her sanity or her capacity for joy to factors beyond her control.

"I wasn't going to let it break me because if I was ever able to come home, I wanted to be okay, I wanted to be upright," she says, explaining how she knew women who died by suicide, others who ended up in psychiatric wards. "I anchored myself with work and service. If I'm not doing something to help elevate the place, and the people, I feel like I'm part of the problem."

36

THE KINGDOM OF HEAVEN
BECKY

The railing is iced with a thin line of fresh snow as I climb the stairs to Becky Kreider's front door. Inside, I add my wet Nikes to the dozens of similar pairs on the shoe rack and wander into the kitchen where the noise of her younger sons swirls around her as she peers into a cauliflower through pink-rimmed glasses. Standing at a remove from the chopping board because of her expanding belly, she is gouging out the gray spots with a knife before reducing the whole, slowly, to pieces. Becky is pregnant with her seventh child, although it took me too many visits to realize this on account of her tent-like dress. Also, though she is wan and tired, that is normal for a mother of six.

Loisann and Anthony moved into their two-bedroom apartment when the Kreiders moved out. The Lord, it was explained to me, had provided the former with their own home in New York City and the latter with more spacious accommodation nearby for their family of eight. Though the rent costs more than the mortgage on their previous two-acre property in Pennsylvania, the Kreiders now live in one half of a three-story house. The bedrooms are upstairs, the kitchen and family room are on the entry level and the schoolroom and washing machine are in the basement, where Tim's desk sits behind a clothesline heavy with laundry.

Becky does not default to a smile to ease conversation but she will give breath to a quick laugh. She employs it variously—Becky having as many kinds of laughter as there are types of rain; sometimes it functions as punctuation, other times as a gesture of tenderness; occasionally as an axe. Originally from Utah, Becky's family moved when she was young to Providence, Kentucky, which she describes as a back-hills place where nobody can get a job. In Utah, her parents had tried Mormonism. In Kentucky, they joined a Mennonite Church. Becky made her own decision to join when she was fourteen. As with Loisann describing her father, when Becky tells me about her family I understand that not only were they not religious in the way she would have liked, but that this feels to her—insofar as she views it as vital to a child's care, no less than providing food and shelter—like a dereliction of duty. Perhaps even a betrayal.

When Becky tells me this about her family, I will think about my own. My mother was one of four. Her siblings would grow up to become Orthodox Jews, much more religiously observant than they were raised. She would come to believe that she spoke with angels. To believe is to belong. But it is also something else. The word "safety," wrote James Baldwin, brings us to the real meaning of the word "religious" as we use it, by which he meant an internal security as much as, if not more than, a physical one.

"My aunt was a—it slips my mind now—a very liberal evangelical. My uncle very much was a promoter of gay and lesbian lifestyles, a lot of things that would seem not exactly biblical," she says with the quick laugh. "My mother loved the song 'My Old Kentucky Home.' I don't think that's quite as typical in most Mennonite homes, complete CDs of totally non-Christian songs." Secular music is unwelcome at the Kreiders' place. And Becky keeps away from the news. "It's just not interesting to me to read the news or whatever."

It slips my mind now. That laugh that functions like a good stiff broom. Becky has a wonderfully dismissive way of sweeping away anything that she deems foolish or wrong or dangerous.

Her toddler waddles around her legs. "Let Mommy get you something," she says, reaching for a bag of hamburger rolls. I ask her about the process through which children become members of their church. "Douglas is twelve, and he's been a member for a year," she explains of her eldest, rapidly folding ham and cheese into the bread. "That's pretty much on the young side, but it sounded like he understood. It was over the time when we were coming up here, and he was being exposed to a lot more things than what a child at home without much mission influence would have heard. He was hearing stories from people from the city about how God was working in their lives. I think it made him more aware. But it's not uncommon for them to be fourteen, sixteen, and sometimes even older. And sometimes we have children that don't choose to follow that at all."

I ask what happens then.

"Well, we pray for them," she says, with a laugh. Douglas walks in and around his youngest brothers. "So maybe these boys want to eat on the porch," she tells him. "You could pray with them and they could eat their sandwiches a while. You need one, too."

"Get to the porch and I'll meet you out there . . ." Douglas instructs them gently in his serious voice as Becky hands him the lunches. She points one of the other children towards the puzzle he's come looking for and returns to chopping vegetables. I ask if there are people who don't follow the norms in their community—those who come out as gay, for example.

"That can really vary," she replies. "Usually our children know that they're hurting their family or their friends and sometimes it's more comfortable for them to go somewhere else if they want to do something they know is unacceptable. So you have those situations where they just voluntarily leave or disappear.

"We would not allow somebody like that to remain a church member but we would welcome them to come to church if they wanted to just attend. We would probably pray for them, a lot," she says with another quick laugh.

"Ideally we would still show them love because that's the only way they have any hope of—I mean, they need to know what's right and wrong," she says, her voice growing harder. "But they also need to know that we love them and that Jesus came to save sinners. All of us have sinned somewhere along the way, none of us are exempt, of course. We could grade the sin but the fact of the matter is that any deviation is going to keep you from connecting with God because God is perfect and holy. So our goal is to reconcile them to God, but also to make sure they know they're loved even though we know they're not doing the truth.

"Now," she sighs, "I've never had any personal experience with it but I know there are some that if their oldest child would decide to become gay they'd ask them to please live somewhere else for the sake of their younger children, knowing that this is an issue of right and wrong."

Ethan, ten, wanders in. "What was I supposed to do for reading?"

"That astronomy book," Becky answers. "It's upstairs in my room." And then she turns back to me with a proud smile and tells me how much he loves reading.

The most remarkable discovery in all of astronomy, the theoretical physicist Richard Feynman once said, is that the stars are made of atoms of the same kind as those on the earth.

Becky makes time and energy she does not have to sit with me and answer my questions about her beliefs and her family. She shows me the baby books she has meticulously kept for each of her children. She presents me with a family photo, carefully writing the name of each Kreider on the back with a blue ballpoint. She urges me to eat lunch with them. We talk about New York City and food and childbirth and sons and I can see what a good friend Becky would be to those who live in her world. Her eyes when she looks at me from behind her glasses: dark and flat as a wet river stone.

It was the silence of the women during the church service. The lesson that "efforts of population control stand in opposition to God's design." That it is "a joy to submit."

The perception I had of the men in this community was challenged, however, the first time I saw Tim Kreider reflexively go change his baby's diaper. Now at the lunch table he wets a dishtowel to wipe that baby's face, lifts him out of his highchair and steadies him on the floor before returning seamlessly to the conversation in which his older sons are asking what they were like as babies.

"You came out with a little pucker in your brow," he tells Douglas. "Like you were looking around and thinking about the world." Then he and Becky remember the nights they took turns walking Ethan up and down the hallway. The boys take extra helpings of smiley-faced potato chips with tomato sauce before a leftover ice-cream cake layered with frozen custard is brought out. Mennonite food is delicious and much of it is vestigially high in the calories required for farming, which many no longer do. ("Plainly said," Loisann once stated, "there's a lot of fat Mennonites.")

In addition to his duties as pastor of the Bronx mission, Tim does some janitorial work and some work for a software company. His main employment, however, is programming for eMyPeople, a company that offers customized internet filtering and whose mission is *to provide internet and email service customized to the level that your conscience demands.* I ask Tim, who dropped out of school in grade nine, how he learned programming.

"I don't think my scenario's uncommon on that score," he replies. "I got swallowed up in Dad's footsteps before I was old enough to really know what was happening."

"You blew up your first computer at what, four?" Becky laughs.

"Yeah," Tim says, sheepishly. Becky explains how it works with the internet, the polluting potential of which ranges from the annoyingly distracting to the apocalyptically sinful. Use is allowed, but filtered and supervised: each person's internet history, or "log," is shared with another church member, and the church sets the parameters regarding acceptable sites.

"We don't have television," Becky says, "because it was decided years ago that it was more bad than good and not easy to filter. And we're fine with that. But the internet came along, and it actually has been argued that it has more bad on it than television, which is probably true, but it can also be used for more good, and it's more easy to filter. So when the good outweighs the bad, then you try to discern which is which."

Cleaning up, Becky says she is looking for an affordable midwife to deliver her seventh child—the first baby she will have in the city. The Kreiders do not have health insurance. For larger medical costs, however, the church would step in to assist. "The Bible talks about taking care of your own," she explains. "So if a member has a medical issue, we would act as their insurance company and all work together to try to take care of their things. We tend to help pay for emergencies or a big thing like chemo or whatever."

In terms of acceptable medical interventions, whatever is advised by the doctors and chosen by the patient is fine by them. One of their founding members, Rachel—I had seen her comforting one of the older women at church—has chosen a "totally medical" approach to her cancer diagnosis. Others have preferred not to pursue chemotherapy. "Some cancers, I don't know if it really matters what you pick," Becky sighs. "Some things are just inevitable."

37

THEORIES OF FLIGHT
DON

Don has written many books about Roswell. An astronaut wrote the foreword to one of these books, a state governor wrote the foreword to another. "My books have been read by presidents," he tells me as we sit in a café the day before he speaks to a packed room of rapt Melbournians. He explains how when a book that Monica Lewinsky gave Bill Clinton for Christmas was subpoenaed, it was found between a volume on Churchill and Don's book *The UFO Crash at Roswell*, inscribed by him to Clinton.

"I can't emphasize enough that I was a complete skeptic coming into this," Don says, speaking with what I imagine to be the force and precision of his father, a World War II army drill sergeant whom he adored. "I came into it with no preconceived expectations or notions of final resolution.

"I find that so often within the American scientific community, they have a preconceived theory and then they set out to prove it, and to me, that's a faulty premise because you're not allowing the evidence to take you where it will."

Don grew up in a town without bookstores. There were books, however, at the department store where he would accompany his parents while they did the Christmas shopping.

He remembers gravitating towards a particular book there called *Flying Saucers: Serious Business*. "Which was a term taken directly from the air force manual," he explains, taking an accurate sip of green tea. "That was the chapter title—'Flying Saucers: Serious Business'."

Thereafter, young Don was on a quest. "Every UFO book I could get. Not that I was believing most of it, even then. But as one of the books would say, 'Just imagine if even one of these accounts were true.' And that was good enough for me . . .

"In high school, I would have my speech classes, and I was already giving talks on UFOs without so much as a note card, which impressed my teachers to no end," he says. "It was like, 'You need to go into that'—but mostly as a professional entertainer, lecturer, motivational speaker."

Don—who explains that he had been an "art prodigy"— went on to study technical illustration, a career cut short when a car accident during a snow storm resulted in damage to his optic nerve and the loss of his depth perception. But this worked out well. Don met the late J. Allen Hynek, astronomer turned ufologist, right out of college. Went on to work for Hynek as a "special investigator" before becoming the Director of Special Investigations at, and then a co-director of, the J. Allen Hynek Center for UFO Studies in Chicago.

Hynek, the man Don considers his "scientific father," earned his PhD in astrophysics at the University of Chicago and joined the Department of Physics and Astronomy at the Ohio State University in 1936, initially specializing in stellar evolution. In 1948, Hynek was hired by the United States Air Force as a scientific consultant to examine reports of UFO sightings and determine whether the descriptions could be accounted for by known astronomical phenomena. At the time, Hynek was quoted as saying that he found "the whole subject utterly ridiculous."

By 1953, however, Hynek would write in the *Journal of the Optical Society of America*: "Ridicule is not part of the scientific method . . . The steady flow of reports, often made in concert by *reliable* observers, raises questions of scientific obligation and responsibility." In a 1967 article published in *Playboy*, Hynek stated, "As a scientist I must be mindful of the lessons of the past; all too often it has happened that matters of great value to science were overlooked because the new phenomenon did not fit the accepted scientific outlook of the time." By the late 1970s, he was speaking openly about his belief that UFOs were real, and that there was sufficient evidence to defend the hypothesis of extraterrestrial intelligence.

Don is exceptionally proud of his relationship with Hynek. Together, their goal was to conclusively prove what they had come to believe from hearing first-hand the Roswell witness testimonies: the alien origin of the flying objects.

"Most people need everything to be linear, leading to a resolution. I never pattern my research that way. It goes like this," he says, drawing a circle in the air. "I especially love going back to witnesses. New answers then generate new questions. I don't rest in that regard." The witnesses, he explains, appreciate this. They see it as Don looking out for their best interests.

"I have been pallbearers at their funerals," he continues. "There was a counterintelligence agent who was at Roswell, and I went to see him in his final years in Florida. He and his wife had lost their only son. The last time I saw him, he'd withered down to barely a hundred pounds, and I just sat with him at his retirement facility. They were going to carry him back to his room and I said, 'No.' I picked him up and I carried him to his room. And he held on to me and said, 'I'll never see you again,'" Don recalls, his eyes getting glassy. "And when I walked out his wife said to me, 'You became a son to us.' So, I take this personally . . .

"I have to catch myself when I allow a naysayer—and I don't even use the word skeptic, but a debunker, a scoffer, who has their own agenda—when I allow them to influence my thought processes," Don says. "I've given them free rent in my head, so to speak. I just refuse to give them it."

Don is still looking for conclusive proof. "Because I'm a very nuts-and-bolts researcher: I want to be able to kick the tires across the street and then I can say, mission accomplished," he says. His holy grail is a piece of the physical evidence that he can hold. To that end, he's led five archaeological digs at the crash site, hoping to find the storied "memory material" witnesses described—a malleable metal-like substance that always sprang back to its original form. "It would be like seeing God himself handling a piece that was manufactured on another planet, or in another dimension, or a parallel universe, or even time travel."

On the last point, he mentions a doctor he once spoke with who had worked at NASA on the joint Apollo-Soyuz space mission. "He told us they would sit there and contemplate the results of long-term zero-gravity space travel on the human body. How we would start to look the way people describe aliens: our bodies would atrophy, our heads would grow, our eyes would get larger. So then I started to wonder—are we dealing with time travel? Are we dealing with us?"

38

HALFWAY HOME
LYNN

Albany County. Bedford. Albion. Taconic. She lines them up for me in sequence, their syllables cold and hard like hail, the New York State women's correctional facilities where she lived for about as long as I've been alive. Facilities where you had no privacy, where you would sit in your cell eating dinner while someone's cellmate was shitting nearby. Facilities with dental care so poor that her back teeth were preemptively pulled out. Facilities where someone would piss on your mattress if they didn't want you in their dorm; cut your face if the way you spoke did not please them. Facilities where you brushed your teeth next to women who placed their children in ovens or in baths of boiling water, where—seeing their eyes, the rise and fall of their chests—you found yourself unable to pass judgment even on them. Facilities where you could be penalized for hugging, or holding hands, or taking one slice of bread back to your cell should you find yourself hungry in the long night. Facilities where every small kindness stood out. The chaplain who shut his door so she could use his phone to call her dying mother. The nun who never asked why she was a lifer. The petty bitch in the kitchen who suddenly threw a dishtowel across

Lynn's lap to conceal the fact that she had pissed her pants after passing out from the pain when a load of frozen meat fell and broke her leg.

Mostly, though, there was activity, the hum of her own self calling, the refusal to give over the responsibility for her life. This is not to say that under that solidity there wasn't always something else, too. A crack through which a chill wind blew: grief, frustration closer to strangulation as she thought of the child she could no longer protect and to whom she was becoming less real each day. The lie of the clock face laid bare as each hour came once, and vanished forever.

Lynn is in the dining hall when it all disappears, again. The steam from the line of things fried, frozen and canned. The curl of hands around cups. The squeak of rubber on linoleum. The hunch of thin and thick green-clad shoulders over plates. Evaporates, gone. Her eyes pulled towards one point only.

"Please tell me you work here," AJ says.

Lynn can only shake her head. After more than twenty years, here they are, suddenly, in the same room. It is a page from the Book of Marvels. They will be together for the rest of AJ's life.

39

THEORIES OF FLIGHT
DON & COLIN

There is a silver-and-red flying saucer in the Grange.

"This is a really interesting thing, what the council have done with this area," George says to Don as they traipse down a path towards the saucer that sits in an empty playground surrounded by the thin trunks of extraordinarily tall pine trees. "Kids love it."

"In Roswell, we have the only flying-saucer McDonald's in the world," Don says, wryly.

George points out spots of interest while Don nods gravely. The direction of the Westall school, where the boundaries of the park used to be—"That's a new toilet block," he says. "The old one was a literal brick shithouse. They spent a lot of money on the park."

Besides housing sleeker commodes, the toilet block is notable for the murals on its external walls. The left side features a full-color map of the planets, the Hubble Space Telescope explained in an inset at the top corner. The right side of the toilet block is devoted to the moon landing.

"It's a very strange place in spite of all the modernization," George says, looking at his surrounds. "It's still got a strange feel about it."

"So, do the trees look affected at all?" Don wonders, tilting his head all the way back to look at the tops of the pines.

"They're bending in all directions, it's weird," George says. "It came behind these trees and down to the ground, somewhere in here, very close to where they put that," he explains, pointing at the flying-saucer play structure on the tan bark.

"I was going to ask if the saucer location is significant," Don says.

"It was more here, near the toilets," George says. "Where the grass doesn't grow even now." It starts raining, so they return to sit in the car to wait for Colin Kelly.

"Some students said they saw one, some students said they saw three," George says. "Some said there was one big one and two little ones. Others said no, the two little ones were further away. So it depends how people were interpreting what they were seeing . . .

"A week later," he continues, "one of the students who lived on the other side of the school was talking to their parents about it and the dad didn't believe them. They said, 'Come, I'll show you where it was!' And they pointed to these trees, and they were back. A week later. They saw them again flying around this area."

"That isn't generally known," Don says, somberly.

"Right! These are the stories you hear when you talk to the witnesses," George says.

"What else do we *have* but witnesses?" Don asks with emotion. "Especially when you have independent corroboration. I had a doctor in Sydney, he was arguing with me—ten people can't be describing the same thing. And that's the point. When there's something profound, something unusual, and they are describing the same thing. That's what makes it all the more believable."

"They may be describing it differently . . ." George says.

"Based on their backgrounds, their perspective, their angle—we have to take it all into account," Don agrees, "but the point is—something is still there."

George met his first Westall witness about twenty years back while working at a pawn shop. A woman who would come in regularly and buy their entire stock of *Star Trek* DVDs. He eventually learned that she had attended Westall Primary and was there on the day of the sighting, looking at the UFO through her classroom window. "She's got an older brother who was in the high school," George explains, "who won't talk about it even to this day. They were told not to talk about it."

"And there were American suits that came in after," Don says.

"Yeah, there was a lot of military," George nods.

"If it would've simply just been a balloon—" Don starts.

"We wouldn't be sitting here," George finishes. The rain has stopped so they pop the doors and head out for another look around.

Between 1960 and 1969, a joint research program between the US Atomic Energy Commission and the Australian Department of Supply (DOS) called Project HIBAL used high-altitude balloons to monitor atmospheric radiation levels. The balloons were silver. Each was tied to a gondola carrying around 200 kilograms of air-sampling equipment, and occasionally additional payloads of scientific instruments. And every balloon was followed by a light aircraft. Researcher Keith Basterfield writes that when these aircraft "cut down" the balloons via radio signal, the payloads would drop to the ground below a twelve-meter parachute and be retrieved by DOS personnel standing by in chase vehicles.

The balloons were colossal and occasionally unreliable. Reporting in 1962 on one that burst after an unsuccessful flight over Mildura, the *Age* newspaper noted that the payload of instruments "with the balloon's one acre and three-quarters of polythene sheeting tangled about it—crashed on Para station, about forty-five miles north of Mildura." The balloon itself was forty-five meters wide and eighty-six metres from top to bottom: imagine a twenty-six-story building suspended in the sky.

Basterfield has hypothesized that the Westall incident was the result of a HIBAL balloon being carried by the northerly winds on that day into the area: specifically flight 292, which had launched from Mildura on April 5, 1966, the day before the sighting. He notes that no documentary evidence has been located proving that this balloon was near Westall on the morning of April 6. Also that, in response to his inquiry, the National Archives reported that the HIBAL files held by DOS had been destroyed by the Department of Defense in 1996. "On the other hand," he writes, "no documentary evidence has been found to show that HIBAL flight 292 wasn't near Westall on 6 April 1966."

Colin pulls up in his truck and strides over to George, who is waving at him from the playground. Nearly seventy, Colin seems younger; there is more brown than gray in his mustache. Don, folded in half inside the flying saucer, shuffles over to the edge and gladly shakes Colin's hand before dismounting. The three men stroll towards the perimeter of pines.

"Channel Nine were definitely here," Colin says, explaining to Don what he remembers after the sighting, how they interviewed two of his friends.

"I saw the Channel Nine news that night," George interjects, explaining he was eight years old at the time. "I'd just read a book about flying saucers at school. And there's these two schoolgirls saying, 'It was definitely a flying saucer, we saw it . . .' And then you hear this guy off-camera go, 'Okay, this interview is terminated.' And the camera went blank. They put it to air that way." He remembers how annoyed he felt, wanting to see more. No one can find that footage now, he explains.

"That's how it always works," Don says, shaking his head. "Yup yup yup yup." He explains an analogous situation with Roswell. "With the landing, and the depressions in the ground, and the sagebrush—it was still smoldering by the time the police got there."

"Right," nods Colin with interest, his hands in his pockets as he walks lockstep with Don around the grass.

"And then Hynek, my own scientific director who I worked with later, was the one who went to seize everything as ordered by the air force," Don continues. "They took all the photographs, all the interviews, they made sure they had everything. And that's what they do, that's what they do."

"Well, this is what's happened here. I've always been interested—" Colin starts quietly.

"And you don't do that for a balloon," Don says.

"You don't do that for nothing," George adds.

"You don't do that for anything except this!" Don says. "Who interviewed you?" he asks Colin.

"Nobody interviewed me," Colin replies.

Carrying his camera and tripod, George points towards an area between the toilets and the trees where there is scrubby grass littered with pine needles. "No grass has grown for like fifty years," he explains. "That's the best I've seen it in ten years."

While George and Don walk off swapping stories about their investigations, Colin tells me about the day he saw a perfect circle stamped in the long grass that grew where we stand, five streets away from his childhood home. "We found it on the day that the sightings happened," he says, his rectangular Transitions dark in the afternoon glare. "It was perfectly round. Perfectly round." There is awe in his voice.

He mentions how some have tried to argue that the grass isn't long enough to imprint like that. "Mate, we're talking something that happened fifty years ago. Believe me, it was trampled. The ridicule we've gotten is unbelievable," he continues with a deep sigh. "They try to say, 'Youse've all colluded.'"

Colin doesn't talk loudly or for the sake of it or with hyperbole. He listens very closely. He presents as someone constitutionally unconcerned with fame. "They were here," he says, pointing to where he saw the men in uniform swarming the land he thought of as his backyard, cordoning it off and guarding it. "Don't tell me it was nothing . . .

"We've got on with our lives. Lived reasonably normal lives. We just want an explanation."

"The first thing I always say," Don's voice floods the air as he and George walk back over, "is I don't want anyone complaining about being tired. We sleep when we get home, now we work. Let's get a shot," he says, heading over to position himself with an arm around Colin in front of the mural on the back of the public toilets—an artist's rendering of what a saucer may have looked like descending into the trees around us.

Walking over to a marker that's been erected to the Westall incident, George explains that his cousin's husband saw the UFO while working in the market gardens across from the school. When George asked him if it could have been a balloon, he replied that a balloon would have been torn up by the descent through the branches. He also said that it looked like a solid object that changed density as it descended, because the branches did not respond. "It flew past him and then when it went into the trees, it looked like it was being projected rather than being solid and physically there," George says.

"Look, even as thirteen-year-olds, we knew what a balloon looked like," Colin says. "It was not a balloon." He mentions the light planes trailing the object towards the Grange, how they circled while it was grounded. "Then it just took off." He makes the *whoosh* noise.

"Classic," Don says, nodding. "The students that came towards the park, was it still here when they came over the hill here?"

Yes, says Colin, adding that he believes what those students reported—not just about what they saw, but about what happened to Tanya. "You're aware of the Tanya story?" he asks Don. "She turned around and started running back and she was hysterical. She got back and she collapsed."

"She disappeared?" Don asks. He's referring to statements that after the girl was placed in the back of an ambulance, not only did she not return to the school, but when visitors went to her home soon after, they found that a new family had moved in, claiming never to have heard of the previous residents.

"I believe they know where she is," Colin says, "but that she doesn't want to talk." He says that he happened to be walking near the canteen that afternoon. Saw the ambulance parked nearby, its back doors open, a girl inside.

"I'm looking, and I'm going, oh, it's Tanya," he says. "Somebody asked me at a later stage if I was sure it was a girl. I was a thirteen-year-old male. I was interested in sports and girls. That was Tanya. It was Tanya. And she disappeared." He also knew the two students who tried to visit her at home only to find she had vanished. "They were just dumbfounded."

We stand for a time looking at the marker erected by the local government. Arrows on it point towards the school, towards Moorabbin Airport. There are quotes from witnesses:

Like a thin beam of light . . . half the length of a light aircraft . . . It was silvery-gray and seemed to "thicken" at times . . . similar to when a disc is turned a little to show the underside. Andrew Greenwood, Westall High School Science Teacher

No seams, no joins . . . looked like it had come out of a mould . . . one smooth piece of metal . . . Victor Zakruzny, Westall High School Student.

We drive over to the school where the light fittings in the new building are subtly saucer-shaped to pay homage to the big event. Walk down the hall, next to the windows that the younger students pressed their faces up against that day in 1966. Colin looks glad to be back: comfortable. Even though this is where he learned, over fifty years ago, that solid ground isn't to be trusted.

40

THE KINGDOM OF HEAVEN
ANTHONY

Anthony Witmar emerges shyly from his office, which is also the bedroom he shares with Loisann, slightly rumpled: a little bear from a storybook cave. With his Bluetooth in his ear and a leather phone holster on his hip, he sits down next to his wife on the sofa where they lean towards each other like a pair of old boots.

Anthony did not finish tenth grade because in Myerstown you can find a good job with somebody from church without a degree. If you wish to venture farther afield, however, you need an education or a transportable skill or capital for establishing a business in order to support yourself and your family away from the community. Work is also vital for Mennonite missionaries because it brings them into contact with the people they hope to convert. But this has shown itself to be a double-edged sword. Anthony explains that in making the radical decision to move to New York City, they had to deal with some reluctance back home about establishing city missions because of prior examples of over-assimilation. Despite a lack of family approval, they held the line.

"It's very easy to just be comfortable in your life path," he explains. "I read the Bible and see we're supposed to go out and make a difference in people's lives. How do we do that by getting rich off of each other in this prosperous, comfortable community?" He understands, though, where the concerns came from. "There's a younger generation that has a vision to get out more, and yet we have the background on what happened before. How do you bridge cultures without losing everything?"

He refers to other Mennonite churches in the city. "A lot of them would be socially progressive," he says. "Maybe that's too harsh a judgment. In other words, more open to the homosexual agenda than other churches. They don't really have a foundation, so they don't stand for anything."

It's the first time I've heard "homosexual agenda" used in conversation. Instead of sounding like raw meat being twisted from the bone, his tone is particularly frightening in its banality.

Like city life, he continues, higher education is considered to carry an unacceptable risk of assimilation. Moving here, however, meant leaving the Mennonite-owned office supply store he had worked at for ten years back home and he found himself unqualified to apply for most jobs in the city. He ended up getting his high school equivalency degree and, while it helped him secure the job he currently holds, this is not the job he would like to hold.

"We're here to interact with the local people and I have a hard time doing that here sitting at my desk, back in my bedroom," he says with palpable frustration.

While I never get a clear answer to the question, it appears that in the five years the church has had an official missionary presence in the South Bronx, they have successfully attracted about four consistent local members.

What he'd love, he says, brightening, is to have a shop. "That would be a great way to provide a service to the community where you would have interaction. For a while before we moved, we talked about starting a coffee shop and bookstore."

I ask what it would take to do this.

"Number one, funds," Loisann replies. Plus, she adds, "This isn't really a coffee-shop neighborhood."

"Lattes and stuff like that," Anthony explains.

I comment that in certain parts of the city, there would be an eagerness for—and the ability to afford—the authentic Pennsylvania Dutch food that Loisann cooks. That many would admire their lived values of simplicity and non-conformance. But that the people who would come for their shoofly pie would be unlikely to stay for their religious views.

"A café at least gives you an interaction," Anthony replies. "Especially with today's culture. An interesting thing was—a person—that came to church. We called this person a 'her,' but . . ."

Loisann clarifies, for my benefit, that this person was transgender.

"In our minds, something like that, coming from our insulated culture, is just disgusting," Anthony says. "I do believe it's wrong, but does that mean I just look in contempt at that person?

"She came to the church a few times," he continues. "In my opinion, in looking at her, it was a confused person looking for love. The cultural revolution, sexual revolution, that's going on in today's world—we don't like thinking about that. But we need to have answers for people too. If we do believe it's wrong, I'm not going to—In relating to her, this is something that we need to—Our natural instinct is just to avoid people like that . . ."

Hearing Anthony talk about this is like hearing Anthony think about it, furiously and to himself, in circles.

"How did we get on her from the coffee shop?" Loisann asks gently.

"Talking about people coming in for pie that might not have any interest in . . ." Anthony says, drifting off once more. "I don't know if 'hip' is the right word. The people that are post-modern, college-educated, far-left, liberal—I mean, just the whole progressive agenda that we look at with scary eyes. It's *those* kind of people I would like to interact with. Give them the opportunity to see not all Christians are bigoted, far-right, gay haters, or whatever you want to call them."

I no longer understand what Anthony is saying. It started at the sentence level. The fragments that disappointed themselves into retreat. The mismatched tones of tender vulnerability and flinty conviction that blurred like off-register printing.

I am beginning, though, to understand what it might feel like to be Anthony. A not insubstantial amount of frustration, dissatisfaction, resentment, but mostly: conflict. Anthony's conflict comes from the fact that the certainties he received instead of education are poor tools for daily living in the particular kingdom in which he and I and Loisann are currently sitting. His training does not serve his human desire to concretize his feelings into thoughts, his thoughts into words, his words into dialogue, and from there into meaningful action.

"We're studying Genesis in Sunday school right now," Anthony continues. "There's so much in the first couple chapters that are foundational for the way everybody lives life. Seven-day week, the concept of marriage. And a lot of that has been—single-parent homes—dysfunctional homes—evolution versus creation. When you start reciting what the Bible says with all that other stuff, it just opens up a world of—Yeah, if you believe you're the descendant of a monkey or something, it doesn't hurt to believe that I was born a girl trapped inside a boy's body. But I mean, if you can grasp hold of the fact that there's a God that made you—What I'm trying to say is, don't try to convert a transgender person or a gay person to a straight person until they understand the foundation of how God made us and what sexuality's all about. Rather than just saying, 'You should think like I do,' give *reason* to believe that."

Loisann interjects firmly: "We have to give our message and show them compassion, but they need to be taken to truth." The light filters in through the window and over their children playing on the floor between us.

I ask how theological disputes are settled and Anthony, reaching for the anchor of Loisann's hand, explains that some things are decided by individual churches, others at a conference level. "Theology always scares me because it takes the things that seem simple and makes them complex," he says. "I hate saying this is definitely the way it is because then you might meet somebody who seems to be living a very Godly, Christian lifestyle who actually believes something a little bit differently. What do you do with them?"

Occasionally Anthony will take his binoculars and drive out near the airport. He loves planes. Last year he saw an Iranian jet landing. Also one painted in green and white for the Jets foot-ball team, and a yellow one for veterans. Because he maintains a list of the registration numbers of planes spotted or traveled in, he knows he has been in the plane that was shot down over Ukraine and that he saw—at Amsterdam airport on a stopover to a mission in Kenya—MH370, the Malaysian Airlines plane that disappeared. "To be a good plane spotter," he explained to me shyly, when I inquired about his hobbies, "your goal is to catch everything that is painted a little bit differently."

41

THEORIES OF FLIGHT
BEN

Say you were driving in the dark and a great orb of light suddenly appeared over your windscreen, pure luminescence like a star descended and emitting a strange energy that you felt shake your car.

Would you report such a thing? And if so, to whom?

In 1994, the Royal Australian Air Force subtracted itself from the task of collecting or investigating UFO reports from the public. As Wing Commander Brett Biddington informed the Australian UFO groups on behalf of the Chief of Air Staff: "The number of reports made to the RAAF in the past decade had declined significantly, which may indicate that organizations such as yours are better known and are meeting the community's requirements."

To put it another way: should you experience such a phenomenon, those grassroots groups of self-educated enthusiasts would be the closest thing to institutional support for you. They would not ridicule you. They would listen to your story with gravity and respect. And that is not nothing.

The history of these groups in Australia dates back to the early 1950s. There are many of them and they are known—by those who know them—according to their acronyms. The groups operate independently and with their own differences and cultures. For instance, where AUFORN (the Australian UFO Research Network) "believe there is enough circumstantial evidence to prove the existence of UFOs," VUFORS (the Victorian UFO Research Society) emphasizes that they have "held a dispassionate attitude on UFOs, claiming it is a scientific problem deserving closer attention." And it is UFORQ's (UFO Research Queensland) official policy that "there now exists, and has for many years, a large body of well attested sightings that are so unambiguous the only reasonable inference is that extra-terrestrial vehicles are flying through our atmosphere, landing on the ground and entering our oceans."

Driven by a belief that a lack of government transparency and/or engagement with the topic has created an unwise vacuum, the various groups share a concern with DIY UFO research: not only data analysis, but direct data collection by providing an avenue for anyone to report a sighting. They are also a supportive space for those who have been affected by a UFO-related experience. That was what led me, eventually, to VUFOA (Victoria UFO Action): a short comment by an older woman on a Facebook page that simply thanked them for respectfully listening to her husband. It made me look again, that grace which was the twinkle of something appearing from the dark before receding back into it.

ARE WE ALONE? ARE YOU ALONE? Had a sighting or experience you just can't make sense of? Fear of ridicule from friends and family? Afraid? Confused? WE MAY BE ABLE TO HELP!

Victoria UFO Action's flyer continues:

> Well, rest assured there's peace of mind knowing that
> we are here for YOU. VUFOA's dynamic is that it has a
> great team including investigators, Counsellors, Indus-
> try specific professionals, including Chemists, Photog-
> raphy experts, Aviation experts and some of our very
> own members have had their very own sightings and
> experiences. You are NOT ALONE.

Sightings can be reported on VUFOA's twenty-four-hour hot-
line or via a form on their website. This form is comprehensive,
with both free-text and pre-populated options, the latter speaking to accumulated experience with sighting accounts as well as
commonalities in those narratives. So, for example, if the object
you saw changed shape, or was shaped like a cigar or a circle or a
cone or a cross or a cylinder or a diamond or a disk or an egg or a
fireball or a flash or a formation or an orb or an oval or a rectan-
gle or a saucer or a sphere or a teardrop or other/unknown—you
are not alone.

Before I met Ben Hurle, the president of VUFOA, I saw him
on YouTube being interviewed by Sheryl Gottschall, the president of UFORQ. He wore a black T-shirt that said *Seeking the
Truth* and sat in an armchair against a wall of books.

Sheryl asked how he got into the UFO subject.

Ben replied that UFOs have always been part of his
consciousness. "As a child, and to this day, I spent all my
time looking up," he said. "I'm always studying the sky, the

clouds—because they're beautiful anyway—but in the back of my mind, I'm also looking for anything that might be unusual in the sky. Sometimes somewhat hopefully."

The first books Ben read at school were UFO books and certain films influenced him as well.

"For instance," he said, "when I saw *Star Wars* as a child, that blew my mind. It absolutely blew my mind. The cantina scene where you've got all those different aliens hanging around the bar, having a drink, to me, made so much sense. I thought, 'There must be places in the universe out there where that actually happens and it occurs and humans aren't at that level to be able to partake in that yet.'

"*The Hobbit, Lord of the Rings,* that type of thing, from a very young age got me interested in other possibilities, other realms, and that there must be other creatures out there in this great wild world and that we're not living in some unique little bubble here. I personally believe that the universe is teeming with life. And because it's so spread out—perhaps it's a good thing—the ability to interact can only be achieved once you achieve a certain level."

Ben lives one hundred and seventy four miles east of Melbourne. This means that by four-thirty in the afternoon, a winter afternoon, the light will be dwindling as I wave goodbye to him and steer onto the country roads—some just paths between farms—that should deposit me back home three and a half hours later. The feeling of excitement adjacent to anxiety this provokes in me is partly due to Ben's warning about animals jumping in front of the cars, one of which is now mine, that move at speed down these unlit roads. But mostly it is due to the accounts he has told me of things seen in this quickly dimming slab of sky and a specific landmark—key to the rich UFO history of the area—that I will be passing just after sunset.

"First of all, I don't have any scientific training," Ben said when I sat down with him in the office where he works selling recreational vehicles, his small dog, Ivy, resting on his lap. "I am a person who from a very young age had an innate belief that there has to be something other than what we see here, and a whole host of things really point to that in a true and real and tactile way, I believe." Ben has brown hair and large brown eyes; his gaze is intense and seems, at times, unblinking—perfectly suited to his preferred position of looking up. He has one of my favorite conversational habits: finishing the other person"s sentences almost, but not quite, along with them. He is articulate and expansive on UFOs, or unidentified aerial phenomena, a subject he refers to in conversation as "the phenomenon."

In terms of his own encounters, Ben told me that he once glanced up from a Saturday-morning game of basketball with a feeling like he was being watched and saw a dark shape glide around his car to the back of his shed and disappear. "It had sparkles around the edges," he explained. "It was like someone had taken a sliver of night and put it into the daylight." On another occasion, sitting on his back patio on "a silver moonlit night," Ben watched a ball of light wheeling across the treetops, illuminating the upper branches as it went off into the distance over the Great Dividing Range. Once, returning from a sky-watching excursion, he saw a tube of white light over his car. And he has had the frightening experience of waking up in the middle of the night to find the silhouette of a hooded figure peering over his bed and feeling like energy was, somehow, being sucked from him. "It was a bright silver moonlit night," he remembered, "and I had the curtains open so the moonlight could come streaming in." If darkness figures strongly for Ben, it must be said that so too does the light, and this is one of the things I like about him.

Ben specializes in the phenomenon as it manifests in Victoria generally and East Gippsland specifically.

"I wanted to know what was happening here where I live," he said about his decision, ten years ago when he turned forty, to become more involved in UFO research. He found that the information-sharing role formerly played by the UFO groups had diminished by this stage. "The internet killed the old ways of connecting with people. It wasn't so necessary to go to a meeting to find out anything. It's all online."

The educative function of the groups, however, is still relevant; perhaps more than ever, he explained, because of "the amount of white noise and junk and uncritical information that's out there now." In the old days, the UFO groups would have investigated directly—spoken to witnesses, taken photographs, looked at the land—which had a quality-control effect. "But now you can hop on Facebook, and I can post a photo of a streetlamp in fifteen different groups and everyone would be ooh-ing and aah-ing over the lovely UFO."

UFO groups are struggling in this environment, not helped by "the fact that the phenomenon is very fluid, it's everevolving."

When I asked him what that meant, he spoke about changes in how UFOs have been described over time: "We could go back to the late 1880s, where people were seeing mysterious airships," he explained. "Over North America, they were seeing these dirigibles floating around, with seemingly human occupants. They would shout down, talk back. And then through World War II we started seeing foo fighters appearing, the balls of light that would follow the bombers on both Axis and Allied bombing raids . . . Back in 70 BC, they were seeing flying shields in the sky. We've always interpreted it in the context of the times in which we've been living. Moving into the new millennium, I reckon it's quite fragmented now."

You can't google the stories that Ben collects. He's dug through yellow local newspapers to save them from oblivion, knocked on doors to concretize what had previously existed only in the memories of moms and dads, farmers and truck drivers and train drivers. He's collated what can be salvaged of the original VUFORS files, some of which came from a filing cabinet covered in bird shit (from the cage long kept on top of it) that he rescued from going to the tip after its owner died.

"There's so much stuff to go through," he explained. "Really great encounters that no one's going to really know about." Ivy crossed the floor to hop onto my lap as he got up to make us tea. Her sister died recently of a snakebite. It was like losing a child, said Ben. In the office she is safe.

He returned with two cups, saying, with an urgency I recognized, "We need to find all these little stories. They build up into a big matrix of stories . . .

"These beautiful encounters that people have had—whether they're scary or mystifying or puzzling or uplifting—they disappear. They don't get recorded in any way for other people to be able to say, 'Wow, this is really interesting.' Maybe there's some commonalities there, some relationships we can see between things."

"When I think about what the phenomenon is," Ben said a little after that, as we sat there in the late light, "it's the fact that we're not just stuck on this little rock in our boring work for fifty years and then dying. There's bigger things out there. We're a part of some multifaceted system of things called the universe and the universe is a very dynamic place. It has a lot more depth to it than we understand currently . . .

"For all the vast volumes that have been written, for the documentaries that have been made, for all the UFO experts that are out there, we still have very little. No one can tell you what the phenomenon is. No one can tell you where they're coming from. These are basic questions. No one can tell you how the craft operate. No one can tell you why they're here. No one can tell you anything. It's all still unknown . . . You're afraid of what you don't know. You're afraid of what you don't understand . . .

"We interviewed a high-ranking Victorian policeman about a UFO encounter that he was involved in and he said, 'I needed it to be something that I could explain but we couldn't explain what it was. I still to this day live with that, not knowing what it was that we encountered on that particular evening.' I hear that all the time."

Absence of evidence is not evidence of absence, wrote the astrophysicist Martin Rees. In 2018, I saw Rees interviewed by

Claudia Dreifus, science writer for the *New York Times*. Rees is Astronomer Royal—a position, he explained, smiling at the small crowd, whose duties are such that he can continue to adequately fulfill them after he dies. Dreifus asked Rees to give a quick rundown on some current issues in cosmology. For instance, she said, people rightly want to know what are the odds on life elsewhere? Illuminated up on stage, they were both thin, dressed in fine, dark materials; each crowned by a full head of luxuriant silver hair that glowed under the lights.

"Well, of course, that's a difficult question," Rees answered. "It's a biological question. One of the exciting things in astronomy over the last ten or twenty years is that we're realizing that most of the other stars in the sky have planets orbiting around them, just as the sun has the earth and the other familiar planets. And so in our galaxy there are billions of planets and quite a fraction of them are like the earth orbiting a star rather like the sun. And that of course raises the question: life started on earth, so did it start elsewhere?"

While it was not currently possible to answer the question, he continued, in the next decade there would be two strands of progress. The first strand concerned the nature of the origin of life. "Because we don't understand how life *became* here on earth. We understand how simple life via Darwinian selection led to the biosphere that exists now that we are part of. But the transition between complex chemistry to the first metabolizing, reproducing entities we called 'alive'—that transition is not yet understood."

The other strand of progress, he said, is that as we refine our telescopes, it will become possible to gather sufficient light from some of the planets around other stars to learn about their atmosphere. He was confident that these two things would tell us whether there's life elsewhere within ten years.

"But then, of course," he continued, "the next question you're probably going to ask is about *intelligent* life. And there, we have even less idea . . . even if we understand simple life we still don't understand how likely it is to evolve into something like this biosphere. Stephen Jay Gould thought it very unlikely, through evolution, to end up with something like this . . .

"But if you ask me to say whether SETI searches are likely to succeed," Rees said, referring to the SETI (Search for Extra-Terrestrial Intelligence) Institute—a research institute that contracts with NASA and the American National Science Foundation, "I'd say it's not very likely but the stakes are so high it's worth an effort.

"If you ask, 'What will we detect?', I think it won't be a civilization like ours," he continued. "It will be something electronic."

This is because it's taken us three and a half billion years to get from the first life forms to civilization. We've had technology for a few thousand years at most, he said, and it's quite likely that within a few centuries we will perhaps have been superseded by some sort of post-human intelligence in electronic form that will be able to spread beyond the earth and be better adapted to living out there than we are, and then *that* can exist billions of years in the future.

"So if there was life that started elsewhere, it's most unlikely—if we detect it at all—that we detect it in this brief phase when it's organic like us. Far more likely that it be a billion years ahead of us and we detect some burping or malfunctioning machine made by some long-dead civilization," Rees said with a lopsided smile, his long white hands steepling under his chin.

There fell a silence during which my heart ached like someone had placed a toilet plunger on my chest and given it a good yank. *This brief phase.*

It was impossible to listen to this without thinking of the Golden Record. On September 5, 1977, NASA took advantage of a planetary alignment that occurs once every 175 years to launch the space probes Voyagers 1 and 2 on a mission to study the outer solar system. As I sit writing this, forty-three years later, they are still transmitting data back to earth from a distance of thirteen billion miles away.

Embedded in each Voyager probe is a gold-plated audio visual disk intended, NASA explains, "to communicate a story of our world to extraterrestrials." On this disk are photos of the earth and some of its lifeforms, statements from then-US president Jimmy Carter and UN secretary general Waldheim, and an audio soundscape called "Sounds of Earth" with greetings in fifty-five languages, whale song, a baby crying, waves breaking and a ninety-minute selection of music including Bach and Chuck Berry. Azerbaijani bagpipes. A wedding song from Peru. Waliparu singing "Moikoi," about the malicious spirits who try to entice newly deceased souls away from their clan country. Blind Willie Johnson playing "Dark Was the Night, Cold Was the Ground" on his slide guitar, singing the notes; his song so powerful it does not require words.

The Voyagers are gradually losing the power required to let us know what they are seeing. We're unlikely to know whether their diplomacy is ultimately successful or whether it was a re-cord we made, in the end, only for ourselves.

The sun is setting as I drive home, listening to our voices now liberated from the sterile envelope of the caravan shop. Talking about the cantina scene in *Star Wars*, that sentiment I had found surprisingly moving. Everyone together: "I saw that as very much a reality."

"Humans," Ben says, "we're just not at that level for galactic acceptance, because we're very aggressive creatures."

"We're embarrassing," I say.

"We're embarrassing," Ben agrees.

"We can't even take care of our own planet," I say.

"We're at the lower end," Ben says. "We're dangerous, we're egotistical, we're expansionist . . . We are to be treated with cau-tion. But I think the phenomenon is also aware that we have that potential to go through our growing pains. And if we don't de-stroy the planet and blow ourselves up, then if we can get through that, then we might be reasonable entities that can interact with other entities that are on a higher plane of intelligence and soci-etal operation. That's perhaps the big-picture scenario.

"We're bad tenants," he continues. "There are a lot of dumb things that've gotten in the way of humanity getting to where we really should be."

Just after sunset, as Ben predicted, I pass a property near Rosedale where on September 30, 1980, a domed object was seen hovering over a water tank before briefly landing. The caretaker of the property reported that when he approached it on his motorbike, he was almost knocked over by a blast of hot air as it ascended after emitting a whistling noise and an awful scream. When he checked the next day, the circle of flattened grass it left behind was still there and the ten-thousand-gallon water tank was empty.

I can't say I don't look for something as I drive past the tank, a replacement in the same spot as the original. But there's nothing unusual. Just trees and long planes of grass extending towards the horizon as I focus on making it home down a road rapidly dissolving into a void broken only by the push of my own headlights through the dark.

42

HALFWAY HOME
LYNN

AJ is sent farther upstate to Albion County Correctional Facility, a routine prison transfer. Until Lynn fortuitously follows a year later, they keep in touch with calls, letters. When she finally arrives it is freezing.

Lynn comes from a cold place but this is a cold she has not felt before. Upstate the majority of the correctional officers are male. Doing the job because it's there, or because their fathers did it, or for the same reason they have Klan tattoos and tattoos of Black babies in nooses: a locked and freezing compartment behind the belly that originally contained a toddler screaming but came, over time, to be inhabited by something silently roiling like the medieval Lucifer at the dead center of the earth.

These men, in total physical control of the population of female inmates, hate the fact that the person Lynn refers to as her husband is, administratively at least, a Black female prisoner.

They spot each other at breakfast the morning after Lynn arrives. AJ stalls up ahead in the line, letting others go in front so that Lynn can catch up. Before she makes it, she is called over by a correctional officer.

I know who you are, he says. You're Mitchell's girl.

Sir, you have that wrong, Lynn replies, looking up at him. I'm sorry, I don't know where you got that information.

Really? he says. You're gonna look me in the eye and tell me you're not her girl?

I'm not, Lynn says, looking up at him. I'm her *wife*. You have anything to say, say it.

("What did he do?" I ask, across from her at the Ukrainian restaurant down the street from the shelter. A wood-paneled womb that we usually have to ourselves.

"He turned the color of your borscht." Lynn smiles, AJ's ashes in a tiny locket around her neck.)

We don't do that here, says the officer.

What is it you don't do here? Lynn says. I'm looking around this dining room and I see plenty of couples. You would be lucky if somebody loved you one-tenth as much as I love her. I don't know any rule against loving somebody. Now, if you see me do something—kiss or touch her in public—I'll hand you a pen, you can write me up. And until then you will leave me alone.

They had a few more years together before Lynn filled out the paperwork in 2004 applying on AJ's behalf for compassionate leave: to be released before he died of the lung cancer that had spread throughout his body. Only when he was deemed sufficiently sick was AJ released to a hospital on the outside where he died, without Lynn but free, one week later.

We've sat in this restaurant three years in a row and that first year I was about the same age as Lynn was when she was convicted, my son the same age as her son at that time. And even though we talk about many things, at some point it always happens: I watch myself seeing my son slapped off-balance down concrete stairs by the man who hates me now even more than he did the two times he broke my skull, and to whom I will soon be compelled by the full coercive power of the state to hand him over, feeling that I had genuinely exhausted all avenues to the contrary.

Out of my sight, overnight.

I think what I would pack in his overnight bag. The diapers. The blanket. The stuffed monkey. I feel certain that such a bag would never be handed over to such a man, and at this point the imaginary formulation of forward momentum projects at light speed into three-dimensional space and suddenly there I am, sitting in front of me, offering myself a mushroom pierogi.

Self-defense and provocation are old defenses. If proven they will, respectively, exonerate the person who kills; or convert a murder charge into a lesser homicide offence on the ground that the killing in question was a required, or at least a reasonable, human response. They are defenses that arose from the framework of the duel: an instantaneous and justifiable reaction to attack by a person who walked the world already armed with their sword or physical strength. In other words, the defenses are tailored—fit like a glove—to male-on-male violence between social and physical equals. For much of the history of our system of criminal law, when women protected themselves or their children from abusive male partners, the mismatch in physical and social resources meant that their reactions necessarily took different forms. These forms fell outside the traditional legal defenses and were therefore recognized only as "murder." For a long time the law refused to understand such homicides as reactive or protective, labeling them instead using the tidy language of malice, of evil. The worst injustice in a world not known for its fairness is the injustice concealed under good order.

Lynn has PTSD. She will be triggered by a man raising his voice, a finger shoved in her face, crowds around or behind her. There was rage in her, a flood that covered the high hills, but it has long receded into a deeper well of sorrow where the truer feeling resides. Animus—whether rightfully aimed or misdirected—does not guide her or leak from her. Lynn is not an angry person.

"I did that to myself," she says, of the half of her life spent inside. "It was bad choices. It was desperation. And I knew that. Technically, *technically*—Ray wasn't my only victim. I victimized the man who actually did the killing and I victimized my mother because she died alone. I victimized my father because he died without me, I victimized my son—he didn't get to be raised by me. If I hadn't, he might have died, but still.

"I can't be mad at a choice that I made. I can't." Her voice thins out and for one moment there is stillness. "Who would I be mad at? The guy that actually put the rope around his neck—for being weak and talking? Should I be mad at the police for arresting me? The judge for throwing the book at me? Well, you know, there was bad judgment—I think he should've said that I had extreme emotional disturbance and given me manslaughter, as it would be now. But you know something? I helped change the pattern jury instructions," she says, tapping her nail on the tabletop. She is speaking of the discussions she had with law reformers about her case. "I helped change it for those who came after me. It wasn't retroactive but I can sit here and say I did right by everybody that came after me."

The light reflects off her ring. Lynn bought this ring, which originally had a sapphire in it, for her mother with her first pay check at the age of seventeen. After her mother died, Lynn's father smuggled it to her in prison. She was forced, eventually, to get rid of it, jewelery being prohibited inside. So she cut the gem off, filed the prongs down and sent it to AJ's cousin for safekeeping. He recently returned it and she took it to a jeweler for repairs. The band had no shine and didn't sit true, she explains; not that you'd know any of that now by looking at it.

43

THEORIES OF FLIGHT
DON

In the library at Docklands on a freezing November night, about one hundred people are packed into a small theater to listen to Don Schmitt reconstruct in molecular detail his thesis about what happened at Roswell.

George Simpson, in his leather jacket, squints at Don through the viewfinder of a video camera secured to a tripod. Ben Hurle, also in a leather jacket, sits nearby, his VUFOA accreditation dangling from a blue lanyard around his neck. Colin Kelly sits on the other side of the room, arms crossed over his chest, waiting for Don to start.

"We're going to go through it, pretty much like we're in a court of law," Don says. Watching him pace in front of the audience does bring to mind a trial lawyer, albeit the TV version. It's less about the suit and tie; more the impassioned gravitas and fluidity of his sentences as he speaks without notes for the next three and a half hours to a quiet room of rapt ufologists. This is no mean feat since the average ufologist—with his conference T-shirt, fixed gaze and strong opinions strongly held—has his own hair-trigger readiness to speak without notes for three and a half hours.

Don runs the red dot of a laser pointer over a slide of the Roswell debris field that shows only the wide blue sky over scrub grass. "High open range," he says. "Once you're airborne, you can see for fifty miles—wide open."

He goes over the timeline of the incident—the myriad characters coming to the fore and retreating as in a Russian novel, the narrative veering away and back like a spy movie. Looking at the black-and-white photos of airmen and nurses and farmers, the small town and the mesa around it, all as they were in 1947, it is easy to slip into the cinematic, to forget— until you see the later photographs of a younger Don smiling next to these people in their old age—that this was a day in full color that reverberated across lifetimes.

"It took sixty troops three full days to pick up every last piece of debris," Don says, pacing. "On their knees, they looked. Pretty detailed recovery of just a simple weather balloon."

In that room, through Don's steady accumulation of detail, we hear how fourteen-year-old Frankie Rowe saw a piece of that debris when she stopped in at the Roswell firehouse on her way home from the dentist to visit her father, who was a firefighter. How they let her hold the strange metallic substance, a solid that was somehow like water running though her hands as she crushed it up and watched it slowly return to smoothness. How scared she still was, crying, decades later as she told Don about the policeman who threatened to kill her if she ever told anyone what she'd seen.

We hear how the rancher William Brazel was working on a homestead fifty kilometers north of Roswell when he found "bright wreckage made up of rubber strips, tinfoil, a rather tough paper and sticks." Collected enough of it to fill a cigar box. Kept a piece tucked away in his chaps—took it out at dinner and sawed at it with a steak knife, marveling how nothing could stop it from returning to form. How it was confiscated by one of the uniformed men who had descended on the town en masse.

Colin listens intently, his chin tilted slightly upward. When I called him the other day to chat, something weird happened. About two minutes into our conversation, he spoke the word Westall for the first time and the line went funny. He couldn't hear me, then I couldn't hear him. So I hung up, called back.

"Mate," he said, unperturbed, "if we're going to be talking about it, you should know about this. I reckon they're listening in. It doesn't happen when I use the phone for business. But it happens all the time when I start talking about Westall." It struck me as possible but not probable. And though it will happen again a few months later on the phone with Rob Tilley— as soon as I mention the word Westall, the line will cut out altogether—I will still consider it improbable that someone is listening. But the coincidence was striking enough for me to mention it here.

"You have your Roswell here," Don is saying, referring to Westall. "It needs to be investigated further. We need to make every last effort to speak to every person involved and help them out of their fear and intimidation."

There follows one moment during which Don is silent and I feel that I see him, truly, for the first time. In this moment, Don briefly glances at Colin—validating him personally without identifying him, unsure of whether Colin consents in this forum.

There Don is. Not the showman, not the aged wunderkind of UFO investigation gently patting his hair into place with the tips of his fingers, but the guy from Wisconsin who goes to his terminally ill younger brother's medical appointments and is excited about spending Christmas with his family. The guy who will soon fly into the Midwestern winter and despite his jet lag will not miss an upcoming performance with his choir: one voice among many. The guy who will email me and ask after my family, remembering details I mentioned only in passing. So I can see why hundreds of people who told no one else, not even their spouse, about their truth ended up making him its custodian. I can see why it was Don who became the repository of these small-town stories which, believe them or not, all form one story of significant change in the mentality of mid-century America and with it the world.

The air is so close in the packed theater that I can feel the exhalations of the woman next to me. I try to imagine Don singing in his choir; it is not hard. I think of "his" witnesses, how he physically aged alongside them but grew younger, perhaps, in his mind, finding only questions where he once had answers, his voice eventually joining a chorus six hundred strong.

As he concludes and starts taking questions from the audience, an article pops up on my phone about the New South Wales bushfires, which have become terrifying. It quotes a local mayor who just lost her home: "The trees are dying and they are so dry and volatile. We've got no water in our dams, no water in our rivers, no water in our creeks."

Earlier in the night, Don clicked to a slide showing an insect that looked like an enormous ant. Explained that certain witnesses reported seeing the occupants of the crashed saucer, described their large heads and wide-set eyes as looking like a Jerusalem cricket, the insect known in New Mexico by the translation of its magnificent Spanish name: child of the earth. Don is now being asked about an entity that was reported to have survived the crash, and to have been taken into government custody. There was an account, he replies, from a witness about seeing this alien in captivity at a government facility. That witness recounted feeling sorry for it and receiving the distinct message: *Don't have any feelings for me because there's nothing more that can be done.*

I click on more articles about the fires. Read about the prime minister, Scott Morrison, not responding directly when asked whether climate change is responsible for what is happening.

Believe it or not about the captive alien, and I don't, its purported message evokes a dreadful familiarity—the logically extended reasoning of those at the lower end, the bad tenants, the dangerous, the egotistical, the expansionist children of the earth. *So then I started to wonder,* Don had said, sipping his tea, *are we dealing with time travel? Are we dealing with us?*

I put my phone back in my pocket, walk out into the cold night where the lights on the water look like an airstrip. I am thinking about those scraps of debris, how Don described them. The material was paper thin, he said. Weightless in your hands. A bullet wouldn't cut it. A sledgehammer just bounced off it, wouldn't mar it.

Soon Don will be back on the debris field for another archaeological dig, using metal detection and subterranean radar in his continuing effort to recover a piece of his "holy grail." I try to imagine something bright, at once physical and ethereal. Something abiding, self-healing, carrying the imprint of itself so firmly within itself that it is fated to return to form regardless of external influence. Of course it would be called "memory material," this substance which was insistently everlasting if not truly indestructible—shattering, as it did, into so many fragments instantly on impact with the hard reality of the earth.

THE KINGDOM OF HEAVEN
BECKY & TIM

Tim Kreider, baby on his lap, hums the first note. Then his wife and their six sons and Marie, the teenage girl visiting from Pennsylvania to help with the kids, all harmonize around the hymn which starts their daily family worship. Their voices coil like vines in their living room where sunlight coats the battered walls. My god, this music. My love for the sound of it arrived fully formed, announcing itself that first day down in the dirty train station like the discovery of a second heart underneath what was—yes, at first—an ironic amusement. But the sound poleaxed me. And the magnetic attraction that snaps me to it never leaves me and it never diminishes. It is with me months later when I walk down the street listening to it, small and tinny, through shitty headphones and when I sit alone at my desk, watching other Mennonite choirs on YouTube, tears burning my eyes. It can't be the lyrics. I am unmoved, at least in the intended manner, by say, "Trust and Obey" or "There's Power in the Blood" or "There Is a Fountain Filled with Blood" or "Are You Washed in the Blood" or "But for the Blood" or "Paid in Full (By the Blood of the Lamb)." And it isn't a question of technical mastery; the voices are by no means perfect. But each time it causes within me a certain pool of feeling—a tenderness. A vulnerability which, strangely, gives me energy, bends towards strength. Something I have not found words for, and perhaps that is the point.

They don't read music, are liberated from the page in that regard. "They grew up with it," Becky shrugged when I asked once how the harmony is taught. "At church, we don't have a choir because we want everybody to be involved." And that's everything, really. These songs are houses with warm rooms for everyone. *This is what it could feel like.*

Though PS 83 is just down the block, the older boys attend school in their basement, where Becky is now heading to check that they are starting their afternoon lessons. I'm not quite sure how I can do justice to the Kreider kids, sufficiently close in age and similar-looking that they bring to mind a Pennsylvania Dutch matryoshka doll. I can tell you that they are a healthy balance between playful and serious, autonomous and cooperative. Getting closer, now, to what I want you to know: they are kind and thoughtful and, while they are raucous in the sorts of ways that bruise the ceiling and pancake the couch cushions and break foot bones, they are also placid and joyful and loving. I watch their faces when Tim or Becky speaks with them and although the theological content of these discussions is as useful to me as the operating instructions for the Mars Rover, many times it feels as though I am getting a master class in parenting. Perhaps most telling: the character of these children is the strongest proof of a happy home.

Marie is leading the boys in an antiquated (and commensurately offensive) hymn before they open their books. *Jesus loves the Eskimo,* they sing, *In the land of ice and snow* . . . Sprinkled with pimples, reclining in her chair, she then guides them to their work, staying ahead by following the teacher's guide. Like Becky, she is wearing a cardigan and the long dress that I ask about as we return upstairs. "Our conference wants their ladies to wear a dress," Becky answers. "We try to teach our young girls to look sweet and feminine but not to be out to grab attention."

From my discussions with Loisann and Becky, I now know that a girl's or woman's membership status in The Light of Truth Mennonite Church signifies that certain things are more likely than not to be true. She's going to cover her head with a small veil. She'll be wearing a full-length dress that she purchased at a Mennonite op shop or made for herself in about four hours. That dress may be a pleasing shade of purple or pink or peach but it will definitely not be red, which is an immodest color because it begs attention. She will be wearing sneakers, probably some sort of black Nike situation, not because it is cool or for the purpose of exercise but because it is cheap, durable and comfortable for the many hours of standing to perform housework and child care which her days demand. She is going to be somber in church; she is not necessarily going to be somber outside of church, where she might dissolve into giggles should she recall something hilarious that happened once. She is not going to wear makeup or nail polish or jewelery or perfume or pants, pants being masculine and her being mindful of the need to maintain a clear line between the sexes. However, while she can wear a blue dress—the masculinity of the blue being satisfactorily offset by the femininity of the dress—it cannot be said that the reverse is true; her husband, if she has one, and if she is in her twenties she probably has one, is unable to wear a pink shirt, the femininity of the pinkness *not* being sufficiently overridden by the masculinity of the shirt. She may have finished high school all the way through to the twelfth grade like Becky, but more likely only the tenth grade like Loisann; either way she will most definitely not have gone to university.

"We just try to stay out of this kingdom," Becky explains when I ask how a typical Conservative Mennonite family celebrates occasions like birthdays and holidays. "You won't find us celebrating Memorial Day or the Fourth of July because we're not politically active. You won't see any flags or patriotic discussions going on, for the most part." She takes a rare breather, sitting on the couch after putting the baby down for a nap while her three-year-old plays nearby. "You won't find Christmas trees or Santa Claus or anything unreligious-related. A very typical Mennonite thing is Christmas caroling. We'll go around as a church and sing for our neighbors. Of course, in the city, you don't just go knock on someone's door and ask if you can come inside," she laughs.

"We tend to abstain even from social drinking. The Bible says take a little wine . . ." She smiles, explaining that while drinking isn't a sin, it's wiser not to get started. "We've had enough experience with people who were drunkards or alcoholics that've tried to come back." She shifts on the sofa, her skin pale as a page. With her white veil and her dark dress, from the side she evokes the sober image of Whistler's mother and this is how I think of her, though we are the same age.

"As a rule, we tend to stay away from public facilities and do things at home, but we frequent the botanical gardens and the zoo, parks, the beach on the off-days," she says, by which she means the cooler summer days on which it is easier to avoid "the undressed." She nods at one of the older boys coming into the room as she grabs the toddler's coat. Zipping him up, she tells him, "You can go down with the other boys and play chalk." His older brother gently picks him up and carries him outside.

When I ask whether the church has a position on parenting or discipline, I get one of Becky's laughs. "There isn't, like, a paper that you get that says this is how to raise your children—unfortunately. The biggest thing, probably, is the Bible. Just to make sure they see God in their lives.

"Another thing that's probably pretty core if they're going to be able to be successful is self-discipline. The Christian life isn't just a bed of roses. No life is. Adult life just isn't," she says, and laughs mirthlessly.

45

HALFWAY HOME
LYNN

In 2015, Lynn includes in her fifth parole application a thirty-year-old letter from her neighbor saying that she saw Ray backhand the boy down the stairs. Also copies of the Family Court's protection order against him, his arrest record and a letter of support from the prison superintendent. Assessments show she poses the lowest possible risk for felony violence, re-arrest and absconding. Her prison work record and relative lack of "tickets" for rule violations mean that she has been an exemplary prisoner, and there is a job waiting for her as a paralegal for a Manhattan lawyer on her release. Still, she is denied parole as she was in 2007, 2009, 2011 and 2013. The parole board gives her another "hit," concluding that she "would not live and remain at liberty without again violating the law," and that her release "would so deprecate the serious nature of her crime as to undermine respect for the law."

Lynn writes to Columbia Law School's Mass Incarceration Clinic for help, and law students file a petition on her behalf challenging the outcome in the New York Supreme Court. Finding that the decision to deny Lynn's parole was "arbitrary and capricious," the judge orders a new hearing. The sixth time she appears before the parole board it comprises Edward Sharkey, a former district attorney, and Sally Velasquez-Thompson, a former police detective.

"I wanted everything to stop," she tells them, "what was going on in my household and around me. And I wanted my problems to end. And it was just about the most horrible choice I could have made. I was so deluded by the fact that if I did this, I would end my own problems. I would end the abuse. I would end my situation. I would end the threat of my son being kidnapped or murdered . . .

"All I want is to show other women that this would be the biggest mistake of their life to take matters into their own hands. I want to show other women to leave safely. I want to show other women this is what happens when you don't. I want to help other people not make the horrific mistake I did."

"It is not a mistake," Sharkey says, the past swinging into the present like an axe. "It's a crime. And you took someone's life and that's not your place to do."

"It's not a mistake," Lynn replies. "I misspoke."

They approve her release. When she walks out of prison with her purple cane on April 28, 2017, she walks out smiling, her white hair reflecting the sun.

Later, a local newspaper interviews Ray's sister who says, "I hate her with all my being and hope she dies a horrible death. She murdered a good man. A compassionate, caring man."

Her mother is dead, her father is dead, AJ is dead. Her sister wants nothing to do with her, her son remains unresponsive to her letters. She is free in the most absolute and terrifying sense:

no home to return to. She has, however, made arrangements to stay at the apartment of an acquaintance in the city. Arrives to find stolen goods, white powder on the table. The woman asks her to lie to a doctor for prescription pills which she would then hand over for the woman to sell. Lynn refuses and things become tense. The woman's husband yells at her, triggering flashbacks of Ray. In her small room, she moves the chest of drawers across the door before she gets into bed, wakes at the slightest noise, worried about her safety and the terms of her parole. She has little money. She hasn't eaten for a day when she leaves. Heads to a homeless shelter, everything she owns in her hands as she walks down sidewalks where everybody is curved like her cane. Looking down, compulsively poking bright squares or speaking, it seems, only to themselves.

46

THEORIES OF FLIGHT
JAIMIE & ASPASIA

"The myth of the individual is frightening because really we are tribal. We are nothing without each other," Jaimie Leonarder says, smoking splendidly in his recliner with his long legs crossed before him. Jaimie is the vice president of the Sydney-based group UFO Research (UFOR). He is also its media contact. When I first tried to contact him, I learned that he does not own a mobile phone. His landline's voicemail message was: *Hello. The person you've reached is not at home and you cannot leave a message so please call later.*

Jaimie and his wife, Aspasia, were involved in setting up the first support group in Australia for people who believed they had been abducted by aliens. After we connected, I learned that the Leonarders are warm and welcoming in person. Also, that I enjoy speaking with them. Which is good because, contrary to my initial assumption, one cannot just talk about UFOs with the Leonarders. Not possible. To inquire about any one thing in that category is to be led inexorably into the lush global ecosystem of information in which they situate the subject. It is to be guided, with great and traipsing gusto, across undulating contiguous terrain that features Nikola Tesla, Thomas Edison,

Sean Penn in *The Falcon and the Snowman*, yowies and the parallel hominid, Marshall McLuhan and media theory, NASA's shameful absorption of Nazi scientists, quantum coupling, their questions regarding the provenance of both cheetah DNA and the blood type of certain Jewish people, alien-human hybridization programs, the documentary oeuvre of Mel Tormé's son Tracy Tormé, and corporations and the myth of the individual, which is where we are at present.

This particular thought process might be understood in Cubist terms: to quote McLuhan, an "instant sensory awareness of the whole"—the world as they view it. And you might dismiss that trajectory as fairly non sequitur, Dada, absurd.

That would be a mistake. Fellow travelers on this path include the "conspiracy-pop" musician, David Thrussell (invited to speak this year at a UFOR event), whose band—Snog—has posted content on its Facebook page that is antisemitic and anti-vaccination, and which proposes that the 2012 Sandy Hook elementary school shooting, in which Adam Lanza killed twenty first-graders and six adults, was a hoax. The UFOR website described Thrussell as follows: "Beloved by iconic figures like Julian Assange and Russian philosopher Alexander Dugin,[1] David Thrussell is provocative and controversial and has lots to say." Jaimie and Aspasia signed off on the post thus: "For our sake, if for no other reason, please humor him."

---

1. Dugin, a contemporary Russian fascist influenced by Hitler, is the populariser of a Putin-approved brand of 'Eurasianism'—a mix of Russian culture, authoritarian government and worship of a strong leader.

Jaimie imprints as some cosmic combination of John Waters, Nick Cave and a slimline iteration of Gomez Addams. Perhaps you recognize him from when he co-hosted *The Movie Show* on SBS. In an earlier life, he was a psychiatric nurse, a diversional therapist and a youth worker based on the streets of Sydney. He is eloquent and delivers sentences that captivate me, such as: "She is one of the better latter-day UFO researchers" or "I worked the streets—someone with a necrotic toe, I could smell blocks away" or "I will go to my grave with an embarrassment of questions" or "One of the most astounding qualities of the human mind is its capacity to pay attention." He met Aspasia at work: she, too, was a psychiatric nurse. As Miss Death, she co-hosted their Sydney radio show, "The Naked City," until 2010. Now Jaimie and Aspasia, in their early sixties and late fifties respectively, are proud grandparents who DJ at a local pub and show rare films in their home where I am currently sitting, stroking their hairless cat, Lilith, who feels under hand like an enormous dried apricot.

In addition to this cat, their warehouse apartment—which is mostly warehouse and only a bit apartment, rather than some more sleekly integrated version of the two—houses a vast collection of films, books, magazines, music, carnivalesque-psychobilly ephemera and an original painting by the serial killer John Wayne Gacy once given to them by a skint ex-flatmate in lieu of rent.

"I always say, 'Just because you've been abducted doesn't mean you're enlightened,'" Aspasia had said earlier, without removing her eyes from her knitting. However, while personalities differ, there is a thread of consistency between abduction accounts, the Leonarders would have me know.

"This is the way it usually goes," she explained. "One night, something will happen and they'll wake up and remember bits and pieces. So then they want to find out what happened to them. They'll go and have some hypnosis therapy and find out that it's been *going on all their life* from a young child . . . And, this is what they say, that there's some sort of a cloaking, masking, forgetting of what's happened so people aren't traumatized."

"Most people who have a really close sighting—a sighting of the second and third kind—are probably susceptible somewhere in there to have had an abduction experience, whether they remember it consciously or not," Jaimie said.

He continued: "Here's the problem with easily dismissing that. If you have what is purportedly a physical and transcendental experience, where all of a sudden your body—is it your spirit body? Your physical body?—is actually now going through the glass window of your bedroom and up into the sky, how do we, in our perception management, integrate that into our lives? The horror and the fear of it. You're going to see signs of post-traumatic stress disorder. And so, instantly, you're going to be diagnosed as mentally ill.

"Now post-traumatic stress disorder doesn't appear in someone unless they've been removed from their reality. You don't get that easily from a nightmare or a drug experience. It doesn't happen. And it's a generational thing. If it's happened to them, it's probably happened to their parents or could happen to their children."

The Leonarder house is under a flight path and the muffled drone of passing planes wove a sonic thread through all our hours of wide-ranging conversation.

"One of the problems we face now is the homogenization of news and data," Jaimie said when I asked about the dismissive response to UFO accounts. With so much information accessible, we have collectively lost the ability to identify or care about things that are of deep concern.

"We have defense department footage that's been declassified in the public domain showing objects that are not drones moving at a high velocity, stopping at a point which would kill anyone in them and destroy any civilian or military aircraft that were doing that. And it's just seen as like, *The Truman Show*: 'Oh, that's just great, what's happening on the other channel?'

"And it's incredibly consistent globally which puts it out of the league of being debunked as some mental aberration or some falsehood and yet it's not being seen for its value. It could, in a way, deconstruct our notion of cultures and walls and we all start to think in terms of human beings. It's an unfortunate thing."

"Can't have a unified planet, jeez," Aspasia said.

"It's all perception management," Jaimie said a little while later. "And we've ended up in a world with so much distraction that we're not seeing the wood for the trees. Ufology is just one example . . . We're just embedded in so much distraction. Alvin Toffler wrote a book in 1970 called . . ."

"*Future Shock*," Aspasia said.

"It was about the fact that we will end up very soon in an information-rich environment without the ability to actually navigate and use that information in a constructive way," Jaimie said. "And so, to me, the only satisfaction I really get is in trying to push myself beyond my desires and get a bit altruistic or to create an environment where I'm creating and not consuming . . .

"Philosophically," he continued, "it's really important that we think outside of the square. We talk about not bullying people and being accepting of different cultures and religious ideologies. So why is there so much ridicule attached to the topic of ufology?"

Jaimie finds the abductees' perspective on life quite astounding. "They're people that actually have fought, against the system, to see the world in a different way." This is why he takes issue with the word "belief." The semantics are not unimportant, he said. "It's supposition to assume that governments have made us reach this point, but there's a lot of evidence. The Central Intelligence Agency decided that, when it was print and television and film media, on the end of the word "conspiracy" should be placed the word "theory" to devalue anyone doing investigative research. So that instantly weaponized that word and took the value of what we'd call investigative journalism into the realm of the tinfoil hat. It's a semantic ballet. Language engineers thought, creates its own neural pathways and it blocks our ability to expand on our imaginations . . .

"You know, television is not called programming for no reason," he continued. "All of us are aware that looking at a computer screen or a television screen you slowly descend into a very submissive, trance-like state. You forget what's around you. And that's the ability of advertising to be so effective in those mediums."

"Children's mental health," Aspasia said. "Kids are killing themselves, kids are anxious all the time."

Jaimie commented that the idea of private media was something that was sold to us. "Now it's the myth of the individual," he said.

"They want us at home, on our own, consuming," Aspasia said. "How do you entirely destroy somebody?"

"Isolation," Jaimie replied.

The taxi driver who dropped me here today used a Sydway map to find the place, pulling the soft brick of it out from under his seat, saying he preferred it to the GPS. I think of him on my way home, as the Uber driver punches the airport address into his phone, follows where it takes him. And of Jaimie and Aspasia, what it means to be in your early sixties and late fifties. How, over the span of their lives to date, LP records disappeared and then cassettes. Reel-to-reel, Beta, VHS. Carbon copies, typewriter ribbons. The black tongue of film inside a camera, every frame precious. Phone booths. Boom boxes. Unfilled time. The direct gaze of the analogue world, faces replaced by pixels.

On their recommendation, I will get a copy of *Future Shock*. Read how Toffler defined the term as the dizzying disorientation brought on by the premature arrival of the future. Too much change in too short a time. To survive, he wrote, the individual must become infinitely more adaptable and capable than ever before. We must search out totally new ways to anchor ourselves. "For all the old roots—religion, nation, community, family or profession—are now shaking under the hurricane impact of the accelerative thrust."

A few months later, Neil, a mortician in his fifties who owns a funeral parlor on the outskirts of Sydney, sits drinking tea at the Leonarders' kitchen table and discussing the Valentich disappearance while Jaimie warms up pumpkin soup for Aspasia. Neil explains that he was once a pilot, though he later lost his license for failing to meet a physical flexibility requirement. That's how he heard the original Valentich radio transmission.

"It was classified, wasn't it?" Jaimie asks.

"My flying teacher had a copy of it," Neil replies. "We all sat there—about twenty pilots and apprentice pilots—listening to this tape that he had."

Neil asked his teacher what he reckoned happened to the plane. "And he goes, 'A hundred percent that was some type of object.' Because apparently he's seen them since he's been flying."

"Once something goes over a certain speed," Jaimie explains, "they're not going to be seen by radar. Nine times out of ten it's the transponder; it's not actually the craft that they're bouncing the radar off."

"That's right," Neil says.

"That's what happened with MH370," Jaimie continues, setting a plate of cookies between Neil and me.

"He described it as a long object," Neil says.

"Cigar-shaped," Aspasia says, tapping at her computer nearby.

"There is a history in Bass Strait dating back hundreds of years," Jaimie says, "you can go back to the early days of the settlement and find that people in boats there were bombarded by these green, thermoluminescent lights. There were a couple of eyewitnesses to a green object over the Cessna. Even though they remained anonymous, there are credible researchers that have done the research on those eyewitnesses. There also was a photographer that took a series of photos. There's a very interesting photo out there of an object that virtually at the same time appears to have come out of the water."

Neil nods, he's familiar with it.

Neil has a wife, three children, a good sense of humor, a messy car, a preference for dobermans and long gray hair that used to be longer and black. He explains that his father was Cherokee, from Arizona. And like his father before him, Neil explains, he has been repeatedly abducted by aliens over his lifetime.

"It all started when I was around four years old," he says, explaining that he always insisted on having his curtains open at night, loved gazing up at the sky and the object resembling a squashed racing car that he would see floating there.

At around eight years old he woke to discover his first scoop mark: something that resembled a mosquito bite on his arm. He rolls up his sleeves to show me how it compares with a mark on his other arm where he had a melanoma removed.

"They're quite unique and very consistent," Jaimie pitches in, rolling up a pant leg to show his own scoop mark, which he discovered one night in the 1990s after finding himself falling back onto his bed with pain in that leg. "It looks like something's gone underneath the epidermis and removed subcutaneous tissue without scarring. I think they just took one out of me and said forget it," he says drolly.

Neil only remembers bits about what he experienced during his abductions. But rather than feeling traumatized, he felt connected to the aliens as he had not to other humans. "I used to say to Mom when I was young, 'I don't belong here.' I've always had that separation."

"But you're great social company," Jaimie says, warmly. "You're a great speaker, really clear recall. You're very pragmatic in the way you go about approaching this subject."

"I never used to be like this," Neil replies. "I was diagnosed when I was about seventeen as a sociopath, a person who can't get on with society. And I *was* like that. I never used to like anyone sitting near me at school, I was very antisocial. I couldn't function in this society because it was so alien to me, so backward, so not understanding that people could think differently."

"If I can interject here," Jaimie says, lighting a cigarette, "in all my dealings with you, you don't tick one of those boxes. Because you have empathy. You have a conscience. I don't think many sociopaths would be able to work in the funeral business, to begin with."

"I've never looked at the world the way people looked at it," Neil says. "I look at people and say, 'You poor bastards, here you are, going to school, which is crap, going to high school, going to uni, and then you just want to achieve in life. Achieve what?!' When I finished my engineering I never did it ever again. To me it was just crap. Surely life is not just going to work and dying."

Everything changed for Neil when he moved to a farm near Tamworth. At 2:00 AM on a Monday morning near Christmas, he was standing at his fridge enjoying a drink of juice ahead of a drive to the city when he had a strong urge to look out the window. Seeing two strange yellow lights in the sky, he walked outside to get a better view. Because there was no noise, he figured it was a twin-engine airplane that had run out of fuel, looking for a place to land. So he turned on the spotlights, started to guide it in.

What landed was an enormous craft with aliens inside. On seeing this, he asked them silently in his mind, "Are you one of our creators?" and immediately felt the most intense love he'd ever experienced. "It was like we are part of them. We are part of the trees, the planet, the stars, we are all interconnected. That's how I got the empathy," he explains. "That encounter just completely changed my view of the world."

Neil told them that they were welcome to return, no one would harm them. The craft took off, slowly following the valley into the distance. Six weeks later he saw through his lounge-room window four or five crafts landing on his property. This continued for years. He was never tempted to take photos, or get a closer look, and he never felt scared.

Neil says that he met his wife in a flying saucer, though they didn't realize it until ten years later. He believes that this is where genetic material was extracted from them to make human-alien hybrids, and that he has two children in space, whom he has visited. "It's really sad because they cling on to you and won't let you go because they need that love," he says.

"They take eggs from women and sperm from men," Aspasia explains. "They bring them back to get them to interact with the children."

"Well, we're dealing with numerous hypotheses here," says Jaimie, who is more cautious on the subject.

"I know," Aspasia says, "but this is a consistent thing from so many different people."

Neil says that he was told in his encounters—not verbally but in mental pictures that appear like slides—that there are benevolent alien species and ones that are evil, the latter using humans as a food source. He notes parenthetically that many people go missing around the planet, never to be found. Jaimie recommends a number of books on this topic. The aliens told Neil that they are creating a new race of humans. "Because our race is obsolete," he explains, "we'll be replaced by this new race which is more intelligent, more kind to the planet."

47

THE KINGDOM OF HEAVEN
PRAYER MEETING

The only indication that the building is inhabited is a few windows below street level, dirty rectangles glowing gold, throwing light at the dark. The church holds evening prayer meetings twice a month. Like family worship, the meetings open with a hymn which tonight is "Living by Faith":

> Living by faith in Jesus above,
> Trusting, confiding in His great love;
> From all harm safe in His sheltering arm,
> I'm living by faith and feel no alarm.

Three of the church's four families sit in chairs arranged in a circle around the room used for children's Sunday school. The Kreiders and the Witmars are here with their children, as well as the newest and youngest family, the Weavers, who married here a couple of months ago. Rachel is too ill to attend, has stayed home with her husband, Eldon, and their children. There is Oscar, a recent member who also cooks for church events, and the two elderly Latina women. Also a man named Junior who has a mustache like a brush and a trucker cap with an American flag on it.

"How many people around the world haven't heard the gospel," Anthony begins, handing around printouts from an organization called The Joshua Project, which is "a research initiative seeking to highlight the ethnic people groups of the world with the fewest followers of Christ." They do this because "accurate, updated ethnic people group information is critical for completing the Great Commission," given that the Book of Revelation describes how people from every nation, tribe and language will stand before the Throne.

Later, on their website, I will decline to download their Unreached of the Day app but will be entranced by their "Ethnic Peoples Tree," which provides the following human taxonomy: Arab World, Deaf, East Asian Peoples, Eurasian People, Horn of Africa People, Jews, Latin-Caribbean Americans, Malay Peoples, North American Peoples, Pacific Islanders, Persian-Median, South Asian Peoples, Southeast Asian Peoples, Sub-Saharan Peoples, Tibetan-Himalayan Peoples, Turkic Peoples and Unclassified. Each group is further broken down according to language or culture with a one-pager addressing how best they might be converted. For example, missionaries to Iran should "pray that Iranian Arabs would see the Jesus film and hear Christian radio."

Anthony notes that in places like Papua New Guinea and Iraq there are people who have never seen a Christian Bible. "I don't have time to read all the statistics they have—how they get all these numbers, I don't know, but anyway—some sixty-five to seventy percent of the world live in religiously restricted countries," he says, peering into the page. "There are four hundred and fifty-eight villages in India with no Christian presence . . ."

Anthony's lesson reminds me about the story of the Tower of Babel. *Now the whole earth had one language and the same words.* After the flood, the united human race built a tower tall enough to reach Heaven. *And the Lord said, Behold, the people is one, and they have all one language; and this they begin to do: and now nothing will be restrained from them, which they have imagined to do.* God then confuses their language so that they cannot understand one another's speech and scatters them across the earth. What is this? Cautionary tale against hubris? Lament? Excuse? *Nothing more that can be done . . .*

Later I will wonder if I should have brought it up with them—something I admire about the religion into which I was born, the concept of *tikkun olam.* The Hebrew phrase means "repairing the world." I understand it in social justice terms. But the sixteenth-century Kabbalists had a more esoteric take, situating it in their creation story, which begins with God contracting the infinite light of the divine to make room for the material world. He proceeded to decant the divine consciousness into one beam of light which contained within itself everything that would ever exist and which then exploded everything we know into being, scattering it everywhere in the process. The undifferentiated fragments of this paroxysm are called sparks—they contain the true meaning of each thing, its voice in the great symphony. Each spark, however, is trapped in the shell that hardened around it during that originating chaos. Our job, Tzvi Freeman writes, is to see past the shell to the spark within, and to relocate that spark to its rightful place. Once a critical mass of sparks have been reconnected, the entire world is liberated. It becomes a different world, the one it was meant to be.

This is not so different from what Anthony believes he is doing. But I wonder what it might actually look like if our individual lives were arranged around a truer conception of repair and reunion. Where that would actually start.

Chief among Freud's major discoveries, Vivian Gornick writes, was that:

> from birth to death we are, every last one of us, divided against ourselves. We both want to grow up and don't want to grow up; we hunger for sexual pleasure, we dread sexual pleasure; we hate our own aggressions—anger, cruelty, the need to humiliate—yet they derive from the grievances we are least willing to part with. Our very suffering is a source of both pain and reassurance. What Freud found most difficult to cure in his patients was the resistance to being cured.

However they hurt us, our tidy and sclerotic stories—about ourselves, others, the world—are something certain. A railing we can cling to like a bird on a perch as we climb the staircase of our days convinced we will slip off at any moment and fall forever.

Anthony continues in a chipper tone, "It's never been easier to reach the rest of the world. If you want to send a message to someone in the jungle of Africa, it can get there instantly. We can't fix the world but we can help one person. As Jesus said, 'The harvest is great, pray that there are laborers.'"

It is now time to compile the evening's prayer agenda. Mentioning briefly the destruction in Syria, Anthony calls for prayer requests for people in other countries. Notebooks come out and pens are held at the ready as everyone takes turns specifying what prayers are required. I am surprised by the note-taking. It hadn't really filtered down that the purpose of tonight's meeting is not educational or social, it is instrumental. That these people left warm homes, walked into the cold night and gathered here together in some effort to effect change. One of the elderly women asks for prayers for "a brother in prison, sent to Ecuador," and her features crumple like a tissue. Tim names his sisters who work at the mission in Honduras.

"My lead trumpet, he went to California," Junior says. "I'm praying he'll come back for our orchestra. So we can have a group. For the Lord."

"That's not another country but it'll count," Anthony says, smiling. He looks down at his notes, adding his own wish: to be attractive to the lost before it is too late. Then he leads the prayers as everyone bows their heads before singing a slow version of "Since Jesus Came into my Heart," the harmony, as always, no less transcendentally beautiful for being imperfect.

Having dealt with the foreign, it's now time for the domestic. "What should we pray for?" Anthony asks, looking around the circle, eyebrows raised. Rachel and her family are named. Gratitude for the Thanksgiving dinner held at the church last week. Oscar says he would like a place where he can cook for three hundred homeless people on Christmas. Everyone old enough to write does so in their notebooks. "What else?" Anthony calls out.

"The brothers in prison," the elderly woman says again, with quiet urgency. Next to his father, Ethan Kreider brings up a recently injured finger. The presidential election is coming, and the candidates are mentioned.

"My sister," Junior says, explaining how she recently became a Jehovah's Witness. "Pray that she find the right way to Heaven."

Anthony mentions his dream of the coffee shop. Adds that he would like a prayer for "Diane, my sister, who is not a Christian." Loisann notes that a prayer will be required for a young woman she visited on Tuesday with some interest in coming to church. Also, steady work for Anthony. Tim, bouncing the baby on his leg, explains that in telling me about their experience in the Bronx, he recently realized how many prayers God has answered for his family. "In my house, it just seems like God is constantly answering," he says, his voice shimmering with emotion.

And then he prays: "For the coffee shop and restaurant—where it will be—our desire that it would be a way of spreading the word. For the homeless, the ability to feed them and spread the gospel as a way of impacting their lives for eternity."

Loisann speaks loudly, both praying and modeling prayer for her children, sitting at her feet. "Thank you, God—we never worry about anything because everything is in your control. I pray for unity, love for each other, that we communicate well. Show us what you want us to do here, God."

Douglas, twelve, goes next. Reading from his notepad in a voice that is still a child's voice but which will start changing any day now, he hurries through: Thanksgiving; Rachel and her family; the brothers in prison—strengthen them; the hurt finger; the coffee shop; religious freedom; the homeless; the restaurant thing, the new president; people attending faithfully; and the house you gave us. He was truly listening. Then

Anthony prays for his sister and says, quietly, "I'll never be whole without you." And he asks God to help them not to worry but to live by faith.

In that dim basement in a cold building in need of repairs that none of its various occupants can afford, I am pinched by the awkwardness of the exposed vulnerabilities, the openness about molten sadnesses and adult insecurities that range from the essential to the existential. But I, the only one who has neither shared nor prayed, am alone in this regard because vulnerabilities safely expressed are a binding together and a source of strength. So though I am sitting in this room, listening and chatting, I have also been, this long hour, floating around in the darkness outside.

I put my photocopies into a folder alongside the tract I was given that first day down in the subway. "Eternity is of utmost importance," it says. "There is no way to compare forever with a few years here. We will live *somewhere* forever."

And, not for the first time, I am envious of these people. Their refusal to accept absence of evidence as evidence of absence. Their insistence on seeing a perfect pattern embroidered into the fabric of reality, constant confirmation—in the good and in the bad—of a loving presence. To hold themselves separate from this kingdom of broken things, trembling inside its dense atmosphere, where the rest of us will die one day and forever, and where there's very little, perhaps, that can be done with that.

THEORIES OF FLIGHT
JAIMIE & ASPASIA

"SETI's an astounding thing," Jaimie says. "I still wonder why governments and huge institutional bodies throw billions of dollars at the search for extraterrestrial intelligence when they will dismiss all ufological information."

One of the oldest methods employed in the official search for extraterrestrial intelligence is the use of radio telescopes to monitor electromagnetic radiation for artificial signals, the assumption being that these would be communications from other civilizations. Such signals, the logic goes, would be easy to identify due to their repetitive nature and narrow bandwidths. The SETI Institute points out on its website that, in each of its last four decadal reviews, the American National Research Council has emphasized the relevance and importance of searching for evidence of the electromagnetic signature of distant civilizations.

Jaimie mentions the Wow! signal—a strong narrowband radio signal received in 1977 that bore the expected features of extraterrestrial communication and remains unexplained by known natural or human sources. Its name comes from the comment written on the computer printout by the astronomer who discovered the sequence, which lasted for seventy-two seconds, and it remains the strongest candidate for an alien radio transmission.

"So SETI has found what it set out to do," Jaimie says, "which is so improbable, because where is the critical analysis of the assumption behind what SETI is? It's the Drake Equation."

In 1961, Frank Drake, a radio astronomer at the National Radio Astronomy Observatory in West Virginia, presented a serviceable way of estimating the number of technological civilizations that may exist in our galaxy. The resulting equation holds that any practical search for distant intelligent life must necessarily be a search for some manifestation of distant technology. According to Drake's calculus, the number of civilizations in the Milky Way galaxy whose electromagnetic emissions are detectable will be a function of: the rate of formation of stars suitable for the development of intelligent life; the fraction of those stars with planetary systems; the number of planets, per solar system, that can potentially support life; the fraction of life-supporting planets on which life actually does then emerge; the fraction of life-bearing planets on which *intelligent* life emerges, the fraction of civilizations that develop technology which emit detectable signals of their existence into space; and the length of time for which such civilizations release detectable signals into space. There is no agreement on the values of these factors so the resulting number of estimated civilizations has varied from one (i.e. us) to a hundred million.

"There's so much misinterpretation of the Drake Equation," Jaimie continues. "It's not the possible number of *planets* that are earth-like out there. It's the possible number of planets that are earth-like out there that'll be *transmitting on a radio band.*"

They keep on narrowing the criteria, says Aspasia. Dismissing evidence.

Jaimie mentions a debate in the field of psychology regarding the causes of schizophrenia: if it's not nature, then what is it in nurturing? "And they say it could be double-sided messages."

"You're anxious because you don't know if you're doing the right thing or the wrong thing," Aspasia explains, "because you've been told on one hand, 'Yeah, that's fine to do,' and then you get chastised for it."

"Orwell spoke about it as doublespeak," Jaimie says. "Enough of that will create these neurological pathways to a breakdown."

The Leonarders are not infrequently approached by someone who makes a point of stridently informing them that they do not believe in UFOs, before eagerly sharing a bizarre thing they once saw in the sky.

"I think this is the incongruous nature of the Western mind-think without a spiritual template," Jaimie says. "We're in this stasis where, in a way, it's like doublespeak. 'This does not exist'—so I should be able to rationally deconstruct this to a point that will alleviate my fears that something's going on that is out of my control."

There's another reason for Jaimie's disdain for the official approach. "It's transference," Jaimie says. "We're doing it with SETI, we're doing it with Mars. Get the hierarchy of values set before you step off this planet into somewhere else otherwise you're using that blindness to go, 'Well, we'll solve it out there, we can't solve it here.' I can't believe billions of dollars were spent on the space program to begin with when they had so many problems with homelessness and poverty and mental illness. Didn't prioritize those before you thought of lighting the wick on any friggin' rocket . . ." he says.

The Leonarders have an adjacent interest in a parallel hominid commonly known as the yeti, the yowie, sasquatch or Big Foot.

"They evidently live a lot closer to us than has ever been imagined," Jaimie says, explaining how he and Aspasia have identified what could be their tree structures two and a half metres off the ground, just out past Katoomba.

The landline rings with a question about an upcoming cinema night. While Aspasia answers it, Jaimie says, "We have one of the worst feet for an undulating environment possible." He explains that yowie hunters have made casts of its footprints that reveal midtarsal breaks, which humans lack. "Which gives this thing— it would be hundreds of pounds, maybe a thousand pounds—the ability to pirouette like a ballerina on an undulating terrain."

I think for a moment of the failures of our feet, and how the dexterity Jaimie describes was reserved for our brains.

"So these animals or human beings, or cross between the two, are far more suited to dealing with the wilderness than we ever will be. In many ways, the human being, the *Homo sapiens*, is a problem because we have to terraform our environments before we can successfully survive in them. So evolution really had a major problem there, in making us so out of place in that environment."

This has led Jaimie to think that "human beings might've been genetically fiddled with," a subject on which he and Aspasia are admittedly verbose.

"We can go on for days," she agrees, having hung up the phone. After questioning the provenance of cheetah DNA and Rh negative blood, she says, "Our eye doesn't fit. We're the only species on this planet that squints at the sun. We don't belong here. We're not from here. We're not from here. We're a parasite. We're a cancer . . . Why would evolution create a being that needs to wear glasses, that can't look up into the sun, needs to wear shoes, clothes, we need to have our teeth fixed. We've got four thousand diseases . . ." She accepts a piece of lemon poppyseed cake from Jaimie, as do I. It's delicious.

"I think the problem comes if we're to assume things," Jaimie says, settling back into his chair. "All we can do, really, to fight the notion of skepticism and ridicule is to go, 'Explain to me why this is.'"

"Tell me, Science: where did it come from?" Aspasia says.

"Why should an insect have no junk DNA, and we do?" Jaimie asks.

"And why is it called junk?" Aspasia asks. "Because you haven't attributed some function to it, it's junk? No, man, no, it's not. Obviously, whatever it is, it hasn't been turned on." She urges me to take another slice of cake.

Jaimie considers Darwin. "He was a bit of an anti-Semite, there was really questionable stuff about Darwin," he says.

"Now they're saying evolution's been proven," Aspasia says. "No, it hasn't. This is the crux of Darwin's theory: that a bear long enough in the water will turn into a whale. I'm sorry, it's just going to be a waterlogged bear. Because it can only *be* a bear, because its genetic material will only allow it to be a bear. Not a whale."

A little while later, Lilith the bald cat wanders in and we all coo over her. "For an animal whose genes are geared completely to go out there and kill," Jaimie says, "their sensitivity and affection is profound when they love you. You know, it's mind-boggling."

Before I go, Jaimie says, "Let me try and round this up. Aspa and I have decided in the final years of existence for us that we take the stand that you've got to respect scientific reductionism but you also have to respect eyewitness accounts. You hold them together and look at the veracity of both. So as much as the academic can assist us in seeing the rules that establish the governing universe, the eyewitness can make us look outside of those rules and see that there might be something else governing reality as well."

He chivalrously walks me out through the Leonarder library with its lightly differentiated optical traffic of books and magazines and DVDs and film reels and sideshow paraphernalia and taxidermy and tiki knickknacks, a great and motley assemblage where the medium is the message.

Jorge Luis Borges imagined paradise as a kind of library. And I always imagined that library as an Eden where all the operating instructions are filed. Not only all the books ever written, but also each of our stories: the past meeting the future, everything indexed and logically related, a return to when the world was as seamless and whole as an apple. I suppose this reflected a belief in the world as a certain kind of text; a faith that, if I could only ask the right questions, I could finally understand.

To believe in the world as this type of text is to believe that all lives—regardless of whether they resolve happily—make sense. To have faith in context and causation. To insist that people for the most part are intelligibly coherent in the sense of being predictably inconsistent and that they are capable, within reasonable bounds, of incredible insight and meaningful growth as they learn, painfully, to bend themselves around reality instead of expecting reality to miraculously bend itself around them.

To repeatedly believe this about people is, to borrow from Philip Roth, to be wrong. But at least it is also to be wrong about oneself. And what other choice do we have?

49

THE KINGDOM OF HEAVEN
TIM

Last year, eMyPeople held their corporate retreat at the Creation Museum in Northern Kentucky; Becky says it was a lot of fun. The fact that Tim works for an internet service provider challenged the preconceptions I had about his community which, due to their way of dressing and speaking, seemed to be from a bygone era. It still surprises me when Tim says he got his computer training simply by being "spoon-fed through life," learning it from his father who bought a computer to do the accounting for his small business.

Programming is not the only language Tim picked up and swallowed whole. "I always had an interest in the Spanish language," he explains, sitting next to Becky in their living room, on a break from his desk in the basement. "But what really pushed it was . . . Okay, I've always had a passion for reaching the souls of people.

"As a youth, we would go into the city and talk to people. So many of them had very sad, frustrating stories. I mean, the section we were in was what one of the locals called Murder Mayhem. And we would tell them, 'You know what? You're struggling. But you're struggling because you have not made hard choices that you need to make. Pick up a Bible. Study it. Read it. Learn what's there because it has answers for life.'"

The idea of teenagers going from a ninety-five percent white rural community into a largely Black and Latino inner-city neighborhood to give older people "answers for life" is less interesting to me than is Tim's voice. He just has a wonderful voice. Burnished. Extremely soft but with profound depth: an almost visible quality of sound shared by a strong, warm breeze. If Tim's voice had a color, it would be bronze. I imagine that voice conveyed the sense of self-possession and deliberate thought that naturally commands authority long before his body, which is very tall and thin, had caught up. Lanky in the way of Lincoln, he bears a face of strong, roughly hewn features that serve an adult, but which no teenager could carry.

"One of our contacts was a Mexican fella, an illegal immigrant by the name of Carlos," he says. "The first time we met him, he was drunk—the typical sob story, being frustrated with life and not knowing where to turn." Tim lost contact with Carlos, but kept asking people about him until he finally found him again in the city. "And he had already on his own just—He was on the job one day, renovating a condemned house, and he says he got to looking around. He says, 'All this dirt. This looks right like my life.' And his testimony is that he saw a little light coming through the window, and he prayed right there and asked God to just come in and change his life. And He did, because when I caught up with him, he was not the same Carlos. He was smiling. He was jubilant. He was reading his Bible."

The cadence of Tim's speech, like his voice, is remarkable. I admire the ways in which some of his words melt into each other and others are stepped apart like stones across a river. But more than the words, I notice the space that hangs between them. These pauses are as frequent as Anthony's pauses but less fraught, more luminous; more like stopping by woods and seeing, between the dense distribution of trees, only clear paths that are all the same path. While others I have spoken to protest loudly about seeing these paths, I believe Tim truly beholds them.

He explains that Carlos moved in with him for a while before Tim helped him move back to Mexico and spent six weeks there, which improved his Spanish greatly; he's returned to visit since.

"We drove all the way down as a family after Ethan was born," Becky adds. "He was five weeks old. We had a lot of fun."

Knowing Tim's pressed for time, I thank him, expect he will return downstairs. But Becky, laughing softly, tells me to ask him one more thing. "The question," she reminds me, "you asked me the first time you were here about how we got to the Bronx? I think you'd like to hear his version of that story." I've spoken with Becky enough to understand that this particular laugh does not signal jocularity; it indicates strong emotion running through like a rip current.

Tim stays. "Our transition here was, I guess you would say, very outside of the box coming from the Mennonite peoples," he starts in. "The experience for most of them is rural Pennsylvania or rural other places. And there are some, I believe, that would take that so far as to believe that's for Biblical reasons. Well, I have to disagree. The only reason they do that is because that's what their grandpa did, that's what their dad did and that's what they're doing. They can't show me otherwise."

A group of young people had started traveling to New York City to pass out tracts, and even though their church was a two-hour drive away, they started holding prayer meetings in the city each month. Tim was approached by the church committee that coordinated these visits because they needed a Spanish translator. Eventually, the prayer meetings became more formal church meetings, held in the apartment where the Witmars currently live.

"Attendance there was anywhere from twenty-five to forty-five. Some mornings it was just totally packed out," Tim says, explaining that families with children drove down as well. I think of that apartment full of white faces, a visiting quorum of their church back home, vastly outnumbering the people they had come to minister to.

The committee eventually decided that the meetings effectively constituted church services without the structure of a church, so it was going to close down the exercise unless it could provide the area with a stable congregation.

"So the question came, 'Who's willing to commit their lives to this work?'" Tim's voice thins out with emotion. No one put their hand up. There was an ordination in train in their Pennsylvania church—a process conducted along biblical lines of nominating potential leaders from the congregation and then casting lots to select among the nominees—and Tim was a candidate. So while they wanted to go to New York, they felt conflicted about leaving. Also, his parents did not support the idea of moving to the city.

"Finally, the morning before that nomination service, I prayed," Tim says. The understanding he reached was that if his name was not ultimately drawn to lead the Pennsylvania congregation, he would take that as a divine call to go to New York. And, yes, in the end another man was chosen.

Tim explains that he had not shared this thinking with his father, who drove him home from church the night another man was selected. Nevertheless, his dad turned to him in the car and said, "You're called to something. I think it's New York."

Tim's eyes well up and his voice breaks on the last words and he pauses here for a very long moment, during which I think of a file my father made for himself when I was not yet sixteen. How he labeled it *Sarah's Writing*, in the beautiful penmanship I have never stopped trying to emulate. What it has meant to me.

Tim clears his throat. Smiles at me. And it becomes clear why Becky preferred to wait for him before answering my question. This is their creation story, the thing that gives them structure and strength, their holy ground.

●

When the Kreiders first moved to New York, they found their neighbors to be kind of standoffish. Normal enough for a big city, they thought. Becky now believes that they've been quietly accepted. "We didn't feel a lot of 'We're Spanish and you're white,'" she says.

Something that surprised the Kreiders about their neighbors was the tenuousness of daily life. "Probably because of the high cost of living, someone will lose their job and just like that they don't have *anything*," was how Becky explained it.

"Whereas if your rent and things weren't as high, you would have a few months of buffer to find a new job. That was a cultural thing that was difficult for us to understand until we moved here—how people can be homeless so fast. But on the other hand there's a lot of homeless shelters so that's at least a small plus," she says with a laugh ascending.

It's staggering in its naivety. Not just about the conditions in many of those shelters but about the long chain that wraps itself around the lives of her neighbors: the consequences of long-standing, structurally embedded educational inequality and employment inequality and housing inequality and health inequality and policing inequality which is the high cost of their lives—but not as she understands it.

Say I hopped in a car right now, outside the Kreiders' place, and drove six miles south into Manhattan. Say I lived on the Upper West Side. I would have a life expectancy of 83.8 years; 74.3 percent of my neighbors would have, at least, a bachelor's degree. Median household income would be $100,746. To the extent that human wellbeing can be measured on a ten-point scale, I would score an 8.61 out of 10 on the Human Development Index.

Now say I lived in Morrisania, the neighborhood where the Kreiders first moved to and where the Witmars live now. My life expectancy plummets to 75.3 years; 10.3 percent of my neighbors have, at least, a bachelor's degree. Median household income is $22,154. On that Human Development Index, I would score 2.88 out of 10.

On the Upper West Side, as in most Manhattan arrondissements, one can buy a thirteen-dollar juice. Residents of the

South Bronx, home to one of the largest produce markets in the world, report the lowest level of fruit and vegetable consumption in the city. Nearly half of the residents live below the federal poverty line. The immediate surrounding area has the highest percentage of incarcerated residents in New York City. The quick subway ride from Manhattan to the Bronx, like the two-hour drive along Interstate 78 from Myerstown to the Bronx, is the distance between sympathy and empathy. Separate planets.

On November 9, 2016, the morning after election day, I visit the Witmar house and then I sit at the Kreider house watching Becky fold laundry.

"If we don't tell them about Jesus, their blood is on our hands," Becky says, talking about her missionary work as she adds a pair of underpants to the gigantic pile at her side. "Everyone is sinful by nature and they will end up in Hell if they don't accept him."

No one brings up the election result. They do not bring up the result because the particular outcome never mattered to them; it being "of the world" and thus merely manifesting the minute ecstasies of triumph and defeat that are transient, distracting and inconsequential: sufficiently small that they don't warrant discussion. I do not bring up the election result because the particular outcome matters very much to me and it confirms my suspicion (long held but, before yesterday, lightly—in the hope for change) that this country, collectively understood, has ceased to care about the common good.

I do not just mean those who actively seek to erode minimum universal standards of education, health care, employment, housing and justice. I also mean those who believed—who actually believed!—that this election could have ended up otherwise in a country where the mass murder of first-graders did nothing to reform gun laws, where people crowdfund their cancer treatments, where adequate parental leave does not reliably exist, where the public schools produce a substantial disparity in basic literacy between Black and white students, where a single mother can work two jobs and earn an income that disqualifies her from public assistance but on which she cannot house herself and her child, and where it is acceptable to jail children of color because they can afford neither bail nor adequate legal representation.

Perhaps it was easier to believe this election could have ended up otherwise if you didn't talk too much about the fact that one kilometer from where you slept, thousands of children lacked medical care. Or that the signs on the subway jubilantly advertising free breakfast programs at school were only ever in Spanish. Or that white faces disappeared entirely after three stops north. Or that seventeen blocks from where you brushed your teeth this morning, things changed abruptly, as if there was a rupture in the space-time continuum through which one stepped, always with prickling fear, into another world where the stores became shittier and then shitty, where gyms disappeared and cafés disappeared and libraries disappeared and vegetables disappeared and people disappeared, to be replaced by payday loan stores and bodegas selling loose cigarettes and cracks in the asphalt of empty playgrounds through which weeds grew long.

So although Becky is at this moment trying to elaborate for my benefit what exactly they mean when they talk about "the homosexual agenda," I am trying to hold in my mind the fact that when one of their members gets cancer, their entire church pulls together to pay those bills. How they use fellowship as a verb. Also, the effect on me of first hearing their choir, when the braiding of voices seemed like a promise of human connectedness. On this morning when I am radiating shame for *actually believing*, I am trying to focus on my work. Though there is a roar in my ears like a plane taking off, I am trying to get closer to the possibility, at least, of a more perfect union.

At my last family worship with the Kreiders, one of the younger boys picks the song. Everyone pairs off. I stand opposite the three-year-old, his tiny hands in mine. He pulls one of my arms towards him and then the other and I reciprocate while everyone sings: *Your work is my work and our work is God's work, When we all pull together, how happy we'll be!*

The theme today is control. Tim asks his children if they think God is big enough to control the future. He looks each of his sons in the face as they answer: "Yes."

"Me too," Tim agrees. "You can't control it, so why worry about it? Okay, what are we gonna pray for?" They decide on Rachel's new cancer treatment. Heads bow, eyes close. I look at Becky's hands, my own, the sky through the glass.

50

THEORIES OF FLIGHT
JAIMIE & ASPASIA

"The UFO Christmas party?" asks the hostess at a bar in central Sydney when I inquire where the function room is. She directs me to the second floor, through the flashing lights of slot machines with names like Moon Race, Fire Idol and Heart Throb, up and into a room where UFOR members sit chatting at circular tables with Christmas-tree centerpieces.

About thirty people have turned up for the Annual Christmas Celebration and Hat Competition. A smaller attendance, Jaimie explains, than is usual at speaking events, and participation in the competition categories (Best Customary Christmas Hat, Most Creative DIY Hat, Best Alien/UFO-themed Hat) has been somewhat perfunctory. Still, everyone appears to be enjoying themselves at the open bar, ducking downstairs occasionally to order a roast from the bistro and making lively conversation. This is now hushed by Jaimie, wearing a black suit, as he takes the mic for a round-up of 2019.

Aspasia, elegant in a black cocktail dress, sits knitting between a friend in a pink Santa hat and a gentleman who has been writing a book on the Pyramids and Pythagorean theory for the last twenty years. The president of UFOR, Maree Baker, is also at the table. Earlier in the year Maree highly recommended I attend a lecture by David Icke, who had not yet been banned from entering the country on character grounds related to his Holocaust denial and his theory that world politics is controlled by a group of alien lizards that includes, but is not limited to, Jewish people. "I know David personally," she wrote, "and can vouch for his integrity." Standing in front of a projector screen showing a flying saucer and the message *Merry Christmas from Out of This World*, Jaimie reports that UFO sighting reports have been up this year.

He checks to see how everyone's been coping with the smoke that's settled over the city since the bushfires started, then takes a quick poll to gauge interest in holding a sky-watch session soon. The screen then moves into a slide showing richly illustrated covers of *Fate Magazine* from the 1940s, while Jaimie lectures—more engagingly than I've ever watched anyone lecture on anything—on the portrayal of UFOs in mid- to late-twentieth-century pop culture.

Soon I am on a plane back to Melbourne, ascending for too long through a yellow-tinged haze over a country that is burning while I read about an upcoming meeting of world leaders in Madrid for their annual bargaining session over how to avert a climate catastrophe.

"As if to underscore the gap between reality and diplomacy," Somini Sengupta reports, "the international climate negotiations, scheduled to begin next week, are not even designed to ramp up pledges by world leaders to cut their countries" emissions. That deadline is still a year away . . ."

We rise above the cloud line into the bright upper air where the view is limitless. Sublime. The sky as abstraction of itself, in blue and white halves, through which a hundred people are hurtling in a metal cylinder, drinking cups of coffee. It is a view which was inconceivable for almost all of human history and which no one is currently looking at, preferring instead to play Candy Crush or revise a social media post infinity times or listen to what is in their headphones while staring at the tired fabric of the seat in front of them.

Back in Sydney, the reindeer antlers and the jingle-bell earrings will come off. Everyone will return to work and family, the smoke suffusing the city as the days slip towards a pandemic that will empty the streets, turn us into ghosts of ourselves, stunned and navigating a new reality in which the old knowledge (that we are each other's biggest threats and only saviors) shocks us like an earthquake, out of the blue and all at once.

The last UFOR gathering for 2019 now over, they will return to feeling comfortable speaking about what they saw or what they feel they must have seen only in select company, in true meetings. While I have loved speaking to most of them, I cannot say that we inhabit a mutually recognizable world. But I can say that if you are a searching misfit, not quite at home where we've ended up and imbued with a capacity for attentive wonder that has been ill-served too many times by what your radar returned—that you are, truly, not alone.

CODA

HERE

51

THE DEATH DOULA
KATRINA & ANNIE

Katrina said she didn't care what happened, funeral-wise, after she was gone. Still, I think she would have loved it here by the bay, her last room, where the walls are clean white frames, water moving at their center.

Annie greets Peter and sits down. She is almost fully recovered from her pneumonia. Ten days of lying low, struggling silently with tight-chested exhaustion to keep up with Lady's diapers and clean up after Missy. Khedup, who doesn't do dog poo, didn't know she was sick; didn't think too much about her car unmoving in their driveway.

Katrina's brother announces to the small group gathered that an accident on the freeway has held up a relative, we'll wait for another fifteen minutes. So staff from the café across the hall come in to take orders for tea or coffee. Katrina—lying on a blanket of lambswool inside a curvaceous birchwood coffin—would have been pleased with this, and how Peter remembered to put in the email a reminder to bring a coin or two for the parking meters outside.

I think also that Katrina would have loved Annie's red lipstick, but Annie's not so sure, asking me to let her know if it transfers to a tooth. She's been busy keeping an eye on her elderly uncle's medical care and pain management, taking Lady and her wheelchair to charity events, registering for a two-day training session on caring for a deceased baby, reading (*Smile or Die: How Positive Thinking Fooled America and the World* by Barbara Ehrenreich); studying (*How to Enjoy Death: Preparing to Meet Life's Final Challenge without Fear* by Lama Zopa Rinpoche); attending a roundtable on spiritual care in multi-faith contexts, and taking fifteen-year-old Missy to an increasing number of vet appointments where she expects soon to be told that the end has come. It never gets easier to hear, she says, squaring her jaw and looking ahead towards the coffin in a way that outlines her elegant profile against the rain-flecked square of sky and sea. She has long untethered her sense of self from her appearance but it has to be said, Annie is beautiful and to look at her in profile is to be reminded of both Renaissance portraiture and the huge-blue-eyed blondness of *Vogue* in the sixties.

Katrina's brother steps up to the lectern. After the Acknowledgment of Country, he explains how we are in a beautiful spot where blue pools once extended down to Seaford: loved by the original custodians of the land for over sixty thousand years. We will have a moment of reflection, he says, in a manner that is both authoritative and nourishing.

Then family photos are projected onto the screens at either side of the lectern. Katrina's music weaves around us. I look at Lachlan in the front row between his older brothers and his mates in their school uniforms. Sixteen. I remember Katrina at the hospice, double-checking with the kitchen that the chips she ordered to surprise him would definitely be ready when he visited after school and I feel the drop of sorrow straight through me like an elevator plummeting.

The next speaker, directing her voice towards the boys, is saying that they will hear Katrina's words inwardly guiding them when they face life's future challenges. Outside, sea birds swoop in a low line over waves and for a single moment the horizon connects their wings like blue thread.

"The eye is the first circle," Ralph Waldo Emerson wrote, "the horizon it forms the second; and throughout nature this primary figure is repeated without end."

Peter stands. Speaks to the guests, to his wife in her casket. I am looping on Katrina, the set of her gaze, her love for her family, her vast equity, how what rankles continues to rankle even when our time is running out because there is no off switch, there is only a great gathering up of all one's pains as one insists on racing ahead anyway. I am looping on her anticipated joy at seeing her Lachie's hands wrapped around a paper cup of French fries, five minutes with Pete in a hot tub, one sip of wine, music always on, the warmth of the sun, the taste of one speck of banana warmed in a pan of syrup. I am looping on the great success that is being loved, and the greater success that is being able to, truly, love.

I am looping on one warm night sitting in the yard with my husband under a salting of stars so thick it reminded me we are floating in space. Us, our child asleep, everything. The perfect joy of it. Then the sudden absurd thought that it will all end. *But we're someone's parents now!*

"Our life is an apprenticeship to the truth that around every circle another can be drawn," Emerson wrote, "that there is no end in nature, but every end is a beginning; that there is always another dawn risen on mid-noon, and under every deep a lower deep opens."

I am looping on Katrina telling me her friend would be sewing her wedding dress into a christening gown so it could be worn some day by any future grandchildren, how this delighted her and shattered her in a way that showed, as clear as a diagram, that our thoughts do not need to blindly follow our longings but that they can be separate wisdoms.

This is what Emerson meant when he referred to the moral fact of the Unattainable, "the flying Perfect, around which the hands of man can never meet." There are no fixtures in nature, he wrote, the universe is fluid and volatile.

I still haven't figured out how we'll go on, Peter is saying, but go on we must and we will.

Soon, he and his four sons will take Katrina's ashes onto a boat, rising and falling. They will launch it from the beach at the end of Dalgetty Road where she played as a child, lay as a teenager with her chin towards the sun. On boards on waves, they will stand pouring her into that water, connected in their grief as by a thread.

But right now, they are feeling the physical fact of their wife and their mother for the last time, threading their fingers through the arched handles of her coffin. They are taking her into their arms into the rain. They are lifting her into the body of a hearse that will drive slowly away as they walk behind it, the road on one side, the deep water on the other.

Being in that room with Katrina was a great teacher. First, one second taught me more about Annie's work—what it takes to be able to do it—than I learned in two years of intimate, on-going conversation with her about how death is a part of life. Second, it taught me something about love.

"Love? What is love?" Annie had asked me to elaborate the first time I used the word casually in conversation. And although I knew it, each attempt to concretize it failed. One second in that room where Katrina was still at home, Peter tending to her between greeting loved ones with an apology about his stubble and giving a quick fix to the oven fan with his screwdriver, his damp hanky in his jeans pocket all the while, pointed at the answer. Love is not reactively pushing away the parts of the picture that don't serve our idealized image; love is truly seeing and truly staying.

And I think that Annie knows this—more than that, I think she embodies it—but I also think that she might need, like any of us, to receive more of it. *I used to think, "Ah, love . . ." I really wanted to have love in my life and I realized that it's so conditional. So, yeah. That was a good teacher.*

A year later I will miss a call from Peter because I have just given birth during a pandemic. When I speak to him I tell him I have been thinking of Katrina a lot lately, speaking with her in my mind.

"Katrina was extremely good at pushing you into places you weren't comfortable with," he replies proudly through his still-thick grief. "And you'd come out saying, 'That wasn't so bad.'"

When I left Katrina's house for the last time, I sent Annie the photo I had taken for her. *Katrina looks wonderful,* she wrote back. *It was clearly a good death because her face is relaxed and not distorted. Perhaps the discomfort you felt was due to the fact that Katrina's eyes are still open.*

52

HALFWAY HOME
LYNN

Lynn is laughing with Sister Ann, an Episcopal nun a few years her senior who is wearing a wooden cross the size of an iPhone around her neck. They are joined by another parishioner who hands the sister a bundle of the *New York Times* sports sections because she is crazy about baseball, barracking beatifically for both the Boston Red Sox and the New York Yankees, traditional rivals. Lynn, now a member of Trinity, is a regular. Will be chalice bearer on Christmas Eve. Attended both the nine o'clock and eleven-fifteen services this morning.

The Christmas decorations are up. Nearly a year has passed since we sat in the lecture on Dr. King's "Letter from Birmingham Jail." It's been a difficult one. Her boss is sick, cancer. Had to cut back his practice, is very reluctantly letting her go. She's philosophical about it, though worried about her income, her lack of savings. She's been sending out feelers to try to find something, isn't limiting herself to legal work given her teaching degree and experience in domestic-violence counseling. Plus, she's bilingual. "However," she says, "I'm seventy-one and disabled and I have a felony conviction. All of which are negatives."

Sitting in the uncertainty, she's used her extra time to be-come more active at Trinity, volunteering at reentry workshops to help formerly incarcerated women, helping pack lunches for those in need, though she is living in a shelter. That's what she's about to do now as she makes her way across the chapel to the card tables set up in a side aisle and spends half an hour joking and chatting with other volunteers while placing boxes of juice and cans of tuna efficiently into brown paper bags for the homeless men and women who will soon stop by to pick them up.

Afterwards, we share her umbrella on the way to a café where "Silent Night" plays while she scans the vegetarian op-tions. We have the place to ourselves. I ask Lynn about her faith, her belief in a just God.

"How did I not say, 'God, if you're supposed to be all good, why are you doing this to me?'" she clarifies. Which is, of course, what I mean.

"I guess there's an element of, 'If not me, who?'" she says. "And I did what I did. And God wasn't happy with that. I mean, clearly it wasn't an action that sat well with God. I had other options—whether they looked viable at the time or not . . ." She pauses. "Some of them didn't. I had no recourse. Like, I could call the cops and they'd do something? No. That wasn't true." She rests her fork next to her salad.

"What it distills into is the fact that pain is part of life. Do you choose to suffer or do you choose to say, 'We all have pain, we all can get through this'? If we are together, it hurts less. It's whether you turn away or turn to. I think everybody has to make that decision.

"I'm not going to tell anybody they have to do this way. Because nobody could tell me that when I was being beaten, so I don't try to tell others that now. It's something I do for me. And if they decide to condemn me for what I do, who am I to take that away from them?"

•

To get to the front door of the shelter, you leave the sidewalk and walk down three stairs to a small courtyard, rubbish bins and the occasional rat to your left, and then down three more steps into a small vestibule where someone recently took a shit. In the front door is a small glass window and I can see Lynn sitting at the reception desk, squinting into a computer screen through her glasses before she looks up and smiles and buzzes me in.

After losing her paralegal position, Lynn was hired as a resident aide by the halfway house where she arrived two years ago seeking shelter. It is July, and she has been in this new role for three months. At the start of the year she moved to a studio apartment at the Brooklyn YWCA, where she has her own door, her own fridge and a table at which to sit and write or make her quilted collages. The move meant a change in parole officers but the new one is more flexible around her work schedule, which changes when she takes on extra shifts. She has joined a writing group, a theater group; has made new friends, has been asked to display her collages in an exhibition. She works doubles and nights at the shelter most weeks, taking the subway there and back.

The director has changed, the resident aides have changed, the case managers have changed. Many of the residents have changed, though some still remain from when she was living here not so long ago. While she has a softer spot for some more than others, she says it and means it: *I am them. There is no me and them. It's us.*

Lately she has been thinking about her upcoming performance with The Theater of the Oppressed, how magnificent it felt to march with the leadership of Trinity Church in New York City's Pride March, one of the youngest residents' recent heroin relapse following the death of her father, the bedbugs that are being exterminated in one of the rooms upstairs, which of her prison collages to include in an upcoming show, and remedying, once and for all, the issue of the shelter's front door that doesn't reliably close, which is now urgent given the open secret that Federal Immigrations and Customs Enforcement agents plan to raid homeless shelters in the city and there are undocumented immigrants living here.

"No one's getting in without a warrant," she says, making a call to the maintenance man. He materializes a few minutes later and stands in the doorway, working swiftly with his screwdriver. When the door shuts with a clean *click*, they hug in shared triumph. Two hours later, ICE agents without warrants will attempt, and fail, to raid a homeless shelter in Brooklyn.

Arranging maintenance is one of her many duties, official and otherwise. She logs exits and entries, inspects bags for drugs, weapons, alcohol. She liaises with the Department of Housing each night to report the final count of beds full and empty. She signs for mail, hands out packages, answers the phone, restocks toilet paper, napkins, dry packets of oatmeal; she makes small talk, hears good news, offers consolation and advice. At night, she does the rounds on each of the shelter's four floors making sure all is well. Mounts the stairs slowly, like when she too slept in those beds, so close their occupants could hold hands.

Weekend nights can be eventful if a resident returns drunk or high or late and after count, forfeiting their bed in a legal process that will then require them to return to central processing for reallocation. Other nights are quiet. Previous resident aides have told me that in those still hours, alone at the reception desk in the two-hundred-year-old building, they've seen the ghosts of previous occupants ascending and descending the stairs, seen faces from a different time in the square of glass in the front door. Tonight we keep looking up at that window with a different fear; but no ICE agents show up and the time moves slowly, Lynn clicking at the computer and chatting with each of the women as they come and go.

I spend six months in this building without realizing I am sitting a few houses away from where my great-grandfather first lived when he arrived in the city. His first New York, when he was young and his family in Poland had not yet been murdered at Belzec, a concentration camp so prodigiously efficient in mass murder that only two Jews, out of approximately six hundred thousand, survived. I wonder what he said about the letters that suddenly stopped arriving from the aunties and the cousins around the time of my grandfather's bar mitzvah. Or whether he stayed silent about the people and the place that had been his home, now gone. And what my grandfather, entering adolescence, made of all that. I research for a living, but there is only so much information I can find using first names and surnames, only so much that can be inferred from patterns and silence.

My great-grandfather's apartment is still around the corner. The kosher bakery I pass each day was open then, and is open now. I have his mother's face, which is also my mother's face. Though all of them are strangers to me, this is how close the remote past is: we live inside it. The light is the same; would have hit just like this, I think each time I exit into the early evening and choose my way home.

Lynn's been crafting. She shows me photos on her phone of what she's been working on lately. Jewelery and snow globes, sweaters and blankets of all sizes. My favorite, however, are her fabric collages. In them, ducks fly into the clear sky above Lake Champlain, cat's tails bowing in the wind. Two hands reach for all that lies beyond a barred window. An owl perches on a branch before a full silver moon. A living room is silent at night, stars filling the navy blue square at the center of parted lace curtains, flowers in a vase, cat on a rug, a fire burning below a mantelpiece on which a real photo of her son sits in a frame. "This is the living room of my longing," Lynn says.

"Can I get my metro card?" a young woman asks, dressed for work on the night shift somewhere. Due to an administrative error no cards are available, so Lynn leaves another resident aide in charge of the desk, grabs her handbag and her purple cane and walks out into the night to buy one from the closest subway station, using her own money.

I walk with her down to Astor Place, where we stand waiting for the lights to change at an intersection in the heat still radiating from the sleek surfaces of the tall buildings I think of as new. I tell her that this was my first New York. How at eighteen I would walk alone and unfindable in the geometry of that place which is both here and not here.

She chuckles, her own first New York, down on Christopher Street, not so far away. And suddenly, I—who was born the same year as Lynn's son—wonder if she and I might appear to passersby as mother and daughter. For one warm and silent moment, I try it on: how the world might feel.

"You know," she says in her teacher's voice, scanning the older buildings around us, "used to be you could only build up five stories around here. They added those other stories later. If you look closely, you can see where that happened. All of them have a stop line before they kept going."

In two months, Covid will hit New York City like a meteorite, cratering the shelters and lower-income neighborhoods where too many of the residents packed densely together will have no place to go but the refrigerated interiors of mobile morgues. Soon after, Black Lives Matter protests will fill the city, looters taking advantage of that necessary moment to smash the storefronts across from the halfway house, those around the subway station. The drugstores, the diner, the kosher bakery. Lynn will write to me that it looks like a war zone. That she is attending online church services but misses being with her Trinity family. She will continue to work long shifts, has no choice. Leaves late, and those are the times that she worries. "The protests remind me of the ones I participated in during the 1960s," she will write. "I don't remember them being as violent. Maybe that's because I was a lot younger then."

All that is in the future, though, and for now Lynn is invigorated by her work, doesn't mind leaving late. She accepts all work she is offered at the shelter, unless it conflicts with her Sunday services, which means she has been keeping a large bottle of Diet Coke in the staff fridge to power her through her twenty-four-hour shifts and the late shifts that end at midnight, after which she zips up her coat, shoulders her bag, and walks up to the sidewalk and down towards the subway.

She rarely feels unsafe; it's the East Village, full of life, eyes on the street. There are always taxis and cars, blinding white lights in bodegas and glowing yellow lights in apartments where she goes in and drops her key neatly in a bowl next to a vase of flowers, where she kicks off her shoes and puts on the kettle and resumes her knitting in a chair that has worn tonsures in the floor, so long has she returned to this spot beneath a mantelpiece populated with framed photos of her smiling with her son and daughter-in-law, their child in her hands.

She will get up to pour her tea and place it by her bed where it will cool while she washes her face in her bathroom and then pulls up her quilt, looking through her lace curtain out the window which is always open a little to let the world stream in. The homes of her longing, none of them hers as she grips the railing down into the station to catch the 1:00 AM train back to the YWCA.

53

THE KINGDOM OF HEAVEN
THE CHOIR

They are caroling down in a hole in the ground, the subway station where I first saw them, except now the weather has turned freezing and the floor is puddled with meltwater. Today they are many. Representatives of the mission families have been augmented by a large group of "the youth" from Pennsylvania as well as a few friends from the Susquehanna Conference with whom they fellowship. A very young man wearing formal pants and a black parka is conducting. Keeping tempo, really: arcing his flat palm from side to side as though petting an imaginary pony.

There is "Joy to the World," "Away in a Manger," "Gloria in Excelsis." There is breath straining for the note which, once found, stays true—unlike words, which are feathers, hollow at their core and liable to shed with time or a change in the wind. As always their voices together are wondrous, and I'm struck by a memory that I wouldn't have thought worth remembering, of being ten, eleven and watching TV alone in the living room. On the screen is a children's program . . . *Sesame Street*, I believe. A time-lapse video of a flower opening set to Pachelbel's *Canon in D*. I am weeping, something inside me that I do not understand and cannot name surging, expanding. And then my mother walks into the room and I hide the fact that I've been crying, somehow embarrassed.

We have feelings for the same reason we have teeth: they support our survival. The neuroscientist Antonio Damasio explains that when we have to make a decision, our brain's emotional center prioritizes considerations for us. Self-awareness—knowing not just what we are feeling but *why* we are feeling it—is crucial for decision-making. The "why" is vital because, just as we cannot always believe what we think, we cannot always trust what we feel in the sense that our knee-jerk reactions—those that extravagantly shout their anger or fear—are warped by our earlier experiences of pain. We damage ourselves and others by trusting these too-loud feelings, these easy and awful repetitive reactions that reduce the world to a dark mirror in which we cannot see our own reflection.

Daniel Goleman, I want to call him a science writer but he is more than this, explains that "the wisdom of the emotions" is a phrase that refers to something that goes on at our depths, the base of our brain. "Our life wisdom on any topic is stored in the basal ganglia," he says. "The basal ganglia is so primitive that it has *zero* connectivity to the verbal cortex. It can't tell us what it knows in words. It tells us in feelings." These gut feelings are the key not only to our ability to make effective decisions but to the moral quality of those decisions. The answer to the question of whether we are about to do the right thing does not come to us verbally, it comes to us through our nonverbal neural system. So the feedback system that keeps us alive is also a "moral rudder"; what keeps us coherent as individuals binds us together as a community. In order to bridge the distance between us, we must get closer, first of all, with ourselves. Truly see and truly stay.

There is a roar inside when we confront the intractabilities of being one among many on shifting ground where we are forced to do all our living and dying. It is an energy that cannot be decanted into the simple stories of anger or fear or blame; it refuses to be purified through the strainer of logic. It can only be felt, ridden like a wave or the wind until it passes, before rising again. Paradise, it turns out, might not be the total library; might just be the water, the air, one bright room in a dark house. More mundane than we could have believed, and there all along.

I chat with a teenage girl wearing glasses, a white puffy coat over her long dress. She speaks softly, seems younger than she is. Her mother is Rachel, the subject of so many prayers. She returns to the choir, twenty-six people now, most of whom will leave the city tonight.

"I think God knows whose shoulder to tap on," Becky once explained about the often-stretched resources of their small community. "We've never been hungry and we never were homeless. But we didn't always know where it was coming from before it came. That's part of the excitement of a missionary journey. God doesn't do miracles for people who don't need them."

While it would make more financial sense for the families of the Light of Truth Mennonite Church to return to Myerstown, economic efficiency is, of course, not the point.

They are here to minister to those who they believe are in need of what their church can offer. But it might not be entirely accurate to call that outward-facing ministry the point of the mission. Perhaps they are ministering to themselves—these people who express their concept of a life well lived using the language of struggle. *It's very easy to just be comfortable in your life path . . . The Christian life isn't just a bed of roses . . .*

And this particular concept of struggle places great emphasis on high helplessness as the ultimate act of faith. *Trust and obey. We never worry about anything because everything is in Your control.*

I can see how the worldview of a lightly educated adult— one who has been taught from birth to see the hand of God in all things from the healing of an injured finger to the death by stoning of a thief's family—may only ever have been a helpless worldview. And I can see, too, how this helplessness, this yielding of agency to an ever-intervening, only-good God, may feel as if it were a type of prayer. And sure, it's hard to walk away from the opportunities for security that society has opened to you. But it is infinitely harder to walk away from opportunities you have had to fight for: opportunities deliberately withheld from communities of color as they have not been withheld from the residents of Myerstown, Pennsylvania.

So, the residents of the South Bronx might regard helplessness in a very different way. They might not feel, now or ever, the holy wisdom of disregarding the education system or the electoral process or medical insurance or housing courts. So it is probable that membership in the Light of Truth Church will remain extremely low and I admit, given their hateful stance

on differences from the religious to the sexual, this feels to me
to be for the best.

"Is there anyone who hasn't handed out tracts that wants
to?" Anthony calls out, scanning the choir. Rachel, who has
been resting in her van, is helped down the stairs. She sits with
the choir in a camping chair, her pale face as white as the hood
through which it peers as she sings along softly. More friends
arrive. The choir swells. One of the new arrivals, a young
blond woman singing "Gloria in Excelsis Deo" in the front
row, smiles at me through the commuters streaming between
us. And I smile back because, though I know now that these
smiles function like a foot in the door, smiling back is mostly
what one does. She walks over with some eagerness.

Though they have internal lives as unique as their finger-
prints, these young blond women are mostly the same young
blond woman. They wear the same type of dress made out of
the same type of material, they have the same immaculate net-
ted veil, the same sturdy sneakers and the same white puffy
coats, but I am referring to the fact that they have the same
look in their eyes when they speak to me. There is something in
the wattage of the smile and the tensing of the features around
it that makes their faces appear mask-like. Part of that something must be the twinge of discomfort anyone would feel in
approaching a stranger in this, the strangest of cities, but the
other part looks like a strain of discomfort close to desperation.

That desperation may be about the state of my unsaved
soul. But it may also have something to do with the pressure
of a constricted world where extemporization is allowed only
within the song that has been chosen for them. This cannot be

each of the young women's first choice about how she would ideally distribute her time and energies but, having considered her options, it may very well be her best choice.

Smiling down into my face with incredible velocity, the young woman asks me how I am and I reply that I am well and return the question. She too is well. And then there is the type of silence which, professionally, I should let hang but that's not who I am and so I tear a hole in it.

"Cold today," I comment.

And her features remain static as she seizes upon the teachable moment to tell me cheerily that Jesus endured discomfort for our sake and so the least we can do is endure some for his. I wave back at Marie from the Kreiders' place, who has just joined the choir, and the young woman is confused: does not know where to place me. When I explain that I am a writer who has been spending time with the mission families, her features rearrange themselves and I can see her actual face. She says it's been nice talking but she better get back to the choir.

It strikes me that, in our time together, I have never seen that mask on Loisann or on Becky. They look at me with something that feels less aggressive, but also less hopeful; more akin to resignation or forbearance. There's judgment there, too, but who am I, who finds them so exotic, to fault them for that? It is true that Loisann and Becky have more children than the hard-smiling young women, and maybe that has something to do with their stark prioritization of energy and emotion. Also, they've been in the city longer than the hard-smilers. Maybe they've internalized a perceptual shorthand for my masculine shirt and my career that tells them I'm a lost cause: that if they try to persuade me "to come to reality," much learned noise will spew forth from my mouth for no gain whatsoever. So while they let me into their homes and make time that they do not have to walk me through the "Mennonite maze," while all our hours together have been pleasant, while I would genuinely love to giggle and gab with Loisann and seek Becky's earnest good counsel, I know that the look on their faces is a door to which I will never use the key. There's nothing more that can be done. And this causes me more sadness than perhaps it should.

The choir launches into "Gloria" for a third time, and it is slightly less entrancing by this stage. At regular intervals, when a train has pulled in or is about to depart, a current of people swells and surges around the singers. Their bodies are tense and hurried. Mostly they avoid taking the tracts offered, which is unremarkable in this city where an offer reliably provokes a reflexive refusal. What is noteworthy is that in every rush there is always someone who willingly accepts, someone who slows to look again.

A young man in a leather jacket covered in bright patches stops on the stairs down to the 4 train and watches the choir for a moment, his hand on the rail. "They Jewish?" he asks me. Mennonite. Like Amish, but not. He nods and stands listening for a moment, his head at an angle. Then is gone.

It's been three decades, but Pachelbel's Canon has never lost its power over me. That song that starts like a heartbeat, ends by coming to rest as though buried in a blanket, and contains in between all the devastating tenderness that feeds a life. My favorite version was played by Wynton Marsalis when he was not yet out of his twenties. His sound is so simple and magisterial—so his own—that it is obvious not that he is headed for greatness, but that he has already arrived. I am talking, especially, about a single note he hits and holds right at the end. You can find it, please, I will wait. *Baroque Music for Trumpets* is the album. "Canon for Three Trumpets and Strings" by Johann Pachelbel—Wynton Marsalis, English Chamber Orchestra and Raymond Leppard. This particular note starts at 5:49. It is, literally, a clarion call and it reaches out, searching, insistently unattenuated and a beat too long as if to say: *Though unanswered, I will go on asking for as long as breath can hold.*

The choir is now thirty-five people strong. Crisply ironed men and boys standing behind a long line of women and girls whose skirts are sheeting down in flags of floral and gingham. And though this tableau is supremely awkward, it is impossible not to be moved by the sound it is making, which is also its message: *Your voice would fit perfectly here.*

The noise of the trains drowns out the choir completely but they do not stop singing, vocal cords silently straining against the walls of noise closing in on them. Beautiful in their insistence and their refusals, down in this damp crossroads, biding their time between kingdoms. Then the trains are gone and the dirty tiles are once again bouncing back the words being sung: *Whatever my lot, you have taught me to say, it is well, it is well with my soul.*

Six different stories, six different notes in the human song of longing for the unattainable. The years I spent writing this book showed me that in order to truly live—with ourselves and with each other—something has to die. Stage models of grief are not new; they were proposed by clinicians back in the 1940s, they are found in the mourning rituals of the world's oldest religions. Kübler-Ross's model is, perhaps, the best known. Five stages: denial, anger, bargaining, depression and acceptance. She originally applied these stages to those suffering from terminal illness, but found they were equally relevant to all deep personal losses: our loved ones, our relationships, our homes; our dreams and expectations and certainties. The stages are not linear, not discrete. Like cyclones, they collide. Like tides, they return. And acceptance is not the euphoric relief one finds on waking from a nightmare, but rather the solidity that comes from embracing the reality that there is much more to the world than wind and wave.

Grief is as individual as it is universal. In our efforts to avoid it, we fabricate bespoke delusions, tailor the terms of our personal negotiations with the intractable. But while we find ourselves washed up on shores so different they could be their own planets, the ground beneath our feet is always the same. I believe we are united in the emotions that drive us into the beliefs that separate us.

Later Becky will tell me she gave birth to her seventh child, a baby girl. I will learn on Facebook that Rachel has died of cancer. I will look at a photo of her with Eldon and their children, at the inscrutable set of her face and how, like me, she had the habit of clutching her thumbs in her fists like a bird on a perch.

A few times, when I am caught at the turnstile, the roar of the train pulling away from the platform beneath me, I will feel I can almost hear them singing. And when a plane flies low, I will think of Anthony looking up. Loisann's students releasing a cloud of balloons into the sky; how they disperse, float away. I will think of the Kreiders driving on that long road pouring down into Mexico, two babies who could grow to be anyone dozing in sunlight. The sisters in prison. Ethan's finger. The unreached. The bad spooks. The great teachers. The long-missing, the never-found. This brief phase. I will be orbiting, and you will be orbiting on top of me. I will think about distance, and how it might all be the work of the devil.

SELECT BIBLIOGRAPHY

PROLOGUE

On the definition of psychological distance see Sergiu Baltatescu, 'Psychological Distance', *Encyclopaedia of Quality of Life and Well-Being Research* (2014), ed. Alex C. Michalos; Yaakov Trope and Nira Liberman, 'Construal-level theory of psychological distance', *Psychological Review* (2010) 117(2), 440.

See C. G. Jung, *Aion: Researches into the Phenomenology of the Self* (1968).

PART 1

CHAPTER 8 IN THE BEGINNING: GEORGIA

... *whose inner coherence defies all factual evidence*, see Finn Bowring, 'Hannah Arendt and the hierarchy of human activity', *Times Literary Supplement*. See also Finn Bowring, *Hannah Arendt: A Critical Introduction* (2011).

Hannah Arendt, *Eichmann in Jerusalem: A Report of the Banality of Evil*, revised and enlarged edition (1977).

Hannah Arendt, 'Thinking and Moral Considerations: a Lecture', *Social Research* 38 (1971).

James Baldwin, 'Letter from a Region in my Mind', *New Yorker* (November 10, 1962).

Donna M. Webster and Arie W. Kruglanski, 'Individual differences in need for cognitive closure', *Journal of Personality and Social Psychology* (2014) 67(6), 1049.

CHAPTER 10 THE DEATH DOULA: ANNIE
Milan Kundera, *The Unbearable Lightness of Being* (1984).

CHAPTER 13 THE DEATH DOULA: ANNIE
Adam Gopnik, 'Writing Nature: Charles Darwin, natural novelist', *New Yorker* (October 16, 2006).

CHAPTER 14 IN THE BEGINNING: ANDREW
Geoff Manaugh, 'We thought we lived on solid ground. California's earthquakes changed that', *New York Times* (July 8, 2019).

Yaakov Trope and Nira Liberman, 'Construal-level theory of psychological distance', *Psychological Review* (2010) 117(2), 440.

CHAPTER 16 THE DEATH DOULA: ANNIE & KATRINA
Martin Buber, *I and Thou* (1923).

Maurice Friedman, *Encounter on the Narrow Ridge: A Life of Martin Buber* (1991).

W. H. Auden, 'The Hard Question' (1933).

CHAPTER 18 THE DEATH DOULA: ANNIE & KATRINA
On 'excruciating vulnerability' see Brené Brown, The Power of Vulnerability, TEDxHouston (2010).

CHAPTER 19 IN THE BEGINNING: TIM

Maria Popova, 'The Life of the Mind: Hannah Arendt on Thinking vs Knowing and the Crucial Difference between Truth and Meaning', Brainpickings.org (2014).

Hannah Arendt, *The Life of the Mind*, vol. I (1978).

CHAPTER 20 PARANORMAL: VLAD

Haruki Murakami, *The Elephant Vanishes* (1993).

David Antin, *Radical Coherency* (1981).

Jennifer A. Whitson and Adam D. Galinsky, 'Lacking Control Increases Illusory Pattern Perception', *Science* (2008) 322, 115.

CHAPTER 21 THE DEATH DOULA: KATRINA

Andrew B. Newberg, Nancy A. Wintering, Donna Morgan and Mark R. Waldman, 'The measurement of regional cerebral blood flow during glossolalia: A preliminary SPECT study', *Psychiatry Research: Neuroimaging* (2006) 148(1), 67.

CHAPTER 22 IN THE BEGINNING: GEORGIA

Julia Kristeva, *Interpreting Radical Evil* (2016).

Joseph Brodsky, *To Urania: Selected Poems, 1965–1988* (1992).

PART 2

CHAPTER 27 THEORIES OF FLIGHT: FRED & RHONDA

Muriel Rukeyser, *Theory of Flight* (1935).

The Valentich investigation file is accessible through the National Archives: VH-DSJ—Cape Otway to King Island 21 October 1978—Aircraft Missing [Valentich].

Two excellent audio documentaries on the disappearance of Frederick Valentich are: Tony Barrell, 'Pilot Frederick Valentich Disappears over Bass Strait', ABC Radio National (2011) and Patrick Stokes, 'Last Light: the Valentich Mystery', ABC Radio National (2019).

CHAPTER 30 HALFWAY HOME: LYNN
'The "robust scepticism that we can know anything or believe anything in these cases" . . .' and 'the impression of even odds . . .' see Kimberly Kessler Ferzan, '#BelieveWomen and the Presumption of Innocence: Clarifying the Questions for Law and Life', *University of Virginia School of Law Public Law And Legal Theory Paper Series* (May 2020). See also Lois Shephard, 'The Danger of the "He said, She said" Expression', *The Hill* (October 12, 2018).

CHAPTER 32 THEORIES OF FLIGHT: FRED & RHONDA
James McGaha and Joe Nickell, 'The Valentich Disappearance: Another UFO Cold Case Solved', *Skeptical Inquirer* 37(6) (2013).

CHAPTER 33 HALFWAY HOME: LYNN
Martin Luther King Jr, 'Letter from Birmingham Jail' (1963).

CHAPTER 34 THEORIES OF FLIGHT: WESTALL
Westall '66: A Suburban UFO Mystery, dir. Rosie Jones (2010).

'UFO Sighting', *Coonabarabran Times* (November 17, 1994).

CHAPTER 36 THE KINGDOM OF HEAVEN
James Baldwin, 'Letter from a Region in my Mind', *New Yorker* (November 10, 1962).

Richard Feynman, 'The Relation of Physics to Other Sciences', *The Feynman Lectures* (1963).

CHAPTER 38 HALFWAY HOME: LYNN

For the concept of refusing to give anyone else the responsibility for your life, I am indebted to Mary Oliver's essay, 'Staying Alive'. See Mary Oliver, *Upstream: Collected Essays* (2016).

CHAPTER 39 THEORIES OF FLIGHT: DON & COLIN

See Keith Basterfield, Project HIBAL—the answer to Westall?—files destroyed (20 April 2014) ufos-scientificresearch.blogspot.com and Westall—document located which shows there was a HIBAL launch on April 5, 1966 (October 5, 2017), ufos-scientificresearch.blogspot.com

'Giant helium balloon bursts over Mildura', *Age* (April 17, 1962).

CHAPTER 41 THEORIES OF FLIGHT: BEN

Alice Gorman, 'Beyond the morning star: the real tale of the Voyagers' Aboriginal music', *The Conversation* (October 3, 2013).

Martin Rees, *Our Cosmic Habitat* (2001).

Stephen Grossberg, 'Towards solving the hard problem of consciousness: the varieties of brain resonances and the conscious experiences that they support', *Neural Networks* (2017) 87, 38.

Daniel C. Dennett, 'Facing up to the hard question of consciousness', *Philosophical Transactions of the Royal Society* (2018) 373(1755).

Tracy K. Smith, 'My God, It's Full of Stars', *Life on Mars* (2011).

CHAPTER 44 THE KINGDOM OF HEAVEN: BECKY & TIM
For Youtube videos showing examples of Mennonite singing, search: 'We are Not Alone' by Pepper Choplin at Sandy Ridge Mennonite. 'Perfectly Broken' sung by Cedar Springs Amish Mennonite Youth Choir of the Richland Mennonite Church sing hymns in the New York subway system.

Hannah Senesh: Her Life and Diary (2007).

CHAPTER 46 THEORIES OF FLIGHT: JAIMIE & ASPASIA
Alvin Toffler, *Future Shock* (1970).

CHAPTER 47 THE KINGDOM OF HEAVEN: PRAYER MEETING
Tzvi Freeman, Who came up with Tikkun Olam?: Don't surrender. Don't escape. Fix the world, Chabad.org.

Vivian Gornick, *Odd Woman and The City* (2015).

CHAPTER 48 THEORIES OF FLIGHT: JAIMIE & ASPASIA
Jorge Luis Borges, 'Poema de los Dones' (Poem of the Gifts), *El Hacedor* (The Maker) (1960).

Jorge Luis Borges, *The Total Library* (1939).

Jorge Luis Borges, *The Library of Babel* (1941).

Marshall McLuhan, *Understanding Media: The Extensions of Man* (1964).

CHAPTER 50 THEORIES OF FLIGHT: JAIMIE & ASPASIA
Somini Sengupta, '"Bleak" UN Report on a Planet in Peril Looms Over New Climate Talks', *New York Times* (November 26, 2019).

CODA

CHAPTER 51 KATRINA & ANNIE
Ralph Waldo Emerson, *Circles* (1841).

CHAPTER 53 THE CHOIR
Jaak Panksepp, 'The Science of Emotions', TEDxRanier (2013).

Daniel Goleman, 'Neuroscience of Emotion and Decision Making', Youtube (2014).

ACKNOWLEDGMENTS

I am profoundly grateful to Annie Whitlocke; Katrina, Peter and their family; the woman I call 'Lynn'; Rhonda Rushton; and everyone who shared their time and their story with me for this book.

I am happily indebted to the librarians and research archivists at the State Library of Victoria; the National Archives of Australia; the Footscray Historical Society; and to the *Coonabarabran Times*. Also, to the archivists at the Manuscripts, Archives, and Rare Books Division of the New York Public Library who guided me to their holdings on women's carceral history which helped to inform the chapters about Lynn's story. Parts of this book were researched while on a research fellowship at the New York Public Library and I will always be deeply grateful for the supportive environment provided by that magnificent building, its exceptional people and its vast collections.

The primary source material found by Bill Chalker and Keith Basterfield, and collated on their blogs, taught me much. I am thankful to them for their research.

I first wrote about Annie Whitlocke and the Ark Encounter in *The Monthly*, and I am grateful to Nick Feik and the editors for their good counsel.

My deepest thanks: to Michael Heyward, Mandy Brett, and my agents Jane Novak, Sarah Lutyens and David Forrer for their wisdom, their dedication and for believing in this book and my ability to write it from its earliest stages. Wait Mandy, there's more (but of course). What a lucky thing in my writing and my life to be in conversation with you. To Masie Cochran, for the type of close read and understanding that writers dream of, and for all her efforts on this book's behalf. To the talented people at Tin House for their wonderful support in sending it out into the world. To Jaya Miceli for such a powerful cover.

To Tali Lavi for her time and her insight and for one letter on silver paper. To Rabbi Kim Ettlinger for introducing me to the work of Martin Buber. To Kris Smith, Tony Jackson, Pamela and Ron Pickering, Liz Coll, Emily Kisyma, Andrea Benegas, Veronica Benegas and my friends (both writerly and not) each of whom made this book possible in their own vital way.

Finally, to Charlie and our beautiful children—our brightest lights—for every minute, for everything, forever.